The European Union
and the Eurozone under Stress

John Theodore • Jonathan Theodore • Dimitrios Syrrakos

The European Union and the Eurozone under Stress

Challenges and Solutions for Repairing Fault Lines in the European Project

John Theodore
Manchester, United Kingdom

Jonathan Theodore
Manchester, United Kingdom

Dimitrios Syrrakos
Department of Economics
Manchester Metropolitan University
Manchester, United Kingdom

ISBN 978-3-319-84867-9 ISBN 978-3-319-52292-0 (eBook)
DOI 10.1007/978-3-319-52292-0

© The Editor(s) (if applicable) and The Author(s) 2017
Sofcover reprint of the hardcover 1st edition 2017
This work is subject to copyright. All rights are solely and exclusively licensed by the Publisher, whether the whole or part of the material is concerned, specifically the rights of translation, reprinting, reuse of illustrations, recitation, broadcasting, reproduction on microfilms or in any other physical way, and transmission or information storage and retrieval, electronic adaptation, computer software, or by similar or dissimilar methodology now known or hereafter developed.
The use of general descriptive names, registered names, trademarks, service marks, etc. in this publication does not imply, even in the absence of a specific statement, that such names are exempt from the relevant protective laws and regulations and therefore free for general use.
The publisher, the authors and the editors are safe to assume that the advice and information in this book are believed to be true and accurate at the date of publication. Neither the publisher nor the authors or the editors give a warranty, express or implied, with respect to the material contained herein or for any errors or omissions that may have been made. The publisher remains neutral with regard to jurisdictional claims in published maps and institutional affiliations.

Cover illustration: Blend-Memento/Alamy Stock Photo

Printed on acid-free paper

This Palgrave Macmillan imprint is published by Springer Nature
The registered company is Springer International Publishing AG
The registered company address is: Gewerbestrasse 11, 6330 Cham, Switzerland

Foreword

The European Union and the Eurozone under Stress: Challenges and Solutions for Repairing Fault Lines in the European Project

Henry the Eighth broke with Rome and therewith also Europe for the sake of a marriage. Not since then has the country faced a divorce issue with serious constitutional implications as Brexit presents us with. The UK has been 'in Europe' since 1972 but anyone who has crossed the Channel and been on the other side will know that we have never been fully a part of Europe. It feels different when you reach Calais or Lille. There you see a single Europe. We British are and have always been semi-detached, if not totally detached. We complained about our contribution and won a rebate. We did not sign up to Schengen. We got an opt out from the Single Currency. We choked at the idea of 'ever closer Union'.

Now we have voted for Brexit. I voted to remain in 1975 and in 2016. I was an enthusiastic Europhile in 1975. I stayed so through the Single Market and until EU 15. It was enlargement which sapped my enthusiasm. A Union of 28 is an ungovernable mess. Even so, UK was not in the Euro and in fact we were never full members like the rest. We had what is now called a Bespoke arrangement.

The most shocking realisation after the Brexit vote has been to find how unprepared the government had been to deal with the result. There were no contingency plans, no scenarios. The treasury produced some dire predictions, but they were statistical exercises not serious scenarios. At the end, it was clear that neither side in the debate understood the complexity of the decision to leave. Apart from the false promises made (hardly unusual in election times), even the Exiters did not know what 'out' entailed.

It is thus welcome that we have a book here which lays out the issues. The authors have crafted a serious analysis of the Brexit decision putting it in the broader context of the crisis in the EU and the Eurozone as well. On the British side, the decision was very much a protest against uncontrolled and uncontrollable migration from the rest of the EU into UK. This was a consequence of enlargement. British people did not object to migration from within the EU 12 or EU 15. Even the immigration from Poland in the first few years of the new century was borne. It was when after the Recession of 2008, migrants came from Romania and Bulgaria that dissatisfaction started. The UK Budget was also under stress and the cuts in public expenditure during 2010–2015 did not help.

One remarkable aspect of the vote is that it is predominantly an *English* vote to exit. Out of the 34 million votes cast (16 million Remain 18 million Leave), as many as 28 million were cast in England. Here, the margin was exactly the same 2 million between Remain and Leave (13 million Remain; 15 million Leave). Thus, the three devolved regions balanced out as to Remain or Leave. Brexit is an English protest vote. It raises longer term questions about our Constitution. Why is England the only region without devolved powers? Is it not time we discussed Federation seriously?

As the authors highlight, the EU has also much to reflect upon. It is clear now that adopting a single currency before a single Federal authority has been a huge mistake. The cost to the weaker economies of Southern Europe has been massive. An entire generation of young people in Greece, Spain, Portugal and Italy will never enjoy adequate income or employment. The Euro mimics the gold standard in its deflationary design. But in the gold standard, there were periodic discoveries in California or Australia which increased the supply of gold. In the Eurozone during the first decade, money flowed in from outside as the markets believed risk was pooled across the zone. After 2008, the investors realised that each country was individually responsible for its debts. They quickly withdrew as much money as they could. The region has not recovered since. Nor can it if the rules of fiscal policy are not relaxed nor is there any move to create a central budgetary authority capable of making transfer payments.

The stories of Brexit are intertwined with the prospect of the Eurozone. There are uncertain times ahead but a good guide is always a help.

It is a moot question of how the twin issues – Brexit and the crisis in the Eurozone – will resolve themselves. But here is a book which will guide you through the maze. Read it and learn.

Lord Meghnad Desai
Member of the House of Lords
Select Committee on EU Financial Affairs

Acknowledgements

We would like to express our deep thanks to all those who have kindly given us their valuable time in helping us to record the events – especially for the insight into the months leading up, during and immediately after the UK Referendum and the migration crisis.

We extend our sincere gratitude to Lord Meghnand Desai, Professor Patrick Minford, Amin Amiri, Professor Jan Gorecki, David O'Brien, Michal Kobosko, Micheal O'Conchuir, Professor Kevin Albertson and many politicians at the Committee of the Regions in Brussels for their insightful observations and views for the writing of this book.

Further thanks go to Barbara, the wife of John, and Anastasia, wife of Dimitrios, who have both provided patience and sympathy in the critical months prior to producing the manuscript, and finally to the many individuals in the UK and in Europe who shared their views on the rapidly changing events in the European Union in 2016.

Contents

1	**Introduction**	1
2	**Europe at a Crossroad**	7
	Background to EU Debt Crisis	8
	Convergence (Maastricht Treaty) Criteria	13
	'Monetarists' Versus 'Economists'	17
	Monetary Union: Stability or Systemic Weakness?	17
3	**The Eurozone Debt Crisis**	27
	Fixed Exchange Rate Regimes – Monetary Union	30
	Fiscal Consolidation and Austerity	42
	An Alternative Approach	50
4	**EU Migration**	57
	Migration – Intra-EU Mobility	60
	Background to the Expansion of Freedom of Movement: From Workers to Citizens	62
	EU Expansion: The Mobility of Central and Eastern Europeans	64
	Freedom of Movement	66

Immigration and the Swiss Experience 72
Migration and the UK 73
Migration into Europe 74
Reactions within Europe 77
Backlash to Open-Door Policies 80
Terrorism and Security Issues 83

5 Brexit and the Referendum Vote 87
What Happens Now? 90
The EU Divorce and Article 50 (Lisbon Treaty) 93
Legal Aspects 94
Exit without Article 50 96
EU Funding Streams 97
SMEs and Start-Up Post-Brexit 101
Venture Capital Funds – The European Investment Fund (EIF) 102
The European Investment Bank (EIB) 103
Reactions in Europe 105
Bratislava 112
The Models for Exiting the EU 114
Hard and Soft Brexit? The Options 114
Northern Ireland and Scotland 118
The Norwegian Model 119
The Financial Services Sector-What about the Banks? 124
The Airline Industry 127
Impact on Tourism 131

6 Brexit and the Economy 133
A Review of the UK Economy, June 2010 to June 2016 136
Exchange Rate Volatility 140
Negative Real Interest Rates 141
The Economic Impact of Brexit – Early Indications 144
Foreign Direct Investment – Bank of England – Interest Rates 150

	Productivity	155
	Effects of Brexit on the European Union	159
	Internal Objectives	159
	External Objectives	160
	The Eurozone Banks: A Threat to the Future and Stability of the Eurozone?	161
7	**The EU and China, Russia and Security Strategy**	167
	Chinese Investment in the Eurozone	170
	Resistance to New FDI Deals	172
	China and the EU without Britain	173
	China's Reserve Currency Status	175
	Trade Imbalances	176
	The EU–Russia and Its Security Strategy	177
	EU Security–NATO Relations	178
	NATO and the UK	181
	Polish Reactions	185
	The Effect of EU Sanctions	186
	EU Policy Inconsistencies	186
	Cost of Sanctions	187
	A Russian Perspective	188
8	**The EU, Taxation and the Multinationals**	191
	Corporation Tax – EU Initiatives on Tax Avoidance and Its Wider Implications	193
	Unpopular with Who?	195
	Luxembourg as a Tax Haven	196
	The Transfer Pricing System	198
	Reflections on Corporate Tax Strategies	201
9	**Conclusion**	203
	Demands for Change	205

Timeline of the European Union 215

Bibliography 217

Index 229

List of Figures

Fig. 5.1 EU Countries – Total 28: Relationship and ties between EU countries 113
Fig. 6.1 UK GDP growth 163
Fig. 7.1 The impact of sanctions on EU member states (in € million) 187

List of Tables

Table 2.1	Qualification for Economic and Monetary Union	14
Table 6.1	UK's GDP in $ and £ terms (trillions)	146
Table 6.2	Summary of UK key economic features, 2013–2019, and two Brexit scenarios	158

1

Introduction

Europe, the birthplace of the industrial and scientific revolutions that made and remade the modern world, is in crisis. The 2008–2009 global financial crisis has morphed into a Eurozone crisis since 2010, a migration crisis since 2015 and the political convulsions that contributed to Brexit.

The process of creating the European Union began in the aftermath of the Second World War (WWII). The EU's founding fathers had visionary zeal but limited expectations confined to establishing a secure, politically stable and *economically* prosperous Europe. The Treaty of Rome in 1957 provided moderate ambitions – ab initio, an *economic* union that eventually grew towards political union in a gradual enlargement to a membership of 28 member states.

The Rome treaty established the European Economic Community, aiming to create a common market a customs union with free movement of capital, labour and freedom of movement. Later landmark treaties, led by the Maastricht Treaty 1992, created the European Union and laid the foundations of a single European currency, the Euro which is examined in Chapters 2 and 3. Further milestones such as the Lisbon Treaty 2007 facilitated not only the EU's enlargement but the strengthening of its political structures. This very centralisation of political power fuelled the perception that democracy in EU member states has been weakened failing to convince voters that member states remain in charge of the 'Treaties' as is clearly the case.

The chief indicators of a healthy economy are high growth, low unemployment and moderated inequalities. Those of a functioning political system are stability and a loose consensus between popular parties on their respective coalitions of Left and Right. Yet the direction of Europe has been precisely the opposite of this in the past decade. The dream of the architects of the European Monetary Union was the creation of an 'island of stability' in a turbulent world. This ambition has, for various reasons, been a singular failure. How and why this has come to be the case will be explored in considerable details.

The manifold crises of the social and economic order of Europe – and the political elites clustered at their apex – will be at the heart of this book. It addresses all the major challenges the EU is facing currently, and the possible paths – good or bad – going forward. As these obstacles are all deeply intertwined, potential solutions need to be based on a comprehensive approach.

In seeking to approach the subject of the European crisis as an integrated whole, this book draws on reflection vital for pursuing the 'right' remedies. Was, for example, the creation of the Euro the crucial factor that provoked the EU's perils? Or is it simply reflective of deeper institutional fault lines, economic issues and social and politics ills?

Two major episodes or processes have undermined the EU's cohesion in the course of the last decade. First is the 'resolution', or at least containment, of the Eurozone's debt crisis according to the terms of a neoliberal and deeply monetarist economic paradigm and second is internal and external immigration. In the latter case, external immigration results from events largely beyond the EU's control, but its resolution has been far from satisfactory. To the disappointment of many of the 'old' EU-15 countries, the East European entrants have largely resisted any attempts to accommodate even a small proportion of the immigrants that arrive on EU soil, claiming asylum status. The German Chancellor's remarks that the German economy would need 5 million more workers exacerbated the situation, as it was widely seen as welcoming new immigrants to Germany. The situation, while calling for an immediate response – on basic humanitarian grounds alone, has been handled in a haphazard and piecemeal fashion, without a coordinated EU policy in place.

We also consider how the implementation of the Maastricht Treaty and the inclusion of 11 East European, formerly Soviet-style command economies – plus Cyprus and Malta, transformed the EU from a predominantly Western and South European trading block of 15 nations and 380 million people into a pan-European supranational institution comprising almost 70% of the entire population of the continent (515 out of 740 million). Their entry has led to massive increases in intra-EU immigration, despite any initial caps or limitations. Has the East European enlargement been a failure, making the EU an unsustainable institution?

The Eurozone crisis and internal immigration are not only related but mutually reinforcing. The solution to the Eurozone debt crisis was a one-sided imposition by the Troika, based on austerity economics, the will of Germany and the orthodox monetarism of the European Central Bank (ECB). Consequently, it focused on the South-Eurozone countries' deficits without addressing the overall Eurozone imbalances and the surpluses in the North. This also meant it led to unprecedented unemployment rates in Portugal, Spain, Ireland and Greece and exceptionally high youth unemployment in Italy.

The situation is perpetuated by the EU's institutional arrangements and the inevitable political instability and social paralysis that follows mass unemployment. As a result, whereas prior to 2014 the increase in EU immigration to the UK was primarily from Poland, Romania and Bulgaria, in 2014–2015 it also saw a substantial increase of over 110,000 national insurance registrations by Italian and Spanish citizens. Resentment to escalating EU immigration was said to be a major factor in determining the UK referendum's outcome.

In this respect, the nature of the problems emanating from the East European expansion needs to be addressed. In 2004, in most Eastern European countries, average wages were substantially lower than wages in the UK and Germany – between the UK and Romania, for example, by a factor of nine. As a result, their accession was bound to attract workers from Eastern Europe that had a very strong incentive to relocate together with their family members. This led to 850,000 Polish citizens relocating to the UK during the last decade, exercising their new treaty rights. This contributed significantly to the emergence of an anti-immigration and anti-EU sentiment (and non-EU) in many parts of the UK, and bolstered the Leave cause ahead of their referendum victory. Was this a profound miscalculation of the UK's New Labour government in the late 1990s and early 2000s, when they provided the main driving force for the Eastern expansion? Why the New Labour government did not apply the same seven-year break to control immigration as Germany and France did? These issues will be explored in our sections on Brexit and Migration.

We begin with discussing the debt crisis: the response to which lacked clarity, and for which the subsequent, sometimes, brutal social costs endured by member states at the receiving end of Troika policies have proven very difficult to justify. Antagonism to these policies has accelerated political change in these countries, reflected primarily in the rise of newly formed parties – parties at the margins of what was formerly considered mainstream politics. Such parties include the left-wing Syriza in Greece, the Portuguese socialist and communist parties and Podemos in Spain. The rise of these populist movements, together with the reduced or collapsing popularity of traditional post-WWII centre-left, centre and centre-right wing parties, has rendered the political governance of Eurozone countries fragile. The influx of immigrants from war-torn countries has also given rise to (extreme) right-wing parties, such as National Front in France, Golden Dawn in Greece and AfD in Germany. Therefore, the combination of unprecedented austerity and immigration has the potential to elevate political fragmentation and discord in Europe to levels not seen since the 1930s. The inability to form a government in Spain since December 2015 too provides a striking example of this.

The bailout policies of the Troika (representing the EU Commission, IMF and ECB) have been instrumental in splitting the Eurozone into debtor and creditor countries, and left a deep psychological divide between the electorates of Eurozone countries. While North Europeans imagined that they have to bail out less hard working

South Europeans, the latter felt they were subjected to fiscal cuts of an unprecedented magnitude they did not deserve and, above all, do not deliver. This division is perhaps the most difficult to reconcile.

The health of the European financial system is intimately tied to the well-being of European states, as manifest in holdings of sovereign debt. Europe is now facing the longest period of sustained unemployment, anaemic growth and financial trouble in its modern history – to say nothing of its tandem social and political problems. Within a global economy poised between recovery and crisis, the Eurozone is performing consistently worse than its neighbours and competitors, and its prospects remain uncertain.

2

Europe at a Crossroad

The European Union (EU) is beset with problems, which include the crises in the Eurozone, its inability to promote economic growth in the wider Single Market and more recently the refugee migration disaster posing an existential threat to its survival.

In order to appreciate the origins of its multiplicity of on-going crises, we need to look back at the economic and political foundations, which crystallised in the Maastricht Treaty (MT) of 1991. The Maastricht resolution to the inconsistent quarter of macroeconomic policy that consists of

i) free trade in goods and services,
ii) free capital and labour movements,
iii) fixed exchange rates and
iv) independent monetary policy

has effectively led to the emergence of a two-tier European Union. The first tier consists of those countries that joined the Euro and the second a tier of nations that did not, but which instead sought specific exchange rate arrangements with the single currency bloc. The UK, Denmark,

Sweden and Poland all opted for retaining monetary independence as a feature of their EU membership. This has rendered the Single Market effectively incomplete, as London is the strongest financial market in the EU capital markets, and as a result capital markets are subject to the £ Sterling/Euro exchange rate volatility. Nevertheless, the status quo was effectively maintained, primarily due to favourable European and international macroeconomic conditions and the absence of systemic international financial shocks from 1999 to 2008: circumstances conducive to relative exchange rate stability between the pound and the Euro.

The onset of the Euro debt crisis in the second half of 2009 set in motion processes that could potentially undermine the effective functioning of one of the key pillars of the EU, the Single Market: the enhancement and effective functioning of which was supposed to facilitate the single currency. Currently, less than 40% of EU markets are regulated entirely by Single Market guidelines, with the remaining subjected to national law. The (Single Market) guidelines include common external tariffs and quotas with the rest of the world, such as common regulations governing industrial production and environmental standards. Broad coordination of macroeconomic policy reduces exchange rate volatility amongst EU currencies and in doing so facilitating enhancement in the volumes of intra-EU trade. At the same time, the Eurozone debt crisis has led to a de facto economic spilt in the Eurozone: the Euro-North consisting of primarily Germany, Austria, the Netherlands and Finland, and the Euro-South consisting of Greece, Cyprus, Spain, Italy, Portugal and Ireland. France and Belgium are difficult to integrate in the two groups, as they have not been directly involved in the debt crisis, in terms of punitive interest rates or heavy austerity programmes. However, their economies are highly indebted and subject to poor growth.

Background to EU Debt Crisis

The Eurozone debt crisis must be seen in the context of the global economic downturn, which was triggered by the US subprime mortgage crisis of 2007–2008 but had its origins in the macroeconomic policies of at least the past decade.[1] As we shall see, a broad-based consumer boom coupled with ultra-loose monetary policy by central banks in the USA and Europe fed a global speculative bubble in real estate and equity markets.[2] The fallout of this gigantic credit bust took its time to unwind across the Eurozone, emerging as an on-going sovereign debt crisis that owes its origin as much to the structural problems of the single currency,[3] and state spending in the Eurozone, as it does to banking leverage, global finance and the securitisation of toxic debt.

It is commonplace to assume that the countries engulfed in the Eurozone debt crisis, most prominently Greece, Ireland, Portugal, Spain (the so-called PIGS) and Cyprus, are victims of their own economic mismanagement and, as a result, invite the view that they are alone to blame for their economic and social hardships experienced. Balancing their budgets through tough austerity policies, without the palliative of currency devaluation, is the associated policy prescription to secure their continued place in the single currency.

The mismanagement of the Portuguese and Greek public finances is beyond dispute. Chronic debt accumulation and sizeable public sectors date back to the late 1970s.[4] It has to be noted though that the social programmes of the time were following from the policies of these countries' dictatorial past.[5] Greece had been living beyond its means even before it joined the Euro.[6] The country was only allowed to join

---

[1] Gros, 'Macroeconomic Imbalances in the Euro Area: Symptom or Cause of the Crisis?' Centre for European Policy Studies, Policy Brief, No. 226, Brussels (2012). Centre for Economic Policy Research 'Rebooting the Eurozone: Step I – Agreeing a Crisis Narrative' Policy Insight, No. 85. Centre for Economic Policy Research-CEPR (2015).

[2] Marsh, *Europe's Deadlock: How the Euro Crisis Could be Solved – and Why It Won't Happen.* Yale University Press (2013).

[3] Lavoie, 'The Eurozone: Similarities to and Differences from Keynes's Plan' *International Journal of Political Economy*, 44:1, pp. 3–17 (1953). Lavoie, 'The Eurozone Crisis: A Balance-of-Payments Problem or a Crisis Due to a Flawed Monetary Design?' *International Journal of Political Economy* 44:2, pp. 157–160 (1953).

[4] Syrrakos, 'On the Greek National Debt' (2017).

[5] Crafts and Toniolo, 'Economic Growth in Europe Since 1945' (1996).

[6] De Grauwe, 'The Governance of a fragile Eurozone' *Australian Economic Review*, 45:3, pp. 255–268 (2011). Pento, *The Coming Bond Market Collapse, How to Survive the Demise of the US Debt Market.* Wiley (2013).

the Euro by inaccurately – registering the equivalent of €10 billion in debt. In a now notorious financial manoeuvre, Goldman Sachs helped the country hide the true extent of its debt – limited by Maastricht Treaty rules to 60% of GDP and a 3% deficit – through a credit swap scheme that engineered a public deficit within the maximum entry criteria.[7] After the country joined the single currency, public spending soared. Wages in the public sector rose by over 50% between 1999 and 2008. The 2004 Olympic Games in Athens cost around €10 billion. As money flowed out of government coffers, tax revenues were hit by an endemic culture of tax evasion on an extraordinary scale, one that is estimated by the OECD to account for at least €20 billion in lost revenues each year.[8]

The Greek economy had grown steadily throughout most of the 2000s in an apparent economic boom, but the financial crisis meant the gaping hole in the country's budget could no longer be contained or concealed. In January 2010, the European statistics agency, Eurostat, issued a report on the debt statistics of the Greek government, pointing to 'severe irregularities' and 'institutional weaknesses' in the way the data had been collected, and suggested political interference in the process.[9]

A month later, the government of George Papandreou (elected in October 2009) admitted a flawed statistical procedure existed. In April, the official measure of the deficit was raised from a prior estimate of 6–8% to 13.6% of GDP – the second highest in the world behind Iceland.[10] This move rang alarm bells in international markets. Greek bonds began their rapid slide to junk status as yields soared, and USA

---

[7] http://www.spiegel.de/international/europe/greek-debt-crisis-how-goldman-sachs-helped-greece-to-mask-its-true-debt-a-676634.html

[8] http://diepresse.com/home/wirtschaft/international/500632/Korruption-und-Steuerhinterziehung_Griechenland-versinkt-im-Sumpf- Christine Lagarde remarked in the summer of 2012, to much criticism, that she felt more sympathy with children in Africa than tax evaders in Greece.

[9] European Commission, 'Report on Greek Government Deficit and Debt Statistics,' January 2010, p. 4, pp. 27–28, quoted on Simitis, *The European Debt Crisis*. Manchester University Press (2014).

[10] http://www.bloomberg.com/apps/news?pid=newsarchive&sid=aUi3XLUwIIVA.

and European stock indices plunged as a Greek default and widespread debt contagion appeared to be drawing near.[11]

By contrast, Spain and Ireland had no such problems.[12] Both countries experienced low deficits and debts, and were cited by the European Commission (EC) as examples of sound public finances (see Chapter 4).[13] However, the substantial increases in both countries' deficits and debts post-2010 led to the view that systemic and long-term mismanagement was the root cause of their problems. This has added to confusion over the origins of the crisis and led to growing scepticism over the solutions put in place.

Much of the worst of the Eurozone debt crisis was stimulated by credit-financed wage and public spending increases over the last decade. The Euro brought the nations of southern Europe low interest rates and easy credit, and they borrowed to finance increased public spending, government wages, and real estate programmes. Both the wage increases of the construction workers and the government employees were largely credit financed. Low interest rates in southern Europe meant that these countries could borrow very easily but failed to add to their productivity.[14] Prices increased with this inflationary credit bubble, which had the knock-on effect of depriving these countries of their competitiveness. The decline in profits in the productive sectors of the economy was counterbalanced by the increase in profits in the unproductive, and highly protected, sectors fuelled by the explosion of cheap credit in the Euro's early years.[15] A process, which was not only an EU phenomenon, that would itself lead to the credit crunch and worldwide recession. Until 2008, credit markets did not substantially reflect the economic differences between the countries of the Eurozone. This resulted in a

---

[11] http://www.nytimes.com/2010/04/28/business/global/28drachma.html?_r=0, http://news.bbc.co.uk/1/hi/business/8647441.stm.

[12] Centre for Economic Policy Research, 'Rebooting the Eurozone: Step I – Agreeing a Crisis Narrative,' Policy Insight, No. 85. Centre for Economic Policy Research-CEPR (2015).

[13] De Grauwe, 'The Governance of a Fragile Eurozone' *Australian Economic Review* (2011).

[14] Gros, 'Macroeconomic Imbalances in the Euro Area: Symptom or Cause of the Crisis?' Centre for European Policy Studies, Policy Brief, No. 226, Brussels (2012).

[15] Centre for Economic Policy Research, 'Rebooting the Eurozone: Step I – Agreeing a Crisis Narrative,' Policy Insight, No. 85. Centre for Economic Policy Research-CEPR (2015).

reduced interest rate spread on debt servicing, as reflected by the spread on the ten-year bonds. This apparent 'convergence' of Eurozone nations' interest rates reversed itself from 2008 onwards.

The competitiveness issue was exacerbated when the post-2004 Accession states of Eastern European, with significantly lower wages, were absorbed into the EU. For comparison, Poland has wage costs of about €7 per hour – less than a third of (now unemployment-wracked) Spain, where they are at €23. No dream of any politician in Europe can overcome this fundamental problem of such wage discrepancies. This is a fundamental long-term structural problem, as opposed to a purely cyclical one of boom-and-bust finances, that can (potentially) be suppressed or mitigated by tempering regulation and economic policy.

The cost of debt servicing came at the heart of the economic debate in the European Commission. The lack of a fiscal union, that is, the lack of a union with the power to tax and spend on a pan-European level, or alternative institutional arrangements combined with the Maastricht Treaty's clause not permitting the ECB to provide lender of last resort facilities (articles 101 and 103) prevented the bailing out of Greece, Portugal, Ireland, Spain and Cyprus. This led to mounting speculation during 2011–2013, as to whether countries were in danger of imminent departure from the single currency.[16] A vicious cycle of financial instability and interest rate increases was created.

Rather than pinning the blame for the crisis on national governments, we suggest blame lies in the wider context of the growth of the fiscal and political institutions of the EU.[17] When the Maastricht Treaty came into force in January 1992, there were four countries with excessive debt levels in relation to the 60% of GDP benchmark, as set by the treaty. These were Italy with a debt ratio of 130% of GDP, Belgium with a ratio of 128%, Ireland with 115% and Greece with 105%. Therefore, when the Maastricht Treaty agreement was signed it was widely expected

---

[16] Micossi, 'The Monetary Policy of the European Central Bank (2002–2015)', CEPS Special Report, No. 109 (2015).

[17] Lavoie, 'The Eurozone: Similarities to and Differences from Keynes's Plan' *International Journal of Political Economy*, 44:1, pp. 3–17 (1953). Wyplosz, 'The Eurozone Crisis: Too Few Lessons Learned' (2016) http://voxeu.org/article/eurozone-crisis-too-few-lessons-learned.

that these four countries would not meet the conditions necessary to join the European Monetary Union (EMU) due to commence on 1 January 1999. In other words, only the creation of a 'small' EMU was apparently attainable. However, it was the flexible interpretation of the debt criterion by the European Commission, according to which countries would be allowed to participate in the single currency provided their national debt was converging at a satisfactory pace towards the 60% benchmark, which allowed these countries to join the EMU.[18] A flexible interpretation was introduced to pave the way for Italy to join the Eurozone.[19] Such a generous interpretation of the Maastricht Treaty debt criterion allowed Italy and Belgium to join with the first wave of 11 countries that acceded on 1 January 1999 – despite their debt-to-GDP ratios of 121.6% and 122.2%, respectively, in 1997. The debt data of these different nations in relation to the accession criteria is presented in Table 2.1 below criteria. Greece joined the Euro in 2001.

Convergence (Maastricht Treaty) Criteria

The Maastricht Treaty criteria, presented below, are a mixture of tight macroeconomic conditions on monetary convergence (criteria 1 and 2), fiscal performance (criteria 3 and 4) and exchange rate stability (criterion 5).

1. National **inflation rates** were not to exceed **1.5%** of the average rate of the three best performing countries.
2. **Interest rate differentials** were not to exceed **2%** of the average of the three countries with **lowest inflation rates**.
3. **Budget deficits** were not to exceed **3%** of GDP.
4. The **public debt** was not to exceed **60%** of GDP.
5. The exchange rate parity had to remain within the narrow band of the Exchange Rate Mechanism (ERM) of 2.25% for at least two years before admission to the final stage was granted.

---

[18] Eijffinger and de Haan, 'European Monetary and Fiscal Policy' (2002).
[19] Galli, E. and Padovano, F. *Sustainability and Determinants of Italian Public Deficits Before and After Maastricht.* Società Italiana di Economia Publica (2004).

Table 2.1 Qualification for Economic and Monetary Union

MT criteria	Inflation rate 1997(%)	Interest rates (%)	Government budgetary position		Exchange rate (in ERM, March 1998)
			Deficit, 1997 (% of GDP)	Debt (% of GDP)	
			<3	1997 Change from 95	
				<60	
Target	2.7	7.8			Yes
Members of EMU					
Luxemburg	1.4	5.6	−1.7	6.7 1	Yes
Finland	1.3	5.9	0.9	55.8 −3.7	Yes
France	1.2	5.5	3	58 9.5	Yes
Germany	1.4	5.6	2.7	(61.3) 11	Yes
Portugal	1.8	6.2	2.5	(62) −1.8	Yes
Austria	1.1	5.6	2.5	(66.1) 0.7	Yes
Ireland	1.2	6.2	−0.9	(66.3) −22.8	Yes
Spain	1.8	6.3	2.6	(68.8) 6.2	Yes
Netherlands	1.8	5.5	1.4	(72.1) −5.7	Yes
Italy	1.8	6.7	2.7	(121.6) −3.3	Yes
Belgium	1.4	5.7	2.1	(122.2) −11.2	Yes
Did not qualify for EMU					
Greece	(5.2)	(9.8)	(4)	(108) −0.7	Yes
Political decision not to join EMU					
UK	1.8	7	1.9	53.4 3	No
Denmark	1.9	6.2	−0.7	(65.1) −13.1	Yes
Sweden	1.9	6.5	0.8	(76.6) −2.4	No

Notes: Figures in brackets indicate that a member state did not meet the convergence criteria as set out in the Maastricht Treaty. Belgium and Italy convinced their EU partners that their debt ratios were converging to the target at a sufficient rate in order to qualify for the single currency.
Source: European Commission (1998).

Upon signing of the Maastricht Treaty, countries seeking to join the Eurozone placed emphasis on meeting the first two criteria relating to monetary conditions, namely inflation differentials and interest rates differentials. These two criteria were of competitive nature as they were considering a country's performance in relation to that of the others. However, the long-term consequences of sustained divergence in inflation – even small divergence – was not considered.

By the mid-1990s, after registering improvement with inflation and interest rate convergence, countries also aimed at either meeting or improving their fiscal conditions concerning criteria 3 and 4, depending on their starting positions in 1992. As a result, criteria 3 and 4 were of an absolute nature, as countries either met them or not, and progress was registered against their past performance. The criteria were applicable from 1993 to 1998 for the Eurozone countries that joined with the first wave in 1999 and for countries that have joined since. They are also still applicable to non-Eurozone countries that have (and wish) to join, e.g. Poland, Bulgaria, etc. Given that criteria 1 and 5 cannot apply to Eurozone countries, as the Eurozone's interest rate is set for the entire area by the ECB, and there is no exchange rate volatility, only the fiscal criteria are still applicable under the Stability and Growth Pact (SGP).

As a result, of the flexible interpretation of the debt criterion, the reduction of 3.3% of the Italian debt-to-GDP ratio, from 1995 to 1998, made it impossible to refuse entry to Belgium, as it successfully managed to reduce its debt-to-GDP ratio by 11.2% in the same period (Table 2.1). Likewise, the remarkable reduction of the Irish debt-to-GDP ratio by 22.8 percentage points, to 66.3%, justified the moniker of 'Celtic tiger' that was commonly used to describe the Irish economy in the second half of the 1990s.[20] Quite remarkably, both Germany and the Netherlands failed to meet the 60% debt criterion in 1997, albeit at narrow rates of 61.3% and 72.1%, respectively. Overall, out of 11

---

[20] Nolan, 'Ireland's Rapid Economic Convergence: The Role of Government Policy and European Union Structural Funds for Ireland's Boom Economy During the 1990s' (2003) http://www.celtic-irish.co.uk/news/wp-content/uploads/irish-economy.pdf.

countries that joined in 1999, only three – namely Luxemburg, Finland and France – met the debt criterion. Germany, Portugal, Austria, Ireland and Spain maintained a debt-to-GDP ratio below 70%. These countries, together with the Netherlands, could form a 'small' Euro (Euro-9), as envisaged by Germany. Indeed, in 1992 Germany anticipated that only six countries would satisfy the MT criteria, as Portugal, Spain and Ireland were not expected to meet them. This would have made the management of the Euro much easier and would provide an incentive for other countries to join once they reduced their debt-to-GDP ratios below a threshold to be decided at a later stage, e.g. 75%.[21]

The flexible interpretation of the 60% debt-to-GDP criterion therefore set a precedent for high-debt countries to join the single currency. The underlying assumption behind this was that countries with high debts would keep servicing them successfully, as they had done prior to joining the EMU, by taking advantage both of the low interest rates set by the ECB and the reserve currency status acquired by the newly formed currency. Given that this was not the case, and in the absence of debt mutualisation, the EMU has been running the risk of stagnation and a sustained debt crisis – while also rendering it politically impossible for some countries to maintain their place in it. The origin of the EMU debt problem therefore goes back, at least in part, to the flexible interpretation of the 60% debt criterion of the Maastricht Treaty. Had such an interpretation not been adopted, Belgium, Italy and Greece and possibly Ireland, Spain and Portugal would not have been able to join. In essence, a 'small' Eurozone would have been created, as envisaged by Germany. This was, ardently advocated by the German authorities, in the mid-1990s prior to assigning Eurozone accession status to countries. It is in this framework that the current stringent stance of the German authorities must also be evaluated.

---

[21] Commission of the European Communities, European Commission. Annual Economic Reports and Reviews: (1995a) 'Convergence Report 1994'; (1995b) 'One Currency for Europe: Green Paper on the Practical Engagements for the Introduction of the Single Currency"; (1995c) 'Report on Convergence in the European Union in 1995'.

'Monetarists' Versus 'Economists'

The conflict between a 'small' and a 'large' Euro currency reflects the long-standing dispute between strict 'monetarists' and 'economists' within EU, concerning the process of European monetary integration in the 1970s and 1980s. According to 'monetarists', led by France, the creation of a 'large' European Monetary Union would provide the necessary macroeconomic framework for less wealthy European countries to achieve high growth rates, facilitated by EU's regional funds, and catch up with the richer ones.[22] Italy, Spain and Belgium supported this approach to monetary union. On the other hand, 'economists' led by Germany have maintained that countries should be allowed to join the single currency only after they have undergone protracted fiscal consolidation. Not surprisingly, the Netherlands, Austria, Sweden, Denmark and Finland have formed the 'economists' group. In summary, then, the argument focused on whether or not economic integration is a necessary pre-condition for a successful monetary union.[23]

Monetary Union: Stability or Systemic Weakness?

The Stability Pact (renamed the Stability and Growth Pact) was agreed in the second half of 1996 and made effective in 1997. The Pact ensured the application of the 3% deficit-to-GDP and the 60% debt-to-GDP criteria, respectively, in the Eurozone countries. Overall, the Euro was created in accordance with the monetarist position, with 11 countries joining in the first wave in 1999 and another eight countries joining from 2002 to 2014. No particularly strong and certainly no measurable *real economic* convergence was registered for the countries joining. The

---

[22] Dinan, *Ever Closer Union: An Introduction to European Integration*. Macmillan Press Ltd. (1999) See also Szasz, A. *The Road to European Monetary Union*. Macmillan Press Ltd. (1999) (In this context monetarists need to be distinguished from monetarism).

[23] Ungerer, *A Concise History of European Monetary Integration: From EPU to EMU* Quorum Books (1997).

crucial nation, in this perspective, is Italy. With Germany being the main export market for both France and Italy, and many Italian and French products being homogenous and price sensitive, a 'small' Euro, which would have excluded Italy, would have provided her with an immense competitive advantage over France in the case of a European recession.[24] The potential loss to French companies of their market share in Germany would have rendered the task of reducing unemployment in France almost impossible. As such, Italian participation to the single currency was vital not only for Italy but for France as well. A very strong Italian desire to join the single currency (with the exception of the President of Banco d' Italia for this very reason), the compression of the Italian debt-to-GDP from 1993 to 1999 and the reduction of the country's deficit increased the chances of her joining. The only remaining obstacle was the country's debt-to-GDP ratio, which despite its reduction still far exceeded the 60% benchmark imposed by the Maastricht Treaty. The flexible interpretation of the debt criterion saw Italy joining the Euro.

This decision had far-reaching implications that dramatically shaped the single currency's current form. Italy joining effectively meant that Belgium and Ireland could accede, as they managed to reduce their debt-to-GDP ratio in the second half of the 1990s. Low-debt (but high-deficit) Spain and Portugal could have not been refused entry either, as they achieved a remarkable reduction of their deficit as a percentage of their GDP. Reducing the deficit was seen as the central step to ensuring a sustainable debt-to-GDP, and thus providing a solid foundation for a successful performance in a monetary union, even according to the 'economists'. However, the potential creation of a 'large' Euro, as was clear by 1997, meant that a number of countries formerly planning to participate changed their attitudes. Denmark in particular, following the flexible interpretation of the 60% debt criterion, decided not to join followed by Sweden, though both countries maintain a fixed exchange rate regime with the Euro, and in this respect differ from the UK, the

---

[24] Karagounis, Syrrakos and Simister, 'The Stability and Growth Pact, and Balanced Budget Fiscal Stimulus: Evidence from Germany and Italy' *Inter-economics*, 50(1), pp. 32–39 (2015).

only EU country in a flexible exchange rate regime with the single currency. In order for Germany to acquiesce to the creation of a 'large' Euro, the application and adherence to fiscal discipline by all Eurozone countries was essential.

The dream of the architects of the European Monetary Union was the creation of an island of stability in an economically and financially turbulent world. Whatever the debateable achievements or blunders of the single currency experiment, it is undeniable that the existence of a single currency, without the corresponding fiscal integration or political union normally underpinning a currency union, has introduced massive new sources of strain to the region.[25] It has given the European arena of the global crisis its own particular flavour of financial trouble. Countries crippled by the burden of sovereign debt, such as Greece, have not been able to devalue their currency to reduce the load in real terms. Indeed, surges in strength in the Euro at critical junctures, most notably in 2009 and late 2010, have wreaked havoc on their ability to service their debt, triggering repeated fears of impending default.[26]

At the heart of the financial infrastructure of the Eurozone lies the European Central Bank (ECB), an institution whose primary task is to keep inflation under control and whose scope of monetary policy is defined almost exclusively as 'maintaining an environment of stable prices'.[27] The ECB explicitly makes the objective of employment and growth contingent to maintaining inflation below but close to 2%. This implies that it would not give priority to other objectives or permit any trade-offs amongst them.[28] The strong currency stance of the Eurozone's

---

[25] Baskaran and Hessami, 'Monetary Integration, Soft Budget Constraints, and the EMU Sovereign Debt Crises' University of Konstanz, Department of Economics Working Paper Series 03 (2013). Hinarejos, 'Fiscal Federalism in the European Union: Evolution and Future Choices for EMU' *Common Market Law Review*, 50, pp. 1621–1642 (2013).

[26] Gros, 'Adjustment Difficulties in the GIPSY Club' Centre for European Policy Studies, Working Document, No 326, Brussels (2010).

[27] 'The Scope of monetary policy' as defined by the ECB, available online at http://www.ecb.europa.eu/mopo/intro/role/html/index.en.html.

[28] Micossi, 'The Monetary Policy of the European Central Bank (2002–2015)', CEPS Special Report, No. 109 (2015). Stiglitz, 'GDP Per Capita in the UK Is Lower Than It Was Before the Crisis. That Is Not a Success', *Guardian* (2015). http://www.theguardian.com/books/2015/may/24/joseph-stiglitz-interview-uk-economy-lost-decade-zero-growth 25/05/16.

institutions and, in particular, the ECB reflects the member countries' need to erase their external imbalances.

The EU elites, of course, hoped that the SGP criteria would not be violated by any Eurozone country. But we know this was not the case, and indeed the elites knew this as they massaged the Eurozone countries statistical financial regimes prior to joining the single currency.

The anti-inflationary reputation of the Euro relied on tight monetary policy so the lack of budgetary control was bound to bring problems. Keeping price stability was a key principle for the ECB to control inflation. But the ECB failed to cope with the wider implications of this policy on the global financial system relating to international exchange rates: in particular, the impact of the fluctuating exchange rate with the weak dollar, which ultimately made most Eurozone countries barring Germany and the Netherlands uncompetitive in world markets and key export industries.

Germany has been the main beneficiary of the Euro prospering at the expense of its southern Eurozone neighbours.[29] It is because of exceptionally low interest rates that Greeks, Spaniards and Cypriots have bought German good and cars, fuelling a massive credit boom in their countries. Before 1999, Germans may have complained about the loss of the Deutschmark, but they stopped when cheap credit skyrocketed its exports to these countries – its Eurozone partners – that now are paying the price for profligacy. Germany has also kept a tight grip on wages. Its GDP is driven by its massive export market representing nearly 50% of GDP so remaining competitive was vital to its domestic economic policies. Indeed, Germany is so competitive *for the same reason* that southern Europe is now uncompetitive – because, in the credit inflation of the 2000s, the southern Eurozone increased their prices relative to Germany. The South did not follow Germany's example and allowed wage inflation to rise and coupled this with a spending boom largely centred on the commercial and retail property markets (Spain, Portugal,

---

[29] Cesaratto, 'The Implications of TARGET2 in the European Balance of Payments Crisis and Beyond' *European Journal of Economics and Economic Policy: Intervention*, 10:3, pp. 359–382 (2013). McKinsey Report, *The Future of the Euro, An Economic Perspective on the Eurozone Crisis*. Germany, McKinsey & Company, Inc. (2015).

Cyprus and Greece). With the global recession, these countries found the level of debt they had acquired unsustainable – with an equally unmanageable rise in borrowing costs. As a result, they faced austerity through the bailout provisions *and* internal devaluations causing cuts in wages, benefits and overall living standards. Greece provides the best illustration of how devastatingly the level of spending and salary cuts has affected the everyday lives of its citizens.[30] As a result, Greek unemployment stands at over 25%, with youth unemployment closer to 40%, wages, welfare benefits and in turn living standards have plummeted by up to 50% and public debt increasing to 175% of GDP. It stood at 120% before the first austerity programme of 2010 and rose to over 175% by 2015. While not all economic malaise in Greece can be attributed to austerity, what is certain is that the austerity agenda failed to provide a viable economic solution.

While Germany's post-crisis recovery is presented as an example of a country that made the short-term sacrifices necessary for long-term success, Germany did not apply to its economy the harsh, pro-cyclical austerity measures that fell on countries like Greece – even as it has benefited from the low interest rates facilitated its thriving export markets in manufactured goods.[31]

---

[30] Joseph Stiglitz (in The Guardian, 17 August 2012) argued that 'No large economy has ever recovered from a downturn as a result of austerity. It is a certain recipe for exacerbating the recession and inflicting unnecessary pain on the economy. Any additional spending should address the longer-term problems – inequality and industrial restructuring – and target the neediest in society who, because of the downturn, are suffering the most. A more progressive tax structure – higher taxes at the top, lower taxes at the bottom – would stimulate the economy. Taxing the excessive speculation that goes on in the financial sector would also be a good thing.'

[31] A Bloomberg editorial entitled cast the role and responsibility of Germany in the debt crisis in this light: In the millions of words written about Europe's debt crisis, Germany is typically cast as the responsible adult and Greece as the profligate child. Prudent Germany, the narrative goes, is loath to bail out freeloading Greece, which borrowed more than it could afford and now must suffer the consequences.... By December 2009, according to the Bank for International Settlements, German banks had amassed claims of $704 billion on Greece, Ireland, Italy, Portugal and Spain, much more than the German banks' aggregate net capital. In other words, they lent more than they could afford.... Irresponsible borrowers can't exist without irresponsible lenders. Germany's banks were Greece's enablers.' It concluded that 'Europe's taxpayers have provided as much financial support to Germany as they have to Greece.'

http://www.bloombergview.com/articles/2012-05-23/merkel-should-know-her-country-has-been-bailed-out-too.

From this perspective, Euro's debt crisis is far more complex in nature than simple conflict of management of the Euro area between France and Germany or even the debate between the monetarist and economist positions. This is the case as all Eurozone countries have different and specific stakes in the successful performance of the single currency. France's position in the Euro is sustainable only to the extent that Italy maintains its place in it. Italy in turn is sensitive to developments in Greece as it is the second most indebted Euro area country. Portugal is closely attuned to developments in Greece and Italy. The Eurozone debt crisis has evolved to a much broader disagreement or even 'conflict' concerning the direction the EMU and the EU need or ought to take. The United Kingdom referendum forms part of this debate: whichever direction EU takes, it would have to be without the UK.

At present, the functioning of the Eurozone post-2009 seems to vindicate economists' aversion to the creation of a 'large' Euro. From this perspective, the policies put forward, based on bailouts, are part of the old 'large' Euro approach that is simply not sustainable without prior economic convergence or, even worse, an economic convergence based on unsustainable policies. And the contrast between the condition of North and South illuminates the key weaknesses at the heart of an austerity-driven scheme for recovery. The whole point of the structural reforms enforced under the terms of the Troika – the triad of institutions that includes the International Monetary Fund (IMF), the European Central Bank and the European Commission – is to make these troubled, debt-ridden Eurozone economies leaner and more competitive. But what makes an economy competitive in an international marketplace? After all, the term is relative.[32] Ultimately and finally, it is prices for a product or service which are not higher than elsewhere. The southern countries of the EU inflated under the credit bubble that the Euro brought them. Undoing this inflation is a very different matter. Cutting nominal wages in a safe manner is extraordinarily difficult: as the example of Greece proves, it puts armies of protestors in the streets,

---

[32] Gros, 'Macroeconomic Imbalances in the Euro Area: Symptom or Cause of the Crisis?' Centre for European Policy Studies, Policy Brief, No. 226, Brussels (2012).

destroys confidence and shatters the social cohesion necessary to maintain a functioning socio-economic order. It is, in essence, the same policy prescription pursued in the UK in the aftermath of the First World War. In particular, from 1920 to 1925 when the then Chancellor of the Exchequer, Winston Churchill, insisted that the UK should return to the fixed exchange rate regime of the time, namely the Gold Standard, at the pre-war parity of $4.86 to the pound. Massive unemployment ensued.[33]

Conversely, the very existence of the Euro makes currency devaluation impossible for individual nations. This removes the main policy instrument for correcting these competitive variations. Underpinning the rationale of these policies, therefore, has been the notion that Greece – as well as Ireland, Spain and Portugal – must instead recover by means of an internal pricing devaluation to replace the currency devaluation that a single currency straitjackets away as an option. This means increasing unemployment so much that wages fall enough to make the country more internationally competitive. The social costs of such a move, however, are extremely high and the evidence it works thin. Unemployment has doubled in Greece (to 25%), more than doubled in Spain (to 21%) and more than tripled in Ireland (to 15%). The biggest problem facing a government in an austerity-driven economic spiral is how it can service debt repayments from an ever-dwindling source of revenue instead of investing in infrastructure and economic development. In Greece, small businesses (SMEs), the main drivers of a modern economy, have been down at a rate of 5000 per month, not to mention the 100,000 that have gone bankrupt since 2008. Those SME businesses that are actually able to trade and do business cannot grow as interest rates on loans are so prohibitively high in Greece and the Mediterranean, in contrast to what are effective 'negative' interest rates in Germany: a scenario in which German banks are in effect paying the debtor to borrow. These circumstances are rather ironic, considering the EU's treasured ambition to enable the private sector to regenerate employment in Europe.

---

[33] Keynes, *The Economic Consequences of Mr. Churchill*. Essays in Persuasion, Macmillan, London (1931).

Whether in fact it would have been easier for Greece to exit the single currency – aside from the crisis in the Eurozone and its likely contagion effect – and devalue its new currency is an important question to ask when looking at the calamitous effect of a single currency on the southern states of post-financial crisis Europe. EU ministers warned of a sharp increase in Greek debt from such devaluation if it were to have left Eurozone.[34] But the fact is that Greece could not pay this debt, as Argentina did not pay two-thirds of its foreign debt after its devaluation and default in 2001–2002.

Clearly, the Argentinean experience is of relevance. The one-to-one fixed exchange rate between the Argentinean peso and the US dollar from 1991 to 2001 provides an excellent case for judging the costs and benefits of a potential exit of Greece from EMU. Argentina and Greece faced significant differences in their economies. In Argentina, for example, the agricultural sector is quite important whereas in Greece services (e.g. tourism) and the shipping industry are significant in terms of growth and employment. However, both countries share striking similarities in terms of their experience from participating in fixed exchange rate regimes.

Both Argentina and Greece defaulted on their debts after participating in a fixed exchange rate regime for a period of ten years, from 1991 to 2001 and from 2001 to 2011, respectively. The participation of both countries' economies on fixed exchange rate regimes had a very positive impact on their macroeconomic performance in the early stages, followed by catastrophic consequences in the latter stages. Indeed, reductions in inflation and interest rates and prolonged growth rates were the key features of both economies from 1991 to 1997 and from 2000 to 2007, respectively. However, both countries faced severe recessions after participating in these regimes for a period of seven years. At which point, both countries' participation in the fixed exchange rate regimes under perspective and their inability to devalue became a major obstacle in

---

[34] When, on May 6th, 2011, Der Spiegel reported that the Greek government was threatening to stop using the Euro, the currency suffered its worst two-day plunge since December 2008. The report is available online at http://www.spiegel.de/international/europe/athens-mulls-plans-for-new-currency-greece-considers-exit-from-euro-zone-a-761201.html.

restoring their balance of payments deficits. Eventually, inability to meet debt repayments effectively led to disorderly default in Argentina in December 2001 and in an orderly Greece in July–October 2011.

Indeed, a reason for Argentina's rapid recovery was that it was finally freed from adhering to fiscal and monetary policies that stifled growth. For more than three and a half years, Argentina had suffered through one of the deepest recessions of the twentieth century by losing almost 20% of its 1999 output. The Argentines took loans from the IMF and cut spending as poverty and unemployment soared. Then, Argentina defaulted on its foreign debt and cut losses from the dollar. It then grew 63% over the next six years, albeit in an inflationary environment, and received a substantial boost from the devaluation's effect on the trade balance, making its exports far more competitive.[35]

Of course, the infrastructure of the single currency renders the Argentine option impossible for member states such as Greece. The nature of the fixed peg was different in the fixed peso-to-dollar exchange rate regime, involving only two countries that maintained their national currencies. In contrast, the Eurozone involved 17 countries (in 2010) that had replaced their national monies with the single currency, and no one could predict the outcome of a disorderly Grexit, for either Greece or the entire Eurozone. However, notwithstanding the different international context of both crises, the Argentinean experience demonstrated the short-term help that can be provided by devaluation.

In the long-run, the second Argentinean default of 2014 reflects the long-standing implications of reneging in international agreements and the inflationary pressures arising from devaluations/depreciations.

The lesson from both the Argentinean and the Greek experience demonstrates that austerity leads to a severe contraction of economic output, which compromises both nations ability to both function as an economy and to pay the very debts such cuts are meant to facilitate. The realignment of relative prices that Greece and perhaps other countries

---

[35] For more on this subject see Mark Weisbrot and Luis Sandoval, 'Argentina's Economic Recovery: Policy Choices and Implications,' published by the Centre for Economic and Policy Research, October 2007.

need cannot really be achieved within the Euro, because it would either mean significantly higher inflation in the core and/or deflation in southern Europe.[36] According to the economics department of Goldman Sachs, a German inflation of 70% would be needed to make southern Europe competitive without price cuts there. That is 5.5% annual inflation for ten years in Germany or an average inflation of 3.6% for the Eurozone. Both scenarios are incompatible with the mandate of the ECB. It may be that a true recovery in the Eurozone requires an eventual realignment of relative prices – meaning inflation in Germany and/or deflation in southern Europe.[37] Yet the entire region is now faced with deflation as a universal and homogenous economic threat.

---

[36] Krugman, 'Crash of the Bumblebee' *The New York Times*, July 29 (2012).

[37] Nechio, 'Monetary Policy When One Size Does Not Fit All. Federal Reserve Bank of San Francisco' (2011) http://www.frbsf.org/economic-research/publications/economic-letter/2011/june/monetary-policy-europe/ downloaded 25/04/2015. Darvas, and Merler, '-15% to +4%: Taylor-Rule Interest Rates For Euro Area Countries' (2013) http://www.bruegel.org/nc/blog/detail/article/1151-15-percent-to-plus-4-percent-taylor-rule-interest-rates-for-euro-area-countries, downloaded 25/04/2016.

3

The Eurozone Debt Crisis

The sustainability of the European Monetary Union (EMU) has been a question of concern since its foundation and a frequent source of criticism. A default by a Eurozone country on its debt, for example, could initiate a chain of events leading to the demise of EMU.[1] Two different, though not necessarily mutually exclusive, sets of arguments provided the basis for questioning the durability of a monetary union like the EMU. First, there are arguments with a predominantly economic focus.[2] They emphasise differences in market rigidities, particularly in labour markets, amongst the European Union (EU) member economies – a variation which makes some countries' exports highly uncompetitive.[3] It has also been argued that the EU is not an optimal

---

[1] Strobel, 'Leaving EMU: A Real Options Perspective', *Applied Economics*, 37, pp. 1449–1453 (2005).

[2] Friedman, 'The Case for Flexible Exchange Rates', in *Essays in Positive Economics*, 2015. Feldstein, 'EMU and International Conflict' *Foreign Affairs*, 76, pp. 60–74 (1997). Friedman, 'EU to Collapse Within 10 Years', *EU Observer* 17th July (2002). http://euobserver.com/news/6944.

[3] Boltho, A. and Carlin, W. 'EMU's Problems: Asymmetric Shocks or Asymmetric Behavior?' *Comparative Economic Studies*, 55:3, pp. 387–403 (2013).

currency area; hence, labour market rigidities, combined with asymmetric shocks, could potentially foster economic developments that would be politically unacceptable for some of the union member countries, such as excessively high unemployment – at that point, EMU may cease to be politically sustainable and collapse.[4] For example, Friedman (2002) has predicted that

> *The EU and its single currency euro will exist for some 5–10 years and then will just break up. EU Observer 12 July 2002*

The second set of arguments posited that monetary union could not endure without a complimentary process of European political union;[5] Congdon (1998) asserted that

> *EMU could indeed prove to be a catastrophe for the integrationist project. It can work if it leads quickly to a comprehensive scheme of political union. But without European political union, it will prove impractical to the point of impossibility.* (p. 6)

Along the same lines, Issing (2000) observed that

> *There is no example in the history of a lasting monetary union that was not linked to one state.* (p. 28)

Added to this picture is the incomplete nature of the Eurozone, as only 19 EU countries out of 28 have joined. Furthermore, the prospect of creating a European political union, to accommodate monetary union, has influenced the attitude of right-wing governments in Poland and Hungary, which have less appetite to do so now knowing that the Euro can only be successful with closer political union. This has effectively led

---

[4] Feldstein, 'EMU and International Conflict' *Foreign Affairs*, 76, pp. 60–74 (1997).

[5] Congdon, 'A Maoist Leap Forward? The Single Currency and European Political Union' The Selsdon Group: 1–8 (1998). Issing, 'Europe: Political Union though Common Money?' *Economic Affairs*, Occasional Paper 98 (2000). Syrrakos, 'A Reassessment of the Werner Plan and the Delors Report: Why Did They Experience a Different Fate?' *Comparative Economic Studies*, 52:4: 575–588 (2010). doi:10.1057/ces.2010.12.

to an emerging paradox. The long-term permanency of the Euro can only be guaranteed by creating a Eurozone fiscal union that ultimately requires a political one in tandem, which many EU countries openly dislike.[6]

In summary, the current environment features an EU that is tripartite, with three countries opting out from the Euro, nineteen joining and six (Poland, Hungary, Czech Republic, Croatia, Romania and Bulgaria) not joining *at present* but legally required to do so. Further, only Bulgaria out of these six countries wishes to enter at the current juncture or in the near future. This divide is compounded by the splits within the Eurozone, with nations now effectively shoehorned into a core and periphery; or, more colloquially, a North and South.

In the context of this complex structure, proponents of the diagnosis of the need to create a European political union have not identified the salient features of such a union, which the EU must proceed towards if the EMU is to endure. A monetary union can be defined unambiguously, but this is not the case with political union. The rejection of the European Constitution by the French and the Dutch electorates in 2005 and 2006 led to the dismissal of the only concrete proposal put forward so far, that of the creation of a European fiscal union. As a result, it appears that the European Central Bank (ECB) functions in a political vacuum: it is independent of the EU member countries' governments and is constitutionally charged with the responsibility of securing price stability within the union, while restricted in its ability to providing 'lender of last resort' facilities up to March 2015. The ECB determines EU-wide monetary policy, while the member countries' governments retain control of national fiscal policies. Monetary policy is assigned the monetarist objective of price stability, but fiscal measures are still available for more Keynesian counter-cyclical policies – though EMU member countries are subject to the fiscal constraints of the Pact for Stability and Growth. Nevertheless, this results in a stark contradiction in policy paths at the national and European levels. This inherent tension in the

---

[6] Notable exceptions to this are Eichengreen and Wyplotz (2016) that maintain that a banking union and a European deposit guarantee scheme will suffice to ensure the Euro's viability.

Eurozone compromise partly explains the conflict between democratically elected governments – in particular in the South – and the ECB, which is not answerable to the EU electorate but has the power to frustrate policies initiated by national governments. The emergence of these conflicts and the divergence of member countries' objectives have been steadily raising the pressure on the EMU and may push it past breaking point.

Fixed Exchange Rate Regimes – Monetary Union

The exchange rate is the rate at which a currency, e.g. the domestic currency (£), translates or converts to another currency. Broadly, there are two types of exchange rates: the bilateral and the real effective exchange rate. The former expresses the value of the domestic currency in terms of another currency, e.g. 1.26 USD to the £ Sterling. The latter is based on a weighted average of the exchange rates of the most important trading partners of the country under perspective. As a result, the real effective exchange rate provides an objective way of judging the relative strength of the domestic currency against a basket of other currencies. For example, by focusing only on a particular bilateral exchange rate, e.g. the £ Sterling to South African Rand, it is very difficult to assess the impact of the Brexit vote on the £ Sterling's performance. In this way, the effects of an 'outlier' bilateral trend are minimised.

Under flexible exchange rates, the adjustment to an economic shock comes directly from the nominal exchange rate that fluctuates daily in foreign exchange markets, without requiring an immediate adjustment to the price ratio of exports to imports. As a result, the adjustment of the UK economy to the Brexit outcome of the EU Referendum, 23 June 2016, is facilitated by the significant depreciation in the value of the £ Sterling leading to more orders for domestically produced goods and services.

The determinants of the exchange rate should not be seen in isolation. Assume for example there is persistently higher inflation in the UK than in France. This imply means that year-on-year producing the same product in the UK would gradually become more expensive than producing it in France. As a result, sales of the product made in France in international markets will increase, at the expense of the sales of the product made in the UK. This would have a negative impact on the volumes of UK exports, and therefore on the terms of trade, in particular, the current account of the balance of payments. It would also have a negative impact on the UK growth potential. This would cause the value of the pound to depreciate.

As with any product, when the Bank of England supplies more £ pounds to the economy, its value would decrease, assuming constant demand. Increasing the supply of money therefore presumes a free-floating exchange rate. Countries that chose to join a fixed exchange rate regime with at least, another country's currency, surrender monetary independence in the sense that they cannot increase the money supply for domestic policy objectives.

Despite the loss of monetary independence, there are two powerful motives prompting countries to join fixed exchange rate regimes. First, inflation-prone countries have an incentive to peg the value of their own currency to that of a country with an anti-inflationary reputation, such as Germany. Doing so enhances the authorities' anti-inflationary credibility and convinces markets that authorities will not succumb to temptation and engage in 'creating' surprise inflation by printing money, which is incompatible with maintaining the fixed rate. Argentina serves as an example, where rampant inflation in 1989 exceeded three thousand per cent and two thousand per cent the following year! Instead of winning the trust of the markets by building a reputation for low inflation policies, which can take a lengthy period, countries can borrow credibility from their anti-inflationary partner in the fixed exchange rate regime. This is the case, as when a country joins a fixed exchange rate regime it signals to the markets, including foreign exchange markets, of its intention not to increase the money supply, while party to the regime. In order to maintain the fixed rate exchange they cannot engage in expansionary monetary policy, without the consent of their partner(s) in the regime. The more they honour the regime, the more their anti-inflationary stance becomes more credible. Argentina joined a fixed exchange rate regime with the USA in 1991, on a one-to-one conversion rate between the Argentinean peso and the dollar, precisely for that reason. As a result, inflation was reduced to 133% in 1991, to 12% in 1992 and −1.5% in 1993. High inflation also provided the main incentive for Italy to join the Euro.

Second, countries have an incentive to join a fixed exchange rate regime with their biggest trading partners. France, for example, has a strong incentive to fix the value of its currency with that of Germany, as this is its primary export market. However, this incentive alone does not fully justify why both countries have replaced their respective currencies, namely the Franc and the Deutschmark, with the Euro on 1 January 2002. In order to understand why this was the case, we need to focus on trade theory, which identifies three stages of trade relations countries can form:

- First, that of a **Free Trade Area**. The European Free Trade Association (EFTA) is an example, which includes non-EU members Norway and Iceland. A free trade area allows for common internal tariffs and quotas. For example, if the UK and France form a free trade area, there would be common tariffs and quotas for both UK exports to France and French exports to the UK. However, different tariffs and quotas will still apply to UK and French exports to the rest of the world (according to World Trade Organisation rules). This means that there would not be common external tariffs and quotas. The North American Free Trade Area (NAFTA) forms such an arrangement.
- Second, a **Customs Union**. This implies the adoption of both internal and external tariffs and quotas. In relation to the UK and France, moving from a free trade area to a Customs Union would involve both countries agreeing to common internal and external tariffs and quotas. The 1957 Treaty of Rome, a cornerstone of what became the EU, created a Customs Union in the European Economic Community together with a Common Agricultural Policy.
- Third, countries could further their integrated trade relations by forming a **Single Market**. This includes agreeing on common laws

and regulations pertaining the Single Market, in competition policies, in particular industrial policies. Single Markets can also be extended to include coordination of macroeconomic policies and exchange rate policies. In its most advanced form, a Single Market would incorporate common macroeconomic policies and the adoption of a fixed exchange rate regime. The Maastricht Treaty in 1992 created a Single Market in the EU, to function in tandem with the European Monetary System (EMS), a 'quasi' fixed exchange rate regime that was in place since 1979.

The set of all these conditions in a Single Market act to maximise the volumes of trade amongst the participant countries. In this environment, therefore, exchange rate volatility is a barrier towards enhancing the volume of trade, as it reduces the predictability of currency parities and therefore the reliable cost of buying and selling goods and services, and also limits the time horizon of contracts amongst entrepreneurs. Limiting exchange rate volatility is therefore a cornerstone to a functioning Single Market. This leads to the question of which type of exchange rate regime is most appropriate for Single Markets. This also leads to the core difference between the UK and the Eurozone: the UK has maintained its place with the Single Market while also preserving its flexible exchange rate relationship with the Euro countries.

In order to address this dilemma, and consider the most suitable regime within the framework of a Single Market, exchange rate theory becomes relevant. Exchange rate economics and economic theory on monetary unions draw attention to four types of fixed exchange rate regimes. These include

1. A *fixed exchange rate regime*, e.g. European Monetary System 1979–1992/1993–1998.
2. A *free inter-circulation area of national currencies*, e.g. European Monetary Union 1999–2001.
3. A *free inter-circulation area of national currencies and a common currency*.
4. A *monetary union, where a common currency could replace national currencies*, e.g. Euro.

It needs to be noted that the establishment of a monetary union does *not necessarily* imply the automatic adoption of a single currency. But this may be deemed desirable. As stated in the Delors Report (1989):

> The adoption of a single currency, while not strictly necessary for the creation of a monetary union, might be seen – for economic as well as psychological and political reasons – as a natural and desirable further development of the monetary union. (Paragraph 23)

The first type of fixed exchange rate regime involves a high level of cooperation between the participant countries – in particular, their central banks in maintaining the exchange rate parities of the countries' currencies within specified permissible bands of fluctuations. The main operational difficulty encountered in such systems relates to the use of foreign exchange reserves by central banks, while trying to ensure the parities do not violate the upper/lower bands of fluctuations. This of course gives raise to speculative attacks against currencies that funds or traders consider the 'weakest link': that is, that are most likely to violate the lower band of fluctuation due to continuous depreciations, reflecting the poor economic outlook. This is exactly what the UK Bank of England experienced in September 1992 when the pound was subjected to massive speculative attacks, spearheaded by George Soros: the notorious 'Black Wednesday' event, which triggered its ejection from the Exchange Rate Mechanism.[7]

In order to reduce the likelihood of the emergence of such pressures in foreign exchange markets, the participant countries' authorities aim at maintaining public finances in a sound condition.[8] However, asymmetric shocks could potentially destabilise the status quo of a fixed exchange rate regime.[9] Suppose, for example, there are only two

---

[7] De Grauwe, 'European Monetary Unification: A Few Lessons for East Asia' *Scottish Journal of Political Economy*, 63:1, pp. 7–17 (2016). George, *Policy and Politics in European Union*. Oxford University Press (1996).

[8] Gros and Thygesen, *European Monetary Integration: From EMS to EMU*. Third Edition, Longman, London (1998).

[9] Copeland, *Exchange Rates and International Finance*. Prentice-Hall (2008).

countries joining such a regime, e.g. the UK and France. An oil shock could influence both countries' economies in a different way based on their relative dependence on foreign energy. Alternatively, obstacles to the effective management of the regime could have political origins, such as the election of a centre-left government in France, pledging to increase government expenditure to levels considered unsustainable by foreign exchange markets or a referendum in the UK over the country's membership in such a regime.

The justification for austerity is that too many Eurozone countries have lived beyond their means for too long and now need to take responsibility for their profligacy. Reducing or rather eliminating budget deficits would, at least in theory, ensure that countries live within their means. This is often supported by a reduction in public services and is part of the formula for governments to 'balance the books'. Under the watchful eye of the Troika, governments have introduced such measures by slashing welfare and infrastructure budgets: an approach that has fuelled a recessionary spiral that makes the relative sovereign debt burden worse, not better. Internal devaluation in respect of wage cuts, pensions and job losses in overmanned public sectors has not proved sufficient to restore competitiveness failing to promote growth in the rest of the Eurozone.

At the epicentre of this story have been the fortunes of Greece. The announcement of the conservative Greek government, in February 2009, that the Greek *current account deficit* for 2008 had reached 14.3% of Greek GDP signalled the beginning of the crisis in economic terms. However, markets paid little attention at the time – in March they entered rally mode, as the so-called Great Recession came to an end. It took a while for markets to realise, however, that in an environment of extremely tight credit conditions and fixed exchange rates current account deficits would very soon make their way into balance of payments deficits, as capital was rapidly drying out. The condition of EMU nations' current and capital accounts is therefore pivotal to the debt crisis story.

In February 2010, the newly elected Socialist government announced that the *balance of payments deficit* had reached 13.6% rendering the country the weakest link in the Eurozone. The subsequent revision of the deficit to 15.4% later that year only added to this perception of a looming 'Grexit' or the imminent departure of the country from the single currency. The impasse reached in Greek finances was the event that triggered the crisis rather than the cause of it. Markets turned sceptical over the authorities' ability to reduce such a deficit, without being able to devalue significantly, given the political and social obstacles involved in such a process. This change in markets' attitude lead to punitive interest rates in April. The European debt crisis had struck.

On 2 May 2010, the IMF and a partnership of Eurozone nations – with Germany heading the negotiations – agreed to a three-year, €110 billion loan, at an interest rate of 5.5%, relatively high, but far lower than the spiralling value of bond yields. Such a loan was conditional on the imposition of an austerity package without precedent in the tough nature of its terms. To make the mounting Greek debt pile sustainable, it included €30 billion of additional cuts over three years and the privatisation of €50 billion of state assets, including the near-monopoly telecom and electricity operators, the country's two main ports in Piraeus and Thessaloniki, several small islands and its best-capitalised financial asset, Hellenic Postbank. Paul Thomsen, who headed the IMF negotiating mission to Athens, stated in defence of these measures that 'The alternative would be much worse for the Greek people and the Greek leaders know that.'

The Greek public appeared unimpressed by this logic, and the subsequent austerity package was met by massive protests, civil unrest and a national strike. With rating agencies, such as Moody's and Standard and Poor's (S&P), immediately downgrading Greek government bonds even further down the definition of 'junk', the ECB on 3 May announced, in an unprecedented offer of support, that it would accept as collateral all debt instruments that were guaranteed by the Greek government, suspending the minimum credit-rating threshold for all such debts in an effort to maintain the solvency of its banks. Such a proactive shift in policy came from an institution otherwise grounded in draconian monetarist principles.

The features of the first Greek bailout (May 2010) are worth considering. It included bilateral agreements between the country and the other 16 Eurozone countries at the time. The recognition of EU institutional deficiencies led subsequently to the creation of the European Financial Stability Facility (EFSF) aiming to accommodate the needs of the Irish, Portuguese and Greek (second and third) bailouts and ensuring the prompt payments of these three countries' matured bonds, while securing their continued place in EMU. However, the lack of these arrangements in 2010 meant that the rate of interest demanded by capital markets to buy Greek debt reached punitive levels, leading to the need for a second bailout involving a 'haircut' of private Greek bondholders. A 'haircut' means in this context losses to bondholders of Greek sovereign debt.

The financial assistance to Greece, as part of the first bailout, equalled €110 billion, which exceeded 60% of Greece's GDP at the time – out of which the Greek Loan Facility in 2010 provided €52.9 billion. The ECB offered help equal to €27.1 billion, and the IMF offer equalled €21 billion. Out of the €52.9 billion of the Greek Loan Facility, Germany has contributed €22.66 billion. Subsequently, in 2012 the EFSF contributed €151.6 billion and further €86 billion were offered under the terms of the third bailout package. This brought the total aid to €336.6 billion, as €11 billion were transferred from the second to the third bailout package.

Two additional issues need to be borne in mind in relation to external financial assistance to Greece. First, the funds for the second and the third Greek bailouts received from the ESFS/ESM have not been raised from tax revenue but from bond issuance, on behalf of the rest of the Eurozone countries. That is to say, not a single cent has been provided by levying higher taxation in Germany, Austria or the Netherlands. Second, 89% of the total help (€299.6 billion out of €336.6 billion) has, in effect, been received by European (French in particular) banks to roll over Greek debt. This leaves only €37 billion that have reached/will reach the real sector of the economy in Greece.

Second, as only €22.66 billion was raised by higher taxation in Germany, and with the country's labour market equal to 40 million people, the help comes down to €566.5 for each German worker (the estimation excludes pensioners). This is a cost *only* if Greece defaults and does not repay. No help was raised via higher taxation for Ireland and

Portugal either. While this help is vital for Greece, Ireland and Portugal to serve their debts, it is against the background of immense current account surpluses that Germany has accumulated since 2009. Obviously, these surpluses can be partly attributed to a very efficient labour force, efficient production lines, IT, strong industrial base and a social consensus that brings together the government (central and local), academia, financial institutions and trade unions. However, the surpluses also emanate from the country's Eurozone membership.[10] The single currency ensures that other Eurozone countries cannot devalue, and the low value of the Euro makes German products very competitive in international markets. As a result, in 2014 Germany registered a record current account surplus equal to €215.3 billion or, alternatively, equal to 7.4% of GDP. In 2015, current account surpluses were further increased to 8.5% of GDP. To put in context, just in 2014 alone Germany's surpluses were almost ten times higher than the country's financial assistance to Greece (€215.3 billion in relation to €22.66 billion).[11]

The first Greek bailout (2010) was followed by turbulence in financial markets. It was only a question of who was next in line to suffer the consequences of high deficits without the ability to devalue. Investors did not have to wait long, as the Irish government's rescue plan for Anglo Irish Bank plus recapitalisation of Allied Irish and the Bank of Ireland led to the balance of payments *deficit* ballooning to 33% of 2010, causing a massive increase in the country's debt-to-GDP ratio. Eventually, this led to Ireland becoming party to a bailout agreement.

Hence, for reasons different from Greece – primarily having to do with the collapse of the Irish housing market, causing immense capital losses to banks – a bailout of (eventually) €85 billion was agreed in autumn 2010 between the Troika and the Irish government that guaranteed repayments on Irish debt from 2011 to 2014. The value of the bailout came to almost 50% of the Irish GDP at the time, ensuring Irish

---

[10] Cesaratto, 'The Implications of TARGET2 in the European Balance of Payments Crisis and Beyond' *European Journal of Economics and Economic Policy: Intervention*, 10:3, pp. 359–382 (2013).

[11] Syrrakos, D. (2017) 'On the Greek National Debt' *Economic Review*, 34:5, Forthcoming.

debt repayments for a period of three years. It differed from the first Greek bailout as it did not involve the privatisation of Irish assets. In the spring of 2011, following the first Greek and the Irish bailouts, Portugal officially requested financial assistance from the EU. The outcome was the Portuguese bailout of €78 billion, equal to 42% of the Portuguese GDP at the time, ensuring Portuguese debt repayments for a period of two years.

While negotiations were taking place for the Portuguese bailout, and the first Greek bailout did not seem to deliver the anticipated results, financial markets became very wary of Spanish financial institutions' exposure to Portuguese debt. If Spanish banks were to be placed at the spotlight of capital markets, given their capital losses following the collapse of the Spanish housing market, the Troika could have ended up also bailing out Spain. However, there were not enough funds, readily available at least, to rescue the fourth largest Eurozone economy. As alarm bells rang on both sides of the Atlantic, markets started questioning the exposure of the French banks to Spanish and Italian debt. It soon became obvious there were simply not enough funds to bailout both Spain and Italy – and so the threat of widespread contagion heralded the broad adoption of the term 'the Eurozone debt crisis'.

The stakes could have hardly been higher. Faced with the potential collapse of the entire Euro area, and as capital flights from the periphery to the core Eurozone countries were under way, financial assistance was provided to the Spanish financial institutions in need. This in aid of rebuilding their capital, while the Spanish banking system was restructured, with a 'bad' bank created to absorb 'junk housing assets' from the Spanish banking institutions. A total of €100 billion became available, but only €44 billion were eventually absorbed by Spanish banks.

It has to be clarified that this financial assistance to Spain did not come in the form of a bailout, but was provided by rescue ECB financial lines – the difference being that bailout funds have to be added to Greek, Irish and Portuguese national debts. Financial assistance to Spain was not added to the Spanish debt load, given that could have prompted Spain to request a bailout.

However, financial assistance to Spain by the ECB elevated the Euro debt crisis and carried out immense consequences for a variety of reasons. First, the ECB seemed to act as the lender of last resort to the Spanish financial sector and thus to the Spanish government – exceeding its stated and long-held mandate as a monetarist institution. If this were the case, why was not help on the same grounds, provided to Ireland less than a year earlier? Questions were raised about double standards – between small and big Eurozone countries by EU institutions and between the dogma attached to the bailout policies and their effectiveness. All this has led to questions about the entire structure of the Eurozone and its supporting institutions, about the lack of appropriate institutional arrangements, such as a fiscal union, and ultimately about the surpluses accumulated in the North Eurozone countries. The questions are pertinent to the entire crisis but unanswered to date.

The first Greek bailout did not salvage the situation for long. Following the bailout to Portugal, in May 2011, it was evident that the economic crisis in Greece had become so severe that the country would be unable to meet its fiscal goals even for the prior aid package. A bilateral EU–IMF audit in June, which called for even more cuts, provoked S&P, the credit rating agency, to downgrade Greece's sovereign debt rating to CCC, the very lowest in the world, and making a default or debt write-down appear inevitable.[12] With major stock exchanges round the world consequently reeling, an extraordinary summit of EU leaders in July in Brussels extended the Greek loan repayment schedule – which they also extended to the Irish and Portuguese – from seven years to fifteen, cut the interest rate to 3.5% and approved the construction of a new €109 billion aid package from the IMF to manage the 'exceptional and unique situation of Greece'. All EU area member states not under special assistance programmes were also required to reduce their deficits to under 3% by 2013.[13]

The situation did not improve under these terms. The brutal recession being endured by Greece, which steadily intensified under the austerity

---

[12] http://www.bloomberg.com/news/2011-06-13/greece-s-long-term-rating-cut-to-ccc-by-s-p-on-outlook-for-restructuring.html.

[13] http://www.european-council.europa.eu/home-page/highlights/a-common-response-to-the-crisis-situation.aspx?lang=en.

programme, made its mounting debt pile harder to pay – and not easier in the way the bailout agreements had intended. A 2009 recession of 3.1% was followed by a 4.9% dip in 2010 and a 7.1% collapse in 2011 – numbers exceeded only by Libya and Yemen.[14]

Unsurprisingly, over 100,000 people took to the streets against these measures in front of the Parliament building on 29 May. Greek debt continued to rise and in the summer of 2011 peaked at €340 billion. In the wake of this spiral, and increased talk of a 'Grexit', or Greek exit from the Eurozone, it became impossible to salvage the country's finances without a substantial 'haircut' to the value of its bonds – the often-used wording for what was nothing less than a default on a large portion of future payments.

On 26 October 2011, with European equities in bear market territory, Eurozone leaders and the IMF came to an agreement with principal European banks to accept a 50% write-off of 'notional Greek debt held by private investors' – the equivalent of €100 billion – while also guaranteeing an additional €100 billion in a multi-financing programme by the EU and IMF.[15] This Private Sector Involvement (PSI) or debt-restructuring deal was ratified by the Euro group in February 2012, with the European System of Central Banks agreeing to buy Greek bonds at this debased rate until 2020. At that point, with the debt crisis still spiralling, the European Union Council abandoned its earlier decision in favour of a more severe plan – one that was initially 50%, but went on to reach 76% of the value of holdings of Greek sovereign debt. Private investors and financial institutions were also forced to accept an additional devaluation of 53.5% on the face value of Greek government bonds, which added to the haircut in October brought the overall loss to just over 75%. This decision required, and received, the unanimous agreement of all Eurozone governments.

---

[14] According to data compiled by the World Bank: http://data.worldbank.org/indicator/NY.GDP.MKTP.KD.ZG.

[15] A summary of the summit meeting was published on the 26th October 2011, and is available online at http://www.consilium.europa.eu/uedocs/cms_data/docs/pressdata/en/ec/125645.pdf.

Fiscal Consolidation and Austerity

The biggest sovereign debt restructuring deal in history culminated in Greece wiping some €100 billion in debt off its books. It effectively asked – or rather compelled – private bondholders to forgive bad debt on a scale never before seen by a sovereign nation. The final terms of the deal forced a 75% haircut on its creditors, an event factored in by Standard and Poor's when they downgraded Greece's sovereign credit rating to 'selective default' – the first Eurozone country in its 13-year history to receive such a rating.[16] Holders of €177 billion of the €206 billion of PSI-eligible debt securities, totalling 83.5% of the bondholders, signed up to the deal.[17] Banks and large pension funds fell meekly in line. Those who did not respond to the bond-exchange offer, or the holders of around €29 billion of bonds – mostly hedge funds – which actively opposed it, were forced to accept these terms.

Whether this arrangement constituted a debt 'default' in the technical sense is a matter of debate. Technically, the nation never missed a bond payment, but this achievement may be a purely semantic one. The International Swaps and Derivatives Association, a collection of large financial institutions, euphemistically described Greece's debt deal as a 'credit event', triggering payouts on CDS contracts associated with a Greek default.[18] But, whatever the outside world would call it, panic did not ensue. French, German and American banks that held Greek debt did not topple, markets did not crash, and contagion did not spread. Yields on troubled sovereign debtors, such as Spain and Italian, ticked up only slightly. The CDS trigger that resulted from a technical default of Greece at least appeared to be a non-event.

Yet the consequences of the Greek bailout for the management of the Eurozone were substantial. As the debt-to-GDP ratio mounted, the recession deepened and the crisis magnified, the Troika became willing to go to

---

[16] http://online.wsj.com/news/articles/SB10001424052970204603004577271383829531576.
[17] http://www.iif.com/press/press+239.php.
[18] http://www.bloombergview.com/articles/2012-03-12/credit-default-swap-time-bomb-failed-to-go-off-over-greece-view.

more extreme lengths to, as they saw it, contain the malaise. The trajectory of the measures taken became ever more aggressive: first in progressively deeper austerity cuts and enforced privatisations and then in the expansion of these programmes to include a direct loss to private bondholders in what was a barely disguised payment default. Each of these steps created its own new set of problems for the Eurozone. In short, austerity added to the likelihood of default, which led to increasingly misguided calls for more austerity. This led to a self-reinforcing downwards spiral.

At least one member of the Troika noted the dangers of the path taken here. In a relatively frank internal report published in June 2013 – released only after its contents were leaked and reported by the *Wall Street Journal* – the IMF admitted to major mistakes in its handling of the bailout of Greece, arguing that it bent the rules on its criteria for debt sustainability, underestimated the damage its prescriptions of austerity would inflict on the economy and made overly optimistic projections on the Greek recovery.[19,20] On the latter point, the report acknowledged that 'there were... notable failures. Market confidence was not restored, the banking system lost 30% of its deposits, and the economy encountered a much-deeper-than-expected recession with exceptionally high unemployment.'[21] It also acknowledged the possibility that 'there is a habitual tendency of Fund programs to be over-optimistic on growth until the economy reaches a bottom (and thereafter to underestimate the recovery),' and at least partly underestimated the impact of fiscal shock.[22]

Regarding the debt management programmes of 2010–2012, the report noted several problems posed by the approach taken: that the Troika arrangement was an entirely novel one in 2010; that public debt was still expected to rise, particularly under the fixed exchange rate imposed by the Euro; and, most controversially, that 'The programme required the IMF's rules for exceptional access to be modified,' with the

---

[19] http://online.wsj.com/news/articles/SB10001424127887324299104578527202781667088.
[20] International Monetary Fund, 'Greece: Ex Post Evaluation of Exceptional Access under the 2010 Stand-By Arrangement,' (Washington DC, June 2013), found at http://www.imf.org/external/pubs/ft/scr/2013/cr13156.pdf.
[21] Op. cit., p. 1.
[22] Op. cit., pp. 22–23.

criteria of 'a high probability that public debt is sustainable in the medium term' being essentially abandoned. The result of this was 'even with implementation of agreed policies, uncertainties were so significant that staff was unable to vouch that public debt was sustainable with high probability.'[23] A point to be added is the near impossibility of a country supporting such a high debt ratio without undergoing an actual economic depression. Doubts about the effectiveness of austerity measures, or the Greek ability to implement them, were exacerbated by a leaked report from the European Commission, which suggested that Greek debt could remain at 160% of GDP by 2020 without substantial additional aid from as early as 2015.[24]

Essentially, the IMF changed its rules to allow countries to get 'exceptional access' to its credit lines. Its actions on the grounds of the extremity of the crisis and the domino threat posed to the Eurozone by a Greek debt default: 'Given the dangers of contagion, the fund judges the programme to have been a necessity, even though the IMF had misgivings about debt sustainability.' In these terms, therefore, the bailout programme was described as a success, despite its myriad problems: 'Greece remained in the Euro area, which was its stated political preference. Spillovers that might have had a severe effect on the global economy were relatively well contained, aided by multilateral efforts to build firewalls'.[25] Furthermore, despite the probability of Greece being unable to manage her debt pile, 'staff favoured going ahead with exceptional access because of the fear that spill overs from Greece would threaten the Euro area and the global economy'.[26] Poul Thomsen, the IMF's lead negotiator in the bailout talks, stated in reference to the signing of the deal in 2010 – despite the lack of any debt relief – that 'If we were in the same situation... we would have done the same thing again.'[27] Thomsen offered a commitment by European leaders to do

---

[23] Op. cit., pp. 9–10.

[24] http://www.nytimes.com/2012/02/21/world/europe/agreement-close-on-a-bailout-for-greece-european-finance-ministers-say.html.

[25] IMF (2013)., p. 1.

[26] Op. cit., p. 10.

[27] http://online.wsj.com/news/articles/SB10001424127887324299104578527202781667088.

whatever it takes to support Greece, Portugal and Ireland with their bailout programmes 'even if the headwinds are stronger than expected.'[28] Christine Lagarde, the Managing Director of the IMF, commented in a separate interview that 'What happened at the time, and it's much easier with the benefit of hindsight, is that not all criteria of exceptional access as defined at the time were satisfied' but that 'there was a crying need at the time for support'; however, she also acknowledged that the IMF's experience 'will probably lead us to reassessing the exceptions to the exceptional access criteria' and that it was aiming to make its debt assessments more rigorous.[29] The logic deployed here is therefore that the desperate nature of the situation justified not only the moves made but any and all mistakes inherent to them. Such questionable reasoning could be used to justify almost any political or financial decision taken in a difficult economic period.

Between 2010 and 2015, the sovereign debt crisis has required three controversial bailouts for Greece, one bailout for Ireland, Portugal and Cyprus, and emergency financial assistance to Spain. Ireland exited the programme in December 2013, after registering remarkable progress, whereas Portugal exited the programme in the spring of 2014. These policies were successful only to the extent they have maintained the Eurozone intact, as they involved austerity measures so extreme they have caused mass riots on the streets and tense games of political negotiation. The muddled and complicated steps towards its resolution have informed national, federal and monetary policy.[30] The fiscal consolidation in Eurozone since 2010 has led to an unprecedented peacetime reduction in peripheral countries' GDP. In 2015, GDP in Greece had collapsed by 26% of its 2009 value. As a result, real per capita GDP in Greece in 2014 was 1% lower than 1999. By 2014, the Irish economy had suffered a cumulative output loss of 9.6% of its 2010 GDP. In Italy, the output loss from 2008 to 2014 reached 12%, whereas in Spain it

---

[28] http://www.ft.com/cms/s/0/78ab958c-c4db-11e0-9c4d-00144feabdc0.html#axzz39oHfUSLk.
[29] http://online.wsj.com/news/articles/SB10001424127887324299104578527202781667088.
[30] Stockhammer, 'The Euro Crisis and Contradictions of Neoliberalism in Europe' Kingston University, Economic Discussion Papers, 2 (2013).

reached 7.5% following a double dip recession in 2009 and 2012. In Portugal, the output loss between 2010 and 2013 equalled 7.5%.

As a result, unemployment levels have reached double digits on average (11.4%) in the European Union and extreme levels in the South – in excess of 25% (with youth employment standing at nearly 40% in both Greece and Spain). Cuts in welfare expenditure, wages and public employment level brought on by austerity restrictions have worsened the living conditions of people dramatically and resulted in a severe economic contraction in much of the South. This is a public discourse about the imbalances within the Eurozone which characterises the divide rhetorically as the problem of 'laziness against effort' or 'Mediterranean corruption' against the integrity and principle of the North.

On the other hand, real per capita GDP in Germany in the same year was 19.4% higher than in 1999. This reflects massive economic benefits accrued to Germany. Such is the scale of the increase that it would be hard to attribute it solely to improvements in the German economy and not at all to the country's participation in the Euro. Indeed, in 2013 Germany registered a current account surplus equal to €189.2 billion, exceeding that of China by 176.7%. In 2014, Germany registered a record current account surplus equal to €215.3 billion or, alternatively, equal to 7.4% of GDP. In 2015, current account surpluses in Germany were further increased to a staggering 8.5% of GDP. On top of that, the country's exports are receiving a further boost from the ECB's Quantitative Easing (QE) programme that commenced in April 2015, which has caused a reduction in the value of the Euro.

This all warrants the observation that although North Eurozone countries are assisting Greece, Ireland and Portugal the help comes only to a proportion of one year's worth of German current account surpluses. Combined with the relative trends of real per capita GDP, it becomes clear that the benefits of the increase in intra-EMU trade since 1999 have not been evenly distributed – if distributed they were at all as discussed in the McKinsey Report (2015).

The creation of the Euro has led to very significant increases in intra-European volumes of trade. However, due to the competitiveness gap between the 'North and South' of the monetary system, the benefits from that enhanced trade have been unevenly distributed. The policies pursued since 2010 as a remedy to this impasse have led to a reversal of the competitiveness gap between the two halves of the Eurozone.[31] This gradual reduction was both based on, and has led to, the collapse of effective demand in southern Europe.[32] If the austerity-driven policies that catalysed this trend continue apace for the near future then most likely the competitiveness gap would be significantly reduced or, as in the case of Ireland, be eliminated.[33]

However, improving competitiveness has come at an unprecedented economic and social cost. The collapse in aggregate demand has increased countries' debt ratios as a proportion of their respective GDP.

As all 'South' EMU countries and Ireland have pursued unprecedented fiscal cuts, causing a reduction in industrial orders in Germany, a process likely to be strengthened by Brexit, it is very difficult to identify new markets for EMU products. The case of Spain provides an excellent example that balancing budgets prior to a recession does not guarantee a smooth fiscal consolidation, if drastic fiscal cuts are applied in a very short time span. The Spanish national debt stood at 45% in 2006. It would most likely exceed 100% in 2016. It violated the 60% benchmark only in the beginning of 2010. A reduction in aggregate demand is quite natural amidst a process of fiscal consolidation aimed at restoring the sustainability of public finances. If, however, the dampening effects on output from reducing government expenditure are significantly underestimated, as it appears to be the case,[34] then the results produced may not be the anticipated ones.

The German authorities enforce policies that aim to rectify the lack of economic convergence of the countries that participated in the 'large

---

[31] O'Rourke and Taylor, 'Cross of Euros' *Journal of Economic Perspectives*, 27:3, pp. 167–192 (2013).

[32] Gros, 'Macroeconomic Imbalances in the Euro Area: Symptom or Cause of the Crisis?' Centre for European Policy Studies, Policy Brief, No. 226, Brussels (2012).

[33] Centre for Economic Policy Research, 'Rebooting the Eurozone: Step I – Agreeing a Crisis Narrative' 'Policy Insight, No. 85. Centre for Economic Policy Research-CEPR (2015).

[34] Blanchard, O., Furceri, D. and Pescatori, A. 'A Prolonged Period of Low Real Interest Rates?' In Teuling, C. and Baldwin, R. (eds). *Secular Stagnation: Facts, Causes and Cures*. London: Centre for Economic Policy Research (2014).

EMU' since its creation.[35] The pre-1999 lack of competitiveness in the weaker economies of the Eurozone has to be rectified. This goes at the core of the economic debate in the single currency region. Germany does not simply 'enforce' a policy aiming to reduce current account deficits: it enforces its own growth export-orientated model to the whole of the Eurozone. As this model seems to be the only one vindicated by the credit crunch in 2007–2008, accentuating Germany's economic dominance in Europe, it equipped German authorities with a 'legitimacy' for its enforcement of hard austerity policies on the South.

This, however, is not one of the original objectives of the single currency. The Eurozone was created to complete the Single Market: not to accelerate Europe, and especially Germany, as the main exporting power in the global economy and nor to promote the reserve currency use of the Euro. The contrast with the economic policies pursued in the USA is striking. The Obama administration managed to restore consumer confidence.[36] If all major economies, including the USA, adopted policies similar to the ones adopted in the Eurozone, then the current slow down on global growth will be difficult to reverse. In addition, this policy places the recovery of the European economy under risk in particular in the light of the slowdown in Chinese growth. India seems to be the only remaining BRICS (Brazil, Russia, India, China and South Africa) country with sustainable economic growth.[37] The moderate decline in Chinese growth rates has already had a negative impact on German exports.

As a result, Germany is jeopardising the recovery of the European economy for the second time in the past two decades. First, in 1990–1991, when huge increases in government expenditure to the eastern regions of the reunified country led to a sharp increase in the rate of inflation, the German authorities responding by increasing the rate of interest in order to

---

[35] Gros, 'Macroeconomic Imbalances in the Euro Area: Symptom or Cause of the Crisis?' Centre for European Policy Studies, Policy Brief, No. 226, Brussels (2012).
[36] OECD Interim Economic Outlook: Global Growth Warnings: Weak Trade Financial Distortions, September 2016.
[37] OECD, 'Global Growth Warning: Weak Trade Financial Distortions', Interim Economic Outlook, 2016.

counter the inflationary pressures, and thereby exporting recession to the rest of the countries in the EMS.[38] Second, German intransigence has led to an unprecedented collapse of aggregate demand in the southern Eurozone, when the opposite is required for the revival of these countries' economies.

The subsequent reduction in real and nominal GDP growth, seen as natural in the process of fiscal consolidation by German officials, would most likely endanger one of the successes of the single currency, namely that of enhancing business cycle convergence from 1999 to 2009. When the Euro was adopted business cycle divergence was thought off as the main obstacle to its viability.[39] For example, Artis and Zhang noted 'we find that the European business cycle is a more elusive phenomenon than we might have expected; whilst some European countries seem to "stick together", there are many which do not.'[40] The remarkable success of the single currency in facilitating business cycle synchronicity is now undermined by the austerity policies enforced in the debt-ridden nations of the South: hammering the growth potential of the Eurozone and provoking a hard divergence in the business cycle of the different states, depending on their respective fortunes. If this split persists in the long run, then the longevity of the EMU is far from certain.

Following the financial crash of 2008, European nations have been busy restructuring and rebalancing their economies, with varying success. Substantial sovereign and bank debt led the Eurozone to fall into a prolonged recession in 2011 as the extent of its problems became fully aware. This is in contrast to the far stronger growth rates being seen in the United Kingdom and the USA. Furthermore, deflation is now a severe and rising threat to the entire Eurozone. The question has been ceaselessly asked since 2010: how and in what form the region can

---

[38] Gros and Thygesen, *European Monetary Integration: From EMS to EMU*. Longman, London (1998).

[39] Artis and Zhang, 'International Business Cycles and the ERM: Is There a European Business Cycle?' *Oxford Economic Papers* 51, pp. 1–16 (1997). Artis, 'Should the UK Join EMU?' *National Institute Economic Review* 171, pp. 70–81 (2000).

[40] Artis, M. and Zhang, W. 'International Business Cycles and the ERM: Is There a European Business Cycle?' *International Journal of Finance and Economics*, 2:1, pp. 1–16 (1997).

survive? Since then the mood for an 'austerity'-based rescue programme has changed dramatically, and the effectiveness of this approach in achieving real growth and debt recovery in the Eurozone is even being questioned by the IMF – its proponent for financial crises round the globe for decades.

Clearly, what has become so urgently at stake since the beginning of the debt crisis in 2010 is not only the survival of the single currency but the entire growth model that they will have to follow to maintain any kind of economic coherence. Currently, Germany imposes its own export-orientated model to the rest EMU member countries, which reflects, as discussed, a significant departure from the policies adopted in the past.

These policies conflict heavily with the objectives pursued by the Obama administration in the USA, in tandem with the Federal Reserve Bank under governors Ben Bernanke and Janet Yellen.[41] Since 2007, the increase in the USA balance of payments deficits means they can no longer absorb shocks to the international economy, while the policies enforced by Germany are contributing to further destabilisation of international monetary relations as they contribute to a continuous dampening of aggregate demand in the global economy.[42] The German-imposed export-led EMU model could potentially provide an answer to the economic malaise of the Eurozone (and the EU in general) only in an environment of sustained global economic growth. This could not have been the case had the USA and China pursued the same policies.

An Alternative Approach

The EMU and its institutions are the outcome of a compromise between France and Germany. It is a compromise which reflects both country's perception over the degree of economic convergence required prior to

---

[41] Wyplosz, C. (2016) 'The Eurozone Crisis: Too Few Lessons Learned' http://voxeu.org/article/eurozone-crisis-too-few-lessons-learned.

[42] Lucarelli, 'German Neomercantilism and the European Sovereign Debt Crisis' *Journal of Post-Keynesian Economics*, 34:2, pp. 205–224 (2012).

participating in a monetary union.[43] France views monetary integration as sufficient for countries to join a currency union. It also believes that participation in such a union will provide the necessary macroeconomic framework for countries to grow over and above those who have not joined.[44] Germany, on the other hand, firmly argued that enhanced growth can only follow the attainment of a high level of economic integration *prior* to the creation of the monetary union.[45]

The EMU, in its current form, consists of a union based on the French-monetarist paradigm. The Maastricht Treaty criteria, as strict as they were for some countries in 1992, were not leading to a framework that could ensure economic convergence either before or after participating in a monetary union. Monetary integration was a prerequisite for joining as reflected by the five Maastricht Treaty convergence criteria.[46] From the moment high-debt countries, such as Belgium, Ireland, Greece and Italy, were granted accession to EMU and countries with low productivity and competitiveness such as Spain and Portugal (that had continuously resorted to devaluations in the past in order to restore competitiveness losses) joined, the region became one fundamentally lacking in economic integration – with economies increasingly locked onto divergent paths.[47] The reaction to the policies enforced by Germany in the South, apart from the brutal social costs, comes from the strong conviction of these countries' electorates that they are the 'wrong' ones, whose profligate spending policies require punishment.

The main purpose of the terms attached to the Eurozone bailouts was to restore productivity after the global recession. Put simply, the idea at their heart has always been that too many Eurozone nations have lived beyond their means for too long and now need to take responsibility for

---

[43] Syrrakos, 'The Franco–German Alliance and Its Role in the Process of European Monetary Integration, 1944–2010 – Lessons for Today' *Olsztyn Economic Journal*, 11:2, pp. 119–135 (2016).

[44] Szasz, *The Road to European Monetary Union*. Macmillan Press Ltd. (1999).

[45] Ungerer, *A Concise History of European Monetary Integration: From EPU to EMU*. Quorum Books (1997).

[46] Treaty on European Union, *Maastricht Treaty*. Luxemburg, Office for Publications of the European Communities (1992).

[47] Artis, 'Should the UK Join EMU?' *National Institute Economic Review* 171, pp. 70–81 (2000).

their profligacy. Budget retrenchment will ensure that countries live within their means while deregulation and privatisation of 'bloated' public services will make them leaner, fitter and more competitive economies. From a creditor's point of view – the view that European Union authorities have apparently adopted – a country that has accumulated too much debt must be punished so as not to encourage 'bad behaviour'. A chief Merkel economic advisor went as far as to say that emergency bailouts to Greece and future EU aid recipients should bring with it harsh penalties. But punishing an entire country for the past mistakes of some of its leaders, while morally satisfying to some, is hardly the basis for sound policy. Indeed, it is worth noting in this respect the special irony that France and Germany were amongst the first countries to break the Stability and Growth Pact (SGP) – an agreement which forbids member states to have more than 3% of budget deficit to GDP, while Spain and Ireland ran surpluses before the 2008 crisis. Germany was in breach of the deficit/debt rule in 1998–1999, 2002–2005 and 2008–2010. Such a fact sits ill at ease with the unyielding rhetoric from the two countries about the indulgent and dissolute behaviour of a profligate South.

An alternative approach that actually aims to resolve the EMU debt crisis has to address the issue of economic divergence in an environment of pre-existing monetary unification. The austerity-driven approach to current account deficits does not facilitate a return to sustainable growth levels. Countries have become competitive at the price of lower living standards for years to come through a process of painful internal devaluation.

In effect, Germany has ended up southern countries for participating in the EMU without prior economic convergence – and doing so by enforcing policies that achieve the opposite. Ironically, this is an approach completely different to the one adopted in the German Democratic Republic after unification, when huge transfer of resources took place to increase investment and create employment.[48] It is

---

[48] Gros and Thygesen, *European Monetary Integration: From EMS to EMU*. Longman, London (1998).

arguably that legacy that influenced German politicians in the early and mid-1990s, when they promised that participation in the single currency will not require German taxpayers to bail out high indebted countries in the European south. This background adds to the existing moral hazard in the Eurozone, as France and Germany were the first two countries that violated the SGP during 2002–2005 but were not punished.[49]

The incomplete nature of the Eurozone becomes apparent when compared to the US dollar. This, comprising a unit of currency for all 51 states of the USA, forms a far more advanced monetary union as it is coupled with a broad fiscal union. The USA, with a federal budget accounting for 20–22% of the GDP of the USA, affords significantly more room for manoeuvring; in the case of regional asymmetric shocks, federal funds are directed to those regions or states in need.[50]

In the USA, the Federal Reserve Bank is the lender of last resort for the US government if required. This role has been performed by the Federal during and after the Great Recession, with QE programmes initiated from 2009. On the other hand, the European Central Bank (ECB) only engaged in Quantitative Easing in March 2015, as the Maastricht Treaty prohibited the purchase of Eurozone countries' debt by the more monetarily conservative ECB.[51]

Given the size of the Federal Budget, the US national fiscal automatic stabilisers – Welfare payments, e.g. unemployment benefits and tax revenue – are much more effective than Eurozone's automatic stabilisers. This simply means that the size of the Federal Budget maximises the effectiveness of the US government's spending power in terms of creating employment in US regions or states with high unemployment at the same time as alleviating the destructive effects of economic shocks in these regions/states. Other advantages for the USA are the status of the

---

[49] Centre for Economic Policy Research, 'Rebooting the Eurozone: Step I – Agreeing a Crisis Narrative' Policy Insight, No. 85. Centre for Economic Policy Research-CEPR (2015).
[50] HM Treasury, 'The United States as a Monetary Union; EMU Study' Stationery Office (2003b).
[51] Micossi, 'The Monetary Policy of the European Central Bank (2002–2015)', CEPS Special Report, No. 109 (2015).

US dollar as a reserve currency and significantly the location and nature of the US financial markets, located in New York.[52]

With its strictly monetarist mandate, the ECB has always shunned the kind of quantitative easing so eagerly deployed by the US Federal Reserve. And yet, to save the Eurozone from dissolution, the ECB has adopted measures that far exceed its original mandate and are beyond any previous conception of its proper role.[53] To help bolster the Eurozone's economy, Mario Draghi has kept interest rates low and used cheap-rate long-term loans to pump liquidity into European lenders, promising do 'whatever it takes' to save the currency bloc. In 2014, the ECB began its own QE programme to try to combat potential deflation and jolt sagging growth in the Eurozone (ironically, just as the Federal Reserve in the USA ends its own). This has contributed to the fact that the Euro's value against the dollar has been sinking to levels last seen four years ago. It has, however, resulted exports becoming more competitive: a boon at least for the German economy.

The other major institution of the Troika, the IMF, had also gone a long way to change its tune on the economic path for Europe. Faced with low growth in the global economy, and especially the Eurozone, the IMF has urged governments to start spending again to buoy growth. This supreme *volte face* comes as the evidence piles up that austerity – at least in IMF and Troika – espoused formulation – has run into the ground as a strategy for dealing with debt. 'The global economy faces the prospect of prolonged subpar growth, accompanied by high unemployment and rising inequality,' Christine Lagarde said ahead of the autumn 2014 meetings of the IMF and the World Bank. While she still stressed the need for fiscal discipline, Lagarde strongly suggested a shift in the IMF's focus towards investment and spending to boost economies across the globe. Therefore, Lagarde argues, 'a much higher premium needs to be put across the membership on policies aimed at decisively raising today's actual and tomorrow's potential growth.' In particular, this includes 'more

---

[52] HM Treasury, 'The Five Tests Framework: EMU Study' Stationery Office (2003a). HM Treasury, 'The United States as a Monetary Union; EMU Study' Stationery Office (2003b).
[53] Micossi, 'The Monetary Policy of the European Central Bank (2002–2015)', CEPS Special Report, No. 109 (2015).

growth-friendly fiscal policies' that would 'support job market reforms'.[54] The IMF may technically be the subordinate partner in the Troika, but it is the one that has been calling the shots for the Greek economy these past four years, and it is the one in charge of putting numbers on the page. It repeatedly projected economic recoveries for 2011, 2012 and 2013 that did not materialise. Wages and salaries are estimated to have declined by almost 30% between 2010 and 2016, but this has not been enough to make Greek exports significantly more competitive.[55] Exports have remained weak and have not come close to compensating for the fiscal tightening and reduced domestic private spending. The strategy of 'internal devaluation' has not yet worked for Greece nor – according to the IMF's data and analysis – for the Eurozone as whole.[56]

The IMF was already admitting as early as in June 2013 that it failed to realise the damage caused by the degree of austerity imposed on Greece. This was only three months after imposing draconian bail-in terms on the Cypriots as the price for their Troika rescue programme. The latest challenge following the shockwaves produced by the Brexit decision comes from the Italian banking crisis – where bank shares dived to new lows – requiring government intervention which would likely breach state aid rules.[57]

What makes this different from other bank bailouts is that new EU rules effective from 2016 pass more responsibility for rescuing failed banks onto creditors, as opposed to taxpayers, as a result of huge bailouts to Greece – three times – as well as Ireland, Portugal, Cyprus and the Spanish Cajas (Savings banks). Cyprus had been a test case for hitting savers with a bail-in. In Italy, there was a tradition of ordinary savers purchasing bank (subordinated) bonds as 'safe havens' so any bank rescue by the Italian government would drag over 60,000 retail (bond) investors into paying for the crisis alongside institutional investors.

In Monte dei Paschi di Siena, the world's oldest bank, for example 'ordinary' bondholders hold €5 billion ($5.5 billion) of subordinated

---

[54] http://www.dw.de/imf-calls-for-new-growth-momentum/a-17987184.
[55] http://www.imf.org/external/pubs/ft/scr/2013/cr13241.pdf.
[56] http://www.imf.org/external/pubs/cat/longres.aspx?sk=40820.0.
[57] http://qz.com/728517/in-the-euro-zones-latest-crisis-italy-is-torn-between-saving-the-banks-or-saving-its-people/.

debt. The new EU rules provide that any state bailout rescue must trigger a 'bail-in' from creditors, meaning that bondholders are included in *debt forgiveness* so forgo their share of debt before taxpayer funds are used to strengthen the bank's balance sheets. Although Brexit is not directly responsible for the Italian banking crisis – which is on-going – it is just that its banks suffered as part of the 'aftershock' having been already in a parlous undercapitalised state with *inter alia* high Non-Performing Loans (NPL) portfolio. With Brussels preoccupied with post-Brexit, migration and coming to terms with galloping populism, there is no immediate chance of a head-on clash with Renzi, the Italian Prime minister, as this may influence voters in the upcoming Constitutional Referendum, making Renzi's mandate more vulnerable.

By mapping the origins of monetary policy through the early years of the EU and the establishment of the common currency for those members that joined, we can start to take a view on possible remedies. In a recent interview[58] (on SKY, TV, 31 August 2016), the eminent and Nobel prize-winning economist, Joseph Stiglitz, commented that 'the Euro was flawed from birth. It was not a question of policy decisions, it was the structure of the Eurozone itself.' The real concern stemming from the management of the various Eurozone crises is that a certain rigidity and uniformity was applied as in handling each case the dominant view of Germany and the IMF prevailed in favour of *Austerity*, a disastrous panacea.

Writing in the FT (17 August 2016), Stiglitz provides an alternative approach and argues that 'A split euro is the solution for the single currency.' This is a bold approach and as he said further

'The hardest problem will be dealing with the legacy of debt. The easiest way of doing that is to redenominate all euro debts as "Southern Euro" debts. Politically decisions will have to be made on what panacea is best. It is certain, that even in the long term, Greece will not be able to service its debt let alone pay off capital. In the meantime Greece as in other Southern Eurozone states (excepting Cyprus) need to increase FDI and introduce further measures to combat tax compliance for both companies and individuals.'

---

[58] On SKY 31st August 2016.

4

EU Migration

The European Union (EU) has struggled to manage its current crop of crises, and the refugee problem drives this problem home. It has surpassed the Eurozone crisis to become the EU's greatest existential threat and the single biggest cause of political instability in Europe at the time of writing. With the migrant crisis, the very boundaries over which free movement should be allowed are being debated – and even what can be meant by the 'free' movement or migration of peoples, both from without and within Europe and the EU.

Exacerbated by the economic plight and on-going conflicts in various African, Asian and Middle Eastern countries, over 1 million people refugees and migrants arrived in Europe between January 2015 and March 2016. Of these, around 47% are documented as Syrian, 21% Afghan and just under 10% Iraqi.[1] According to Eurostat, EU member states received over 1.2 million first-time asylum applications in 2015,

---

[1] 'Monthly Arrivals by Nationality to Greece, Italy and Spain', *Refugees/Migrants Emergency Responses* (Mediterranean, 31 March 2016).

well over double that of the previous year. Of these applications, two-thirds went to Germany, Hungary, Sweden and Austria.[2]

Subsequent events and the rising tide of anti-EU and anti-immigrant populism across the continent have made it clear that the problems of migration pose the greatest challenge and potential threat to the stability of the European project. It concerns the entire EU membership and not just the Eurozone. It has and continues to stir more anti-EU sentiment than the on-going debt crisis, even in countries with less of a Eurosceptic electorate. It continues to be a threat to EU solidarity if left unresolved. In the UK, it became the central theme of the proponents of the Brexit Leave Campaign. When linked to inflow of refugees and economic migrants from outside the EU, it has been one of the main reasons for the growth of right-wing parties in Europe particularly in Germany, France, the Netherlands and amongst most of the post-2004 accession states of central and eastern Europe.[3] Hostile voters and their self-appointed representatives on both left and right claimed that it took away jobs and imposed strains on housing, welfare, education and healthcare: strains felt hardest amongst the poor. Debt-ridden Eurozone states subject to stringent bailout conditions and sporting high levels of unemployment are particularly concerned about preserving the principle of freedom of movement and its strict observance as central to the privileges of the Single Market.[4] Opposition to this fundamental core principle, as enshrined in the Treaty of Rome,[5] has increased sharply with the accession of Bulgaria and Romania in 2007 (Croatia was admitted on 1 July 2013), when it became clear that low wages in those countries would prompt an exodus of the work force to western Europe in large numbers.[6]

---

[2] 'Record number of over 1.2 million first time asylum seekers registered in 2015', EUROSTAT.

[3] COR interviews and Polish commentators.

[4] Austerity in Greece between 2008 and 2013 led to mass migration of many young professional talent denying the country of the very means skills to grow out of recession and contribute to debt repayment.

[5] Article 48 Treaty of Rome and the Directive 2004/38/EC on the right to move and reside freely.

[6] Eurostat figures state 2.12 million Romanians have gone to the EU: Spain 823,000, 888,000 Germany, 160,000 UK 80,000.

Much of the perceived problem lies in the Schengen agreement of 14 June 1985, and 26 European countries (of which 22 were EU member states and the others were part of the Free Trade Association) joined together to form a free movement zone in which internal border checks are abolished, but external Schengen borders are still enforced. It has, therefore, facilitated a scenario by which people entering, legally or illegally, one nation of the EU have much easier access to the entire region. This concern is further compounded by growing security issues facing European cities from international terrorism – especially that sponsored or inspired by ISIS. While a series of debt crises have dominated people's minds, there has been a wake-up call for improved security and migration control.

The prime task for expediting this lies, at least in theory, with the EU Commission: with the cooperation of member states through their own internal security measures. In his mission letter to Dimitris Avramopoulos, the newly appointed EU Commissioner for Migration, Home Affairs and Citizenship, Jean Claude Junker emphasised the agenda by saying

> Migration is one of the most pressing challenges I have highlighted in my Political Guidelines. Europe needs to manage migration better, in all its aspects. A successful migration policy is both a humanitarian and an economic imperative. We need to show that the EU can offer both a compelling case to attract global talent, and a vision of how to robustly address the challenge of irregular migration. We need a new policy on migration that will address skill shortages and the demographic challenges the EU faces and that will modernize the way the EU addresses these challenges.

He went on to state that...

> The other priority of your portfolio (for the new Commissioner) will be to help the Member States to manage and secure Europe's borders. The Common Asylum EU framework needs to be fully applied and operational. We also need to step up the fight against cross-border crime and terrorism. The EU can make a key contribution to citizens' security in an

area with clear ramifications for freedom of movement and fundamental rights.[7]

This was a daunting task for any national government to coordinate, let alone an organisation of 28 states.

Migration – Intra-EU Mobility

The EU–Turkey Agreement (June 2016) contains the flow on Europe's south eastern exposed borders through the Greek Aegean islands. Historically, economic migration from within Europe is nothing new. The origins of free movement stem from the post-war need to encourage rapid economic growth after the devastation of Europe's industrial sector, towns and cities. This could only be attained by encouraging policies of flexible mobility of qualified and skilled workers throughout the European Economic Community (EEC), the forerunner of the European community and the EU. Between 1958 and 1972, work permits were granted to what were colloquially known as 'gasterbeiters' or 'guest workers' in the Benelux countries of Belgium, the Netherlands, Luxembourg, France, Italy and West Germany (the Federal Republic of Germany)[8] Similar schemes operated in the Scandinavian countries.

About 30% of these foreign workers came from what was then referred to as the European Economic Community; from the high unemployment regions of southern Italy, Greece and Spain; but also, in substantial numbers, from Turkey, a country outside the EEC. The latter have moved almost exclusively to Germany's industrial heartlands, with most remaining to this day.[9]

---

[7] Jean-Claude Junker President of the EU Commission, 1st of November 2014.

[8] West Germany signed bilateral agreements with a number of European countries (Italy, Greece Spain) and Turkey which allowed for the recruitment of less skilled workers in West Germany's factories during the boom years of industrial growth known at the time as the German 'Economic Miracle'.

[9] Those from Algeria went to France and the UK continued to receive many from the British Commonwealth.

With the continuing enlargement process from the 1980s, the operation of transitional restrictions on free movement for new members helped to quell concerns that immediate freedom of movement would lead to mass migration (notably, Britain waved these controls under the Blair–Brown governments).[10] But with EU enlargement from central and eastern Europe fears resurfaced of an exodus of large numbers of migrant workers.

Member states do not need reminding that they signed up to this; albeit not foreseeing the extent of an enlargement that has now driven to the very geographical borders of Europe. The right to free movement is enshrined in the founding Treaty of Rome 1957 that established the European Economic Community and will unquestionably remain. The intent and consequence of this policy was that the very borders that had been fought over in two world wars were now permanently open for Europeans to conduct trade through the free movement of capital, labour and services.[11]

In May 2004, the 15 states of the European Union were joined by ten new member states, which was the largest expansion in the history of European economic integration. The new member states included Czech Republic, Hungary, Poland, Slovakia, Slovenia and the three Baltic states of Estonia, Latvia and Lithuania. Cyprus and Malta also acceded at the same time. But unlike in the 1980s, when Greece, Spain and Portugal had joined, significant fears existed of mass migration from these new east European accession states based on the much greater disparity in incomes and living standards enjoyed by their workers over those in the west. Consequently, the accession of the new members was coupled with the imposition of a seven-year transition period to try (somewhat unsuccessfully) and mute this impact.

Only the UK, Sweden, Ireland and Malta allowed citizens of the new accession countries to work in their labour markets immediately, which led to sizeable inflows (the largest of the new accession countries) into these countries, particularly Poland. Since its accession to the EU in 2004, and

---

[10] For Greece (1981) Spain and Portugal (1986) there was a 6 year transitional period.
[11] Freedom of Movement was one of the original Four 'Freedoms' with Capital, Customs and Services.

the Schengen area in particular, around 2 million Poles have emigrated – primarily to the UK, Ireland and Germany. The majority, according to the Central Statistical Office of Poland, left seeking higher wages abroad, while retaining full residency status in their home country.[12]

It is estimated that between 2004 and 2008 Poland's net outflow of citizens accounted for about 1% of its total population. The substantial increase of this outflow, in that nation and throughout eastern Europe, has led to concerns by their authorities of a serious 'brain drain' from the very countries most in need of such skilled professionals – trained at their government's expense in *their* universities. As an example, 2300 Polish doctors now serve in the NHS – an institution in which over a quarter of the doctors are not of British national origin.[13] This development sits ill at ease with the original purpose of the enlargement – which was, and still is, to develop economies of the poorer members of the EU.

Immigration at the time of this enlargement was not perceived as such a significant threat in these countries – in contrast to France, where a fictional character iconised as the 'Polish Plumber' was used to fuel fears on how skilled French workers were soon to be replaced by a flood of cheap eastern European labour. Around 70% of migrants from the post-2004 accession states have gone to Ireland and the United Kingdom. Migrants from Bulgaria and Romania, on the other hand, have mostly chosen to go to Italy and Spain (in the case of Romania, linguistic affinity in a Romance language appears to have played a part).

Background to the Expansion of Freedom of Movement: From Workers to Citizens

Legal Issues: The Role of the European Court of Justice in Interpreting EU law on Freedom of Movement.

---

[12] Anne White. *Post-communist Poland: social change and migration. Polish Families and Migration since EU Accession.* Policy Press (2011), p. 27.

[13] No. of Poles in the UK is 790,000 (ONS estimate 2014) excluding descendants of immigrants after World War 2. No of Polish doctors in the UK NHS 2,300.

Case law emanating from the European Court of Justice (ECJ) expanded on the concept of freedom of movement and enshrined its practical function and forms. A key example of this is the Baumbast case, which specifically gave the children of the migrant worker the right to remain in the UK to complete their schooling.[14] The ECJ was asked to determine whether family members of an economic migrant worker –in this case a German national – could continue to have right of residency under EC treaty law when the migrant worker takes up new employment outside the EC. In this regard (as in other cases), the court referred to Art 8 of the European Court of Human Rights, of which all EU members are signatories.

This right of free movement was originally intended for economically active workers able to support themselves, but the European Court of Justice has, through a number of leading cases, expanded the concept of freedom of movement to cover residency as well as for the broader economic activity of those who were able to support themselves in their destination country.[15]

Accordingly, in this respect it can be said that the ECJ's rulings gradually shifted policy from protecting primarily free movement of *workers* to the free movement of *persons*. In individual cases, the court ruled that a member state of the EEC could not, for example, prevent entry to or take away the right of a citizen of another EEC state, on the basis that they had, but were no longer, an employee of a company within the EEC[16] or even that they had engaged in criminal activity for which they would not be equally punished in the citizens' former member state. In 1990, freedom of movement came to be guaranteed

---

[14] In its determination, the ECJ had to take account of the Article 8 of the European Convention on Human Rights (ECHR) which re-enforced the concept of 'family rights' in freedom of movement rather than the rights of children *per se*.

[15] The Metock case was decided by the ECJ in July 2008 on a reference from the Irish High Court in Dublin concerning the interpretation of Directive 2004/38/EC regarding the rights of EU citizens together with family members to freely take up residence in any other member state. The ECJ made it clear that the right of residency extended to those family members that had *not* been nationals of another member state thereby ruling that the Ireland's regulations were in breach of the 2004 Directive.

[16] The definition of worker was expanded to include seasonal and short term contract employees.

for students,[17] pensioners[18] and the unemployed, as well as for their families.

The process of establishing freedom of movement for all nationals of member states was finalised with the signing of the Maastricht Treaty in 1992, which created the European Union and introduced the concept of a common European citizenship. Two years later, the Schengen rules were incorporated into the Treaty of Amsterdam, and by 1999 European citizens were free to cross most intra-European borders without having to show their passports or identity cards. The Schengen area now applies to 25 European countries (22 in the EU) including Switzerland, Norway and Liechtenstein.

As the process of encouraging migration and easing travel restrictions continued, emphasis was placed on reducing border control formalities within Europe. The Schengen Agreement created a common and essentially (and intentionally) borderless area between Belgium, France, Germany, Luxembourg, the Netherlands, Portugal and Spain, wherein travel credentials were only required at the external borders of this zone.

EU Expansion: The Mobility of Central and Eastern Europeans

In May 2004, the existing 15 states of the European Union were joined by ten new member states, which was the largest expansion in the history of European integration. The new member states included Czech Republic, Hungary, Poland, Slovakia, Slovenia and the three Baltic states of Estonia, Latvia and Lithuania. Cyprus and Malta also acceded at the same time. But unlike in the 1980s, when Greece, Spain and Portugal joined, significant fears existed of mass migration from these new east European accession states, based on the much greater disparity in incomes and living standards between east and west, as discussed above.

---

[17] Directive 93/96/EEC.
[18] Directive 90/365/EEC.

During the accession negotiations, a transitional period of seven years was established so that each old member state could control when they would open their borders to workers from the new members. These restrictions were not applied to Cyprus and Malta, both part of the commonwealth, with strong ties to Britain; and a country where many Cypriots had moved to after the Turkish invasion of Cyprus in 1974.[19] Free movement between all member states was finally guaranteed by May 2011 at the latest for the citizens of those countries that joined in 2004 and by January 2014 for the citizens of Bulgaria and Romania.

Around 70% of migrants from the post-2004 accession states emigrated to Ireland and the United Kingdom. The latter had both removed restrictions for the movement of labour immediately upon their accession. The Blair government in Britain had totally misjudged the numbers who moved especially from Poland to the UK after 2004, sowing the seeds of latter opposition to this move: Nigel Farage, the leader of United Kingdom Independence Party (UKIP), later branding it an 'uncontrolled experiment in mass migration', and for which many of the economic hardships experienced in the UK since 2008–2009 were blamed. Germany, France and Austria, by contrast, used their right to restrict for the full term so as not to open the floodgates. After the 2004 expansion, Poland was the source of the largest number of migrant workers amongst all new member states. In fact, the number of Poles 'temporarily residing' in another EU member state more than doubled between 2004 and 2007, amounting to 2 million and representing over 5% of the country's 38 million people.

Crossing borders within this area has been made incredibly simple by policy, technology, the travel industry, and globalisation. But this reality presents a key problem for those studying European mobility: many forms of cross-border movement within this area remain uncounted by official statistics. European citizens can now cross borders unregistered, often remain essentially invisible in their destination countries, and are

---

[19] For more on this see John Theodore and Jonathan Theodore, *Cyprus and the Financial Crisis: The Controversial Bailout and What It Means for the Eurozone* (London: Palgrave Macmillan, 2015), pp. 19–37.

counted differently depending on their countries of origin and destination. In the United Kingdom, for example, the measurement of immigration mainly relies on the number of residents who were born abroad; while in other countries, such as Germany, it is determined by the number of residents who are not national citizens. Statistics of 'emigrants' are not clear cut either: Austrians are categorised as 'emigres' when they leave their country for more than three months, Belgians after six months, Finns if they intend to stay abroad for more than a year, and Poles and Romanians only if they indicate that they are leaving permanently. The fact that widely different rules are applied makes it extremely difficult to establish consistency in policy across member states. Nor is citizenship itself a dependable method of accounting for mobility; Belgium, for instance, requires three years of residence before citizenship can be granted, while Austria demands a minimum stay of ten years. Children born to foreign citizens are foreigners themselves in some countries, such as in Sweden and Finland, but they automatically become citizens in the country of birth in others, including Great Britain and the Republic of Ireland.

Freedom of Movement

The principle of freedom of movement is a cornerstone of the whole European project so becomes a sticking point for obtaining a 'soft brexit' in future negotiations between the UK and the EU. It is seen as central to the EU's aim since its inception after the Second World War to break down economic and ideological barriers between member nations. It is frequently touted as the crowning achievement of the European Union – ahead of economic prosperity and post-war peaceful coexistence. But the experiment has not satisfied the underlying objective of the European Commission, which is concerned about economic growth in both Eurozone countries and later accession states. Migrants flocking to Germany, Ireland and the UK have helped to fill employment gaps in their workforces – particularly in manufacturing and processing services, hospitality and crucial public services such as healthcare. What is not often appreciated – and, ironically, usually only by the opponents of high levels of immigration on the nativist political right – is that this has typically been at the expense of their home economies, in the 'brain drain' noted above.

However, the majority of foreign workers in Europe continue to come from outside the EU. In 2000, about 5.1% of the total EU members, or 19 million people, lived in a country of which they were not a citizen. The majority of these foreign citizens lived in Germany (37.0%), France (18.4%) and the United Kingdom (10.2%). Only about 6 million of the foreign citizens (1.6%) living in the European Union in 2000 were nationals of another EU member state, and the majority of them also lived in Germany (1.9 million), France (1.2 million) and the United Kingdom (860,000).[20] According to EUROSTAT, the statistical office of the European Union, 31.9 million foreign citizens lived in the EU-27 in 2009, comprising 6.4% of the total EU-27 population. About one-third, or 11.9 million, were citizens of another EU-27 member state.[21]

The effects of the eastward enlargements of 2004 and 2007 are visible, not only in the overall figures for 2009, but also when it is considered that the two largest national groups in the EU's itinerant population were those of Romania (2.0 million EU migrants) and Poland (1.5 million EU migrants). Together, these two groups accounted for 11% of all foreign citizens living in the EU-27 member states in 2009. Turkey, a candidate for future EU membership, had the biggest share of migrants living within the EU-27 when compared with all non-EU and EU countries (2.4 million).[22]

The proportion of foreign citizens living in each country varied from less than 1% in Poland, Romania and Bulgaria to 44% in Luxembourg. In terms of numbers, Germany, again, hosted the largest share of foreign nationals in the EU-27 (2.5 million) followed by Spain (2.3 million), the United Kingdom (1.6 million), France (1.3 million) and Italy (1.1 million).

---

[20] http://www.migrationpolicy.org/article/free-movement-europe-past-and-present.
[21] http://ec.europa.eu/eurostat/documents/3433488/5583732/KS-SF-08-098-EN.PDF/fd0c3fbe-4119-4da6-9b6c-1039024b4e0b.
[22] Although Turkey is a member of the Customs Union, Progress towards acquiring EU membership has met with obstacles and lack of movement in fulfilling the *acqui communitaire*.

When Greece, Spain and Portugal joined the EEC in 1981 and 1986, six-year transitional restrictions on free movement were put in place. All three countries had seen large-scale migration to north-western Europe in the 1960s and there were concerns that immediate freedom would lead to unsustainable mass emigration from those nations. However, both during these restrictions and after they were lifted, migration from Greece, Spain and Portugal to other member states remained low. It could be argued that this low migration rate was due to the economic optimism in the southern countries that followed their EU membership: hope, that is, for a better future at home, and decreasing the need to look for better opportunities elsewhere. In this vein, freedom of movement allowed those who had already migrated to return, knowing that if necessity required they could easily move abroad again.

Despite comparatively low overall levels of intra-EU migration, worries about 'social dumping' – that is, the hiring of workers or subcontractors from other member states to carry out employment for lower wages than nationals – led to the establishment of the Posted Workers Directive in 1996.[23] This directive states that workers posted in another member state should receive the same wage as local workers from the start of their employment.[24] This was to include minimum standards of social welfare but a number of European Court of Justice rulings made it easier for foreign companies not to comply with strict social welfare rules normally applicable to workers based in countries such as France and Belgium.[25]

As discussed above, one of the key commitments made in the 1957 Treaty of Rome that came to define the European Economic Community was 'the abolition obstacles to the free movement of persons, services and capital.' Aside from the bold vision of an open and peaceful Europe, the free movement clause was intended to create a more efficient labour market by increasing the options available to both

---

[23] c.europa.eu/social/main.jsp?catId=471.

[24] A 'posted worker' is an employee who is sent by his employer to carry out a service in another EU Member State on a temporary basis.

[25] https://www.ft.com/content/d6235564-4e6b-11e6-8172-e39ecd3b86fc.

employers and workers across the continent. Gradually, the right to free movement was extended to other groups, such as retirees and students. Intra-EU migration has, however, remained low. While an estimated 3% of population worldwide is an international migrant, Eurostat data show that in 2004 only 1.6% of citizens of the then EU members lived in other member states. Despite the expansion in the EU through the 1980s and 2000s, and contrary to much of the political discourse on the subject, general rates of EU mobility have therefore remained fairly low.[26]

Today the share of EU migrants varies across Europe with about half from new member states, even though these new eastern EU states represent only 20% of the EU population. Destinations of post-2004 migration differ from those of earlier migrants. Whereas Germany, France and the UK had the largest EU-foreigner populations in 2004, by 2013 Spain and Italy overtook France and Germany in this regard. The UK has received the most with circa 1.1 million migrants between 2004 and 2011. In relative terms, Ireland also stands out; in 2013 EU foreigners made up an estimated 8% of the population. In contrast, Sweden received around 70,000 post-2004 migrants and has one of the lowest inflows of all EU-15 states.

Britain and Ireland both had great appeal, because of the language issue and because they had rising economies, the construction sector and public services with chronic long-term staffing shortages, most notably in health and social Care.

Discussions on intra-EU mobility highlight not only the numbers involved but also the economic and social consequences of such movements. Central to the Leave campaign in Britain was the worries of their citizens that migrants from the new, poorer, member states undercut the wages and employment opportunities of local workers and exploit the welfare systems (this was a decisive selling point for the Leave campaign, as highlighted in that chapter). Many seem unaware of EU regulations designed to limit the possibility for wage competition between local and mobile EU workers. According to EU law, intra-EU migrants should be

---

[26] https://www.imi.ox.ac.uk/people/evelyn-ersanilli.

paid and employed in line with the labour laws in the country of work. Workers who are temporarily posted in another member state by their employer are also required to receive the same wage as local workers from the first day of their employment.[27] However, it can be noted that employers have always found ways around these rules by operating via branches in other states or by engaging workers as self-employed sub-contractors instead of employees, an established practice which helps all employers escape employer social security.[28]

Free movement in the EU is conditional on EU citizens being employed, studying or have sufficient resources to be self-financing for themselves and for any family members so as not to become a burden on the social assistance system of the host member state (Directive 2004/38/EC). This means that intra-EU migrants cannot claim social assistance from the moment they migrate, unless they have a job with a wage that qualifies them for certain forms of social security support. There are cases where new migrants or criminal gangs on behalf of 'ghost migrants' have succeeded in abusing the rules to apply for social aid, but in many cases the hosting state has been dilatory in conducting the 'habitual residence test' before granting assistance. This suggests the problem is a lack of enforcement rather than a lack of regulations. Holland, Britain, Germany and Austria are now joining forces to combat the so-called welfare tourism. A junior justice minister Fred Teeven echoed well held views that 'citizens who have never worked in the Netherlands should not be allowed to claim welfare benefits (bijstand).'[29] The Netherlands, Germany, Austria and Britain agreed to take the matter up with the European Commission, calling on it to address their concerns about the abuse of the welfare benefit system by the members of other EU states. Teeven is quoted in the Dutch media as saying that the four countries think it will be possible to declare [welfare claimants who have never worked] undesirable under current EU rules.[30]

---

[27] http://ec.europa.eu/social/main.jsp?catId=471.
[28] http://www.rug.nl/research/portal/files/17752809/Chapter_4.pdf.
[29] http://www.dutchnews.nl/news/archives/2013/03/holland_britain_germany_austri/.
[30] https://www.ucl.ac.uk/news/news-articles/1114/051114-economic-impact-EU-immigration.

The issue is seen as a serious problem in all four countries: Justice Minister Teeven further stated that 4260 non-Dutch EU citizens were claiming welfare benefits by the end of 2011.[31] 'We know a certain percentage are fraudulent but we do not know exactly how many,' he said. The official line from Brussels has stressed that there are effective measures in place to deport foreign citizens who abuse a country's welfare system, with Cecilia Malmström, EU Commissioner for Home Affairs, quoted as saying. '[EU citizens] are allowed to stay for a limited time [in another EU country] and if they cannot sustain or support themselves they must go back.'[32]

Migrants improve not just their own lives but the economies of their host countries. European immigrants who have arrived in Britain since 2000 have been net contributors to the treasury, adding more than £20 billion to the public finances in the first decade of the century. Recent studies by University College London University further demonstrate that intra-EU migrants are in fact net contributors to their new places of residence.[33] Conversely, there is little evidence that intra-EU migrants are disproportionate users of the welfare systems in their countries of residence – let alone that there exists a widespread phenomenon of 'welfare tourism'. European immigrants who arrived in the UK since 2000 have contributed more than £20 billion to UK public finances between 2001 and 2011. It is often forgotten that many of the professional doctors, nurses and skilled workers were educated in their home state (costs borne by their countries of origin) that has lost their services constituting a 'brain drain' of mammoth proportions. The productive human capital value has been calculated at £6.8 billion (between 2000 and 2011)[34] which has been spent on their education by their home country. The research further shows that in the period from 2001 to 2011, European immigrants from the EU-15 countries contributed 64% more in taxes than they received in benefits. Immigrants from the central

---

[31] Op. cit.
[32] Op. cit.
[33] https://www.ucl.ac.uk/news/news-articles/1114/051114-economic-impact-EU-immigration.
[34] Ibid.

and east European 'accession' states paid 12% more than they received.³⁵

Immigration and the Swiss Experience

Although not a member of the EU, Switzerland, which along with Norway and Iceland (and Liechtenstein), is part of an economic area enjoying many of the tariff-free benefits of membership. This, however, comes at a cost – to enjoy these benefits, Switzerland has had to sign up to the principle of freedom of movement and also has to be part of the Schengen agreement. Swiss Eurosceptic credentials are strikingly similar to those of the UK. The electorate have backed curbs on immigration in the same way as the recent UK negotiations with Brussels demanded safeguards in the form of the 'emergency break' clause on immigration. In the UK, the main concern is not just assimilation but also the demands of unregulated immigration, pressures on the benefits and welfare system and the UK's ability to absorb inflows at present levels – all, as polls have repeatedly shown, increasingly unpopular with the electorate.³⁶ In Switzerland, these fears are exacerbated by the fact the population numbers only 8.4 million.

This concern with a loss of identity – and the time-honoured tradition of Swiss neutrality – was raised by Micheline Calmy-Rey, a former social democratic Swiss foreign minister, who stated that 'we are a bit like the British in that we think we are a special case within Europe. We are something like an island.'³⁷ Expectations that Switzerland will be able to negotiate a better deal on the back of the Brexit vote in the UK's referendum are unlikely.³⁸ Brussels is conscious that the deal could set a

---

[35] Research undertaken by Professor Christian Dustmann and Dr Tommaso Frattini of the fiscal consequences of European immigration to the UK, published by the Royal Economic Society in *The Economic Journal.*
[36] https://www.migrationwatchuk.org/briefing-paper/361.
[37] *Financial Time* 22nd April 2016.
[38] http://www.politico.eu/article/swiss-could-become-brexits-latest-casualty-european-union-migration/.

precedent for negotiations with Britain, so any softening in its approach would be counterproductive. 'Basically, Switzerland will get a "Cameron minus minus" deal,' said an EU source close to the process, in reference to the February 2016 Agreement in the Cameron talks to restrict some welfare benefits for migrant workers, in order to sway wavering British support ahead of the referendum.

Without an agreement on freedom of movement, Switzerland would be faced with the same tariffs and loss of trading benefits now confronting the UK. The country is coming under increasing regulatory examination both by the EU and the USA. The need for compliance and transparency is affecting its reputation as a safe haven for the secrecy of its client base. Investigations are moving faster than expected with the release of the 'Panama papers' implicating a number of Swiss banks from a list known to be hiding the wealth of numerous individuals avoiding (or evading) tax liabilities in their domestic tax jurisdictions. The benefits of remaining an important trading partner with the EU may force the Swiss into further compliance mode with Brussels.[39]

Migration and the UK

The image for the year ending June 2015 shows a long-term figure of international migration into Britain of 336,000 – an increase of 82,000 from the period ending June 2014. This is based on the difference between gross immigration of 636,000, less 300,000 (20,000 less than in year ending June 2014) who emigrated over the same period. They were also able to show that the Conservative Government's consistent pledge to cut immigration to 'tens of thousands' was simply unattainable while adhering to the EU principle of freedom of movement.

But if EU net migration into the UK was 180,000 (12 months to the end of June 2015), non-EU migration was even higher at 201,000

---

[39] The 2005 Savings Tax Directive was to curb tax evasion of in the EU (and European households in Switzerland). Under this program, tax evaders holding interest-yielding accounts in Switzerland have two choices: they can either report their accounts to the fiscal authorities of their resident countries or they can pay a tax upfront and keep their anonymity.

(45,000 net emigration mainly to EU). In fairness, the scale of net migration has risen almost exponentially from 2004 to 2014: the implications of the post-2004 enlargement were not fully forecasted by the existing membership.[40] Official forecasts relied on by the Blair government totally underestimated the flow, especially from Poland.[41] In 2007 when Bulgaria and Romania joined the 'club', the UK took the precaution of imposing the official transitional arrangements, delaying the inflow – although by June 2015 figures showed that 219,000 Romanians and Bulgarian citizens had migrated to the UK.[42]

Strengthening the 'Leave' campaign was the notion that uncontrolled numbers put immense pressure on those local authorities responsible for housing and welfare – especially in those locations of greatest migrant concentration. Residents of many small towns and villages bore witness to the pressure on schools, hospitals and other public services such as council housing in short supply for those already on waiting lists – but now facing competition from migrants, with those with large families being prioritised by state tenancy policy (based on need ergo family size).[43]

Migration into Europe

Europe's relative stability has offered a safe haven from the turmoil engulfing the Middle East and North Africa. Problems of the Eurozone debt crisis aside, it is also perceived as one of the richest regions of the world. It must not be forgotten that Syria's (and Iraq) immediate neighbours such as Lebanon, Jordan and Turkey have over the years taken in millions of refugees but are massively overwhelmed and lack sufficient resources to manage what they have, let alone absorb

---

[40] Seen as a counterbalance to the Franco–German hegemony. The first Blair government 1997–2004 was in the vanguard of those advocating enlargement.

[41] 25,000 was the Home office (by Jack Straw) estimate at the time.

[42] http://www.telegraph.co.uk/news/uknews/immigration/11987954/Romanian-and-Bulgarian-workers-top-200000-for-first-time-say-official-figures.html.

[43] https://www.migrationwatchuk.org/pressArticle/64.

more. While providing a measure of financial support, the Gulf States including Saudi Arabia cannot claim to be accepting refugees in any real numbers. The rulers of these wealthy states like Qatar, United Arab Emirates, Saudi Arabia, Kuwait, Oman and especially Bahrain have social, religious and cultural issues with minorities and worry about being swamped by refugees (many of whom will be of the Shia branch of Islam rather than their dominant Sunni variety). Their economies heavily rely on migrant labour with genuine fears that a large influx of refugees would further destabilise demographics. The knowledge that Saudi Arabia has, however, offered to build 200 mosques in Germany, while well meaning, is no substitute for humanitarian assistance.

In response to reports that Saudi Arabia is planning to build 200 mosques in Germany, Ambassador Nugali at the Ministry of Foreign affairs said: 'This issue is not under consideration and no discussions have taken place with the German government about it. Therefore, the reports are without basis or truth.'[44]

But equal criticism has been levelled at the EU and Europe for being less than enthusiastic in alleviating the refugee crisis. 'European and US officials [are] shedding crocodile tears over the plight of Syrian refugees,' tweeted Nasser Al-Khalifa, a Qatari diplomat and a former ambassador to the United States. Like his colleagues in the Gulf, Al-Khalifa accused the west of politicising the migrant crisis in order to deflect responsibility away from Europe and demonise the GCC.[45]

The crisis now engulfing Europe began slowly from 2011 with the convulsions generated by the Arab Spring. At first, Tunisians risked their lives to cross the Mediterranean on unstable fishing trawlers to get to the Italian island of Lampedusa. The fall of the Gaddafi regime in Libya encouraged Libyans and other sub-Saharan Africans to attempt the dangerous journey from Libyan in their tens of thousands. As the Middle East disintegrated and border controls increased, migrants and refugees began to redirect their journeys through the less hazardous

---

[44] http://www.huffingtonpost.co.uk/2015/09/25/saudi-arabia-denies-offering-build-200-mosques-germany_n_8194146.html.
[45] http://www.jpost.com/Middle-East/Analysis-Gulf-states-face-bad-rap-on-Syrian-refugee-issue-444448.

Balkan land routes through Turkey, from which there is a short crossing to the nearest Greek islands off the Turkish coast – but still arriving, technically, in the EU through Greece.

A massive spike in such numbers arose when Germany became the epicentre of the refugee crisis in 2015 with an 'open-door policy' when the German government, headed in this very publicly by Angela Merkel, pledged to accept all Syrian asylum applications, regardless of how they reached or entered German territory. This was a breach of the controversial Dublin Regulations by which refugees (asylum seekers, *not* economic migrants) can only apply for asylum in the very first EU member state they enter. Although Chancellor Merkel had strong humanitarian motives, for which she was praised in pro-Arab publications such as Al Jazeera as 'the loving mother' and 'Mama Merkel',[46] the move backfired when it provoked right-wing protests and anti-Muslim demonstrations by Far Right and Neo-Nazi groups. Merkel's coalition government has suffered a series of losses in regional elections to the right wing (AfD) opposition as a consequence of her sanctuary policy.

If anything has done to shake the foundations of the European project it was the relentless onslaught of refugees 'swimming' towards Europe in their tens of thousands. The open wound of the Eurozone's economic crisis has, at least comparatively, proven less of an existential threat. The cornerstone of the open borders policy enshrined in the Schengen Agreement of 1985, enabling free movements of peoples across the continent, has been thrown into jeopardy. Concerns raised in Brussels did not seem to get urgent answers to the struggles faced by those members on the front line, namely the countries along the Mediterranean coastline – Greece, Italy and (to a lesser extent) Spain – and the transit countries of Serbia (not a member), Hungary and Slovenia – as they attempted to control borders, register and fingerprint asylum seekers, as well as shelter, feed and police such enormous numbers.

With a Syrian civil war that has killed 250,000 people, and displaced half the population, triggering one in five Syrians (4 million people) to

---

[46] http://lifehopeandtruth.com/discern/nov-dec-2015/the-migrant-crisis/.

flee the country entirely, it was feared that this was only the beginning. While the overwhelming majority of migrants were Muslim, not all were refugees from Syria. Taking advantage of the crisis were migrants from other nations, stretching from Pakistan to North Africa. According to the United Nations, just 53% of the migrants are Syrian. Years of warfare and the departure of the USA from Afghanistan and Iraq, where sectarian violence has reigned supreme, has acted as a catalyst for dispossessed people to shift westward towards Europe. Destitute peoples from Africa's shanty towns and from other war-torn territories exacerbated the disaster.

Other immigration policy experts predicted even greater numbers to come. According to Mark Krikorian, Director of the (admittedly Conservative-leaning) Center for Immigration Studies, Washington, DC, 'There are hundreds of millions who would undertake the journey – whether jobs await them or not – to ensure that their children grow up in Germany, France, England, or Sweden rather than Syria, Chad, Afghanistan, or Mali. What we are seeing is the vanguard of those millions calling Europe's bluff.'[47]

Reactions within Europe

Germany's decision to absorb so many refugees sent shockwaves through central and eastern Europe. The Visegrad Group of Czech Republic, Hungary, Poland and Slovakia were vehemently anti-immigration, with apparently little desire to become multi-cultural societies in the mould of their western European partners. They fiercely opposed refugee quotas which Brussels – led by Germany – has tried to impose on them, as contrary to their very reasons for joining the EU. Hungary's Minister for Foreign Affairs and Trade Peter Szijjártó described the crisis bluntly in comments to the *Hungarian Times*. 'It is self-delusion to call this situation a migration crisis,' warned Szijjártó. 'It is a massive migration of

---

[47] http://www.nationalreview.com/article/423339/where-there-no-border-nations-perish-mark-krikorian.

nations, with inexhaustible reserves.' He predicted that the crisis will continue for years and could see an astonishing 35 million migrants heading to Europe.[48] Even beyond the menace of seeding ISIS-inspired terrorism, Hungarian Prime Minister Viktor Orbán warned of the threat to Europe's 'Christian character' because 'everything which is now taking place before our eyes threatens to have explosive consequences for the whole of Europe.'[49]

In the blame game these countries (Austria, Hungary, Poland and Slovakia) focused on the Greek and Italian entry points which, being so overwhelmed, had failed to process refugees adequately for relocation requests. Both countries took the full force of this problem – Italy in 2014 being overtaken by Greece in 2015–2016 of the refugee invasion.

The strongest voice of resentment to the fair distribution and sharing of refugees through imposed asylum quotas came from Victor Orban, the Hungarian Prime Minister, when he referred to the German Chancellor's 'moral imperialism' in attempting to coerce/force unanimity in dealing with the migrant crisis.[50] A referendum on 3 October 2016 gave Orban an overwhelming vote to reject an earlier quota of 1200 migrants demanded by Brussels. "Hungary had a 'democratic right' to a different approach. . . . [for] We are Hungarians however, we cannot think with German minds. Hungary should have the right to control the impact of a mass migration."[51] This statement squared the Hungarian leader in firm, direct opposition to the German Chancellor Angela Merkel's 'open-door' approach.

In Poland, while there were official statements claiming readiness to accept up to 2000 refugees, remarks by Andrzej Duda, the Polish President, rejected the EU's proposal of compulsory quotas, saying: 'I won't agree to a dictate of the strong. I won't back a Europe where the

---

[48] ifehopeandtruth.com/discern/nov-dec-2015/the-migrant-crisis/.
[49] https://issuu.com/discern/docs/discern_november-december_2015.
[50] *Yahoo News*, 23 September 2015.
[51] http://www.telegraph.co.uk/news/worldnews/europe/hungary/11884665/Refugee-crisis-EU-divided-as-Hungary-attacks-migrant-quota-as-unrealisable-and-nonsense.html.

economic advantage of the size of a population will be a reason to force solutions on other countries regardless of their national interests.'[52]

Poland claimed that as a country, – apart from its Ukrainian, with whom it shares centuries of history and culture[53] – it is by and large a homogeneous state with over 90% following the same Roman Catholic faith. Both Hungary and Slovakia – apart from their Roma minorities – are also able to claim a strong homogeneous entity. These are central European states without a recent colonial past, and which had no stake in the nineteenth and the twentieth century's power politics that triangulated around the Middle East, Asia and Africa.

Realisations soon arose of the hard limits to even Germany's capability to absorb such numbers. It was already a magnet for economic migrants as well as asylum seekers. Figures of 800,000 were estimated to apply for asylum in Germany, equal to 1% of Germany's population, and until its own citizens started to dissent[54] it has considered accepting another 500,000 annually for the next several years.

If Germany still had strong economic and demographic growth, it could successfully absorb this influx, at least in economic terms. But this is no longer clearly the case. While German unemployment appears low (4.7%), the economy is only growing at 1.6% annually. For the rest of Europe the ability to absorb a refugee influx is even worse.

Reasons other than altruism influenced Germany's elite to push this policy. Reparations for the guilt of its Nazi past are cited but more relevant for welcoming an influx of refugees is to meet the future needs of its workforce as Germany has the world's lowest birthrate. According to current demographic estimates, the population of 81 million today will shrink to 68 million in a few decades. 'What Germany is proposing,' said syndicated columnist Rich Lowry, 'is undertaking a vast social and demographic experiment, with the rapid, bulk importation of Muslim

---

[52] http://www.bloomberg.com/news/articles/2015-09-08/polish-president-blasts-eu-dictate-of-the-strong-on-migrants.
[53] Pre-1939 Poland included a large part of what is western Ukraine ad % of what is now part of Ukraine, i.e. the Catholic part.
[54] https://euobserver.com/beyond-brussels/131034.

immigrants into a country with an aging population' ('The Refugee Crisis Is Exposing Europe's Folly,' *New York Post,* 8 September 2015).

In the Presidential Elections on 22 May 2016, the hard-right Freedom Party of Austria narrowly lost to the Green party's candidate Professor Van Der Bellen by the narrowest of margins in modern European electoral history – namely 31,000 votes, or 50.7% versus 49.9%. The Freedom party took a hard line on this immigration, opposing the Austrian government's agreement with Brussels for the allocation of its share of refugees. The presidential election was in fact mainly symbolic but the Right's gains reflected the inability of the Austrian ruling elites – namely the coalition of Conservatives and Social Democrats – to meet the aspirations of many working-class voters for jobs – jobs they now perceived to be threatened by new economic migrants and refugees. The outcome of the vote was in major part attributed to a final wing produced by postal votes but was nevertheless welcomed with huge relief by observers outside Austria:

'This victory in extra time may bring some relief to European policy-makers and financial markets as the feared scenario of a populist at the head of a core euro zone country has not materialized after all,' Carsten Brzeski, the Frankfurt-based chief economist at ING-DiBa, said in a note on the results.[55] 'Nevertheless, the result also stresses that almost half of the Austrian voters in fact did vote for right-wing populist Hofer and seem to sympathize with a very strict stance on Austria's refugee policy and a very distant relationship with the European Union (EU),' he added.

Backlash to Open-Door Policies

In Germany, the political change in climate towards continued acceptance and integration of large numbers of refugees – including those that fall under the heading of 'economic migrants' – has been influenced by a number of events. The shift in attitude can be highlighted in the much

---

[55] www.cnbc/id/103653340.

publicised Cologne riots that occurred on New Year's Eve, 2015, when the police recorded 553 criminal complaints by women – of which 45% related to sexual attacks by gangs of North African/Arab men. This provided strong ammunition to more right-wing protesters who blaming these violations on the large influx of refugees in 2015. The main backlash came on 12 January 2016 in Leipzig, Eastern Germany, when the police arrested right-wing anti-migrant demonstrators reacting to the events in Cologne.[56]

With the number of new Muslims in Europe from socially conservative backgrounds increasing dramatically, eastern and central European countries have become concerned about such a radical change to their social demographics. Their reluctance to take in Syrian refugees revolves around worries, fair or unfair, and about the integration of massive numbers of ethnically, culturally, religiously and linguistically different migrants. Reactions by opponents to this influx have oscillated between the religious and the economic. Dutch right-wing politician Geert Wilders called the immigrant surge an 'Islamic invasion,' one that 'threatens our prosperity, our security, our culture and identity.'[57] In August, the Slovak government said it would only accept Christians from Syria because 'in Slovakia we don't have mosques,' according to an interior department spokesman.[58] In Poland, verification of 'Christian' status would have to be certified by clergy at home. Former French President Nicolas Sarkozy focused instead on economic factors, describing as 'folly' the idea of 'taking on dozens of thousands of migrants for whom we have no jobs in Europe.' With an unemployment rate exceeding 10%, France already has had deep problems with the assimilation of Muslim migrants since its colonial control of North Africa.

---

[56] https://www.ft.com/content/7728b140-b90a-11e5-b151-8e15c9a029fb.
[57] http://www.reuters.com/article/us-europe-migrants-netherlands-idUSKCN0RA0WY20150910.
[58] At the Bratislava EU Summit on 16th of September 2016, hosted by the Slovakia, the Visegrad Group called for 'flexible solidarity', a policy by which states that do not want to take migrants could contribute financially with equipment and manpower to the EU's migration policy – as is already the case in the Balkans.

The problems facing the northern French port town of Calais – where the bilateral treaty between France and the UK provided a barrier for UK entry – gives a constant reminder to the British and French public of the failure of immigration policies and lack of positive unified action to remedy the growth of 'ghetto' camps in and around the city. In France, the National Front has been able to leverage on citizens discontent and is likely to capitalise from this in future elections in the Nord-Pas-de-Calais regions and in the presidential elections to be held in the spring of 2017 – which currently jeopardise Francois Hollande's chances of a second term.

The Calais Impasse – criticised in many quarters as a major scandal – arises out of the inability of both the UK and France to resolve what has become a humanitarian tragedy. Reliance has been placed on the terms of a bilateral agreement in 2003 to set up immigration controls in each other's channel ports.[59] This is notwithstanding both countries being subject to UN and EU law in terms of their processing of asylum and refugees applications.

Controlling immigration has become one of the defining election issues in the UK and France – as with other western European members, particularly Germany and Holland. It is dominating the outcome of many local and national elections and was the principal factor in the upsurge of the United Kingdom Independence Party (UKIP), which was able to pull in popular support from both Left and Right by courting the anti-immigration, anti-EU and more general anti-establishment vote. In doing so, it attracted 5 million votes in the last UK general election in May 2015 – though under the British first-past-the-post electoral system, this gave it only a single seat.

Figures supplied to Parliament forecast that up to 3 million more migrants could arrive in the UK by 2030.[60] It is statistics like this that gave ammunition to the Leave campaign. Arguments put forward by government and think tanks claiming that immigration is good for the

---

[59] The Le Touquet Treaty between France and the UK, signed on 4th February 2003 moved the UK border to Calais, but this is under threat if the UK leaves the EU.
[60] https://hansard.parliament.uk/Commons/2016-05-05/debates/160505108000002/EUImmigration.

country-alienated voters in the depressed post-industrial towns and cities of North East England. On the contrary, it is constantly argued by local and regional authorities, including town and city councils, that high net immigration puts greater burden on the provision of local services and infrastructure – especially housing – at a time of austerity, an acute housing crisis and cutbacks in local services by central government. Economic counterarguments that show that immigration – especially highly skilled immigrants – has been a spur to economic growth and created more than 2 million jobs since 2005 fell on deaf ears with the majority of the electorate.[61] Although the Blair government post-2004 underestimated the level of economic migrants from the EU accession states, recent inflows have stabilised and any new surge is more likely from those still in the process of seeking membership (Serbia) or very recently joined (Croatia).

Terrorism and Security Issues

Exacerbating the formidable challenge Europe faces in the migration crisis is the growing security threats to its citizens from terror attacks, such as the coordinated bombings in Paris on 13 November 2015, killing 130, and Brussels in March 2016, which left 31 dead. (The group calling itself Islamic state (ISIL) admitted responsibility in both cases.) What made the attacks particularly alarming in the context of border security is that the terrorists have been able to re-enter the EU in the guise of refugees, as border controls do not track their movements back across the EU's external entry points from the training camps in Syria, Iraq and elsewhere.

---

[61] OECD April 2016 controversial report entitled 'The Economic Consequences of Brexit: A Taxing Decision' suggested that a Brexit vote would be damaging to the UK with a 'knock on' effect on other European countries and also reducing the UK GDP by over 3% by 2020 and 5% by 2030. The report forecasts a decline in foreign direct investment, as the UK would no longer be the conduit allowing for access to the EU internal market. See also the National Institute of Economic and Social Research (NIESR) report to be published on 9th May 2016.

As state authorities are pledged first and foremost to protect their citizens, the very freedoms upon which the EU was established have been increasingly placed under threat. Freedom of movement and travel, cornerstone principles of the EU, coupled with the right to privacy and freedom from surveillance, are challenged by these fears. Increasing the powers of the police and security services may, at least in the short term, help to counter this rising external threat. Investigation has shown that cross-border sharing of intelligence has not been effective and that improving and streamlining these channels through organs such as Interpol are vital to dealing with the problem in future.[62]

The open border policy in the EU does have some important caveats. It allows states to control borders in situations of 'national security', or for matters more vaguely defined as 'public policy'. The regulations were partly suspended during the worst of the crisis in August 2015 when the Merkel government in Germany made use of the 'sovereignty clause' to take on a special responsibility for processing applications for Syrian asylum refugees. This was followed by the Czech government in September, who also agreed that Syrian refugees could have their applications processed in the Czech Republic, even though they had applied for asylum in other EU countries.

In today's crises, the burden of conducting this rests on those countries with external EU borders through the Mediterranean; this overwhelmingly means Greece and Italy, with Greece, pivoted at the edge of Europe, carrying the greatest toll in terms of sheer numbers.[63]

Migration into the EU is not simply a consequence of recent wars in the Middle East or the on-going economic plight of Africa. It is also closely linked to broader processes of globalisation. As a result of the proliferation of the Internet throughout the third world – up from 9%

---

[62] http://www.telegraph.co.uk/news/2016/03/23/european-cross-border-security-years-away-experts-warn/.

[63] In 2008 the Italian and Libyan governments agreed a treaty to stop uncontrolled migration from Libya to Italy which led to the enforced return of migrants by the Italian coast guard authorities, a policy which fell apart with the advent of civil war against the Gaddafi regime in 2011 but which also led to a ruling by the European Court of Human Rights in 2012 that Italy was in breach of the European Convention of Human Rights for expelling migrants to face potential danger from the regime in Libya.

in 2006 to 32% in 2014⁶⁴ – driven by the exponential adoption of smartphones since 2007, the world's poorest citizens can now receive a much better picture of the economic opportunities, or necessities, present in the richer nations of the First World. Migrants do not have to be in war-torn Syria or eking out an existence in 'no go' areas in downtown Bagdad or Mogadishu. And typically, they no longer have faith in their country's ability to stabilise civil disorder, still less raise living standards and economic well-being.

On 20 March 2016, a deal was struck between the 28 EU leaders and Turkey with the aim of bringing to an end the flow of migrants through the Aegean and into Greece and then Macedonia and Serbia. The agreement in Brussels provided that all migrants crossing to Greece would be returned to Turkey (at the EU's expense) – but in exchange for every Syrian returned, one Syrian residing in a camp in Turkey would be resettled in the EU. It is often forgotten that at this point Turkey was already hosting over 1 million refugees.[65] To make the deal more attractive, Turkey was also to be given funding of €3 billion to help with the crisis, and a promise by Chancellor Merkel following her meeting with Turkish President Recep Tayyip Erdogan and Prime Minister Ahmet Davutoglu, to progress its application to join the EU.[66] As a further gesture of goodwill she also agreed to offer Germany's support to speed up plans to ease visa restrictions for Turkish citizens to visit the EU. This 'deal' was not without substantial problems for both politicians. A general election was scheduled in Turkey on 1 November and Erdogan and his ruling Islamic party (AK party) could have been accused by opposition parties for selling short on the country's EU accession issue. Merkel faced opposition at home from her own party as well as from Germans as a whole with support for her ruling conservative Christian Democrats falling below 40%. The Turkish attempted Coup d'Etat on 15 July rapidly put down by forces loyal to the government, and with overall support from the Turkish

---

[64] Data published by the Internal Telecommunications Union, published 25th May 2015.
[65] Lebanon and Jordan as well as in the Gulf states.
[66] EU leaders views on Turkish visas and Acqui Communitaire progression.

electorate new claims arose that democracy may be the real loser. This has soured relations between the EU and Turkey but not to the extent that the March agreement is in jeopardy (at least, not in 2016). Europe was slow and tame in their condemnation of the illegal coup, and EU leaders felt that the Erdogan government has used it as a pretext for clamping down on opponents of all categories.[67]

2015 saw a vast flow of migrants from Turkey to Greece, and Greece across the Balkans into the heart of the EU. These flows all but dried up after the EU and Turkey struck their deal in March. But the arrangement is fragile, which in many quarters is expected to eventually fail.[68] And in any case, the flow of migrants into Europe has not stopped and is on the rise again. According to the International Organization for Migration, more than 106,000 refugees and migrants arrived between July and August 2016 in Italy alone. Another 60,000 continue to languish in camps in Greece.

There are no simple answers to this on-going emergency. As discussed, the factors at work range across the political, social and economic spectrum. But it is unlikely that the fear and intolerance that has been provoked in many quarters is going to provide the correct answers. It is precisely the inability of European nations to coordinate a shared and cooperative approach to the crisis – the very concept on which the EU is founded – that is making the emergency so hard to control.

---

[67] https://eu.boell.org/en/2016/09/19/how-deal-post-coup-turkey.
[68] https://www.ft.com/content/48882f9a-5d48-11e6-a72a-bd4bf1198c63.

5

Brexit and the Referendum Vote

The surprise verdict in the UK Referendum decision on Thursday, 23 June, sent shock waves throughout the UK, the capitals of the European Union (EU) and world markets. Both Cameron's government and the European leadership had totally miscalculated the public mood. Even Leave campaigners were largely surprised at the outcome. Elites in Brussels and across the EU reeled at the news and in the instability it would cause. The verdict was greeted as one of the most momentous events in Europe since the collapse of communism in 1989. It means that both Britain, the EU, and possibly the world were entering unchartered waters. Previous referendums in Denmark and Ireland had been overturned,[1] but the Prime Minister (PM) had declared in advance that this was an 'all or nothing with no going back'. Unlike other referendums, it had the approval of both Houses of Parliament and so it required no additional endorsement through their votes. So to fall back on the claim it was only 'advisory' – in legal terms – would not wash with the electorate, still less with Eurosceptic wing of the Conservative party.

---

[1] Nice and Lisbon treaty.

© The Author(s) 2017
J. Theodore et al., *The European Union and the Eurozone under Stress*, DOI 10.1007/978-3-319-52292-0_5

The post-mortem on such a seismic event in the history of Britain, Europe and the EU will be debated for many years. Deep roots can be found in the growing mood of Eurosceptic since the ongoing Eurozone and migration crises of the region. For years, voters of all the major political parties had grown ever more hostile towards the free movement of people. Polls have repeatedly shown immigration rivalling or leading the economy as the public's biggest concern. It was in this climate that United Kingdom Independence Party (UKIP), a party of relatively trivial status, was able to flourish – coming first with 24% of the popular vote in the 2014 European elections, the first time an outsider party had won a British national election in a hundred years.

It is hard to dispute that Vote Leave ran a far better campaign than their Remain rivals. Its message was tight, focused and simple – with the line 'Vote Leave, take Back Control.' This appealed to both sceptics of European integration on the 'sovereignty' issue, and the large pool of voters – particularly from white working class backgrounds – concerned with the loss of immigration control. Whereas Cameron had, since he first formed a coalition government in 2010, sought to appease voters by pledging to reduce net migration to tens of thousands a year, by the time of the Referendum, the figure stood at a third of a million – an order of magnitude above the stated goal. Furthermore, he failed to secure limits on free movement in his EU negotiations, owing to the objections of Germany and other member states. These failures emboldened Vote Leave's cry to 'Take Back Control' (implicitly, 'of our borders') and enabled them to run an aggressive and immigration-focused campaign.

The Remain side never crafted an effective counter to this slogan. Instead, it misjudged the popular mood in its repeated warnings of economic chaos and technocratic invocations of elite banking and business opinion. But the former claim, inflated sometimes by absurdly speculative claims, was easily dismissed as 'Project Fear' – a label borrowed and retooled from the Scottish National Party (SNP) campaign for Scottish independence in 2014. George Osborne's suggestion that GDP would fall by the equivalent of £4300 per household was simply not widely believed. And nor were the legion of economists, academics and business minds; many of them were charged with failing to anticipate the 2008 crash, or even fuelling it, regarded as credible.[2] Furthermore, Brexiters neutralised the economic argument by moving the campaign onto territory far more comfortable for them – immigration, the migration crisis and Turkey (in the latter case, implying that 75 million would soon have an opportunity to descend onto British shores).

Millions of UK (and EU) citizens have, for a long time, felt disenfranchised from both the political decision-making processes and the supposed benefits of globalisation. Growth for them has, especially since 2008, meant stagnant wages, increasing unemployment and austerity budgets – without any punitive retaliation against the banking or political classes that failed to secure them against the social and economic upheavals of the twenty-first century. These concerns have not been ameliorated by the popular press, who have fed the public with detailed account of the misbehaviour of bankers over bonuses and allegations of criminal behaviour over Libor (culminating in prosecutions) and Forex rigging of the financial markets.[3] These activities have not endeared institutional elites to the public nor to legislators in the Parliament. It is not surprising that sympathy is in short supply from voters to champion the banks as a special case in the Brexit negotiations, even though the financial sector accounted for £67 billion towards UK tax revenues in 2014/2015 – or 11% of total receipts, an enormous sum.[4]

The *neoliberal* elite in Brussels had for years buried its head in the sand against the festering populist discontent, passing the buck to the member states to face off these opposition movements. Could Brexit have been avoided had the pre-referendum negotiations with Brussels given Cameron a better deal on EU immigration? Probably not – as Brussels had no mandate to change the treaties relating to the Single Market – namely, its sacred four freedoms, including Freedom of Movement (FOM). 'Ever closer union' was easier to part with, as it would relate more to political

---

[2] 'The British public has had enough of experts', Michael Gove was able to effectively claim in a Question Time interview.
[3] https://www.gov.uk/government/news/chancellor-confirms-manipulation-of-key-forex-benchmark-to-be-made-a-criminal-offense.
[4] http://www.dailymail.co.uk/wires/reuters/article-3654693/Financial-services-British-economy.html.

extensions for those states anchored to the Euro. But it was also largely ceremonial. If any one factor can be attributed to the success of the Leave campaign then an unreformed policy on FOM with all its implications became the catalyst for the Brexit victory but without any realistic solutions on what form it would take; and with no answers on how the UK economy would function without vital immigrant labour to run its National Health Service (NHS) hospitals, hospitality sector and the high demand for seasonal workers. Recouping full sovereignty may become a very expensive consequence of leaving the EU: inviting an oft quoted phrase that sovereignty is the right to commit economic suicide. What this invites is a reality check: all ideological governments, of both Left and Right, must note that sovereignty, without total political and economic disengagement from globalization, has a more limited meaning in today's world. It begs the question of what is 'sovereignty'in a complex economic global environment governed by the whims and vicissitudes of international markets. The UK government, planning the negotiations for an exit from the EU, is already taking hard lessons on how the economy may fare not only post-Brexit but from now until the time of the *divorce absolute*. In the words of the Chancellor Philip Hammond at the October 2016 Conservative party conference... 'the British people did not vote on 23 June 'to become poorer, or less secure.'[5] Yet investors have started to mark down the value of the UK's asset base by selling the pound sterling – down over 15% since the Referendum outcome in the fall of 2016 – as they price in the implications of a hard Brexit.[6]

What Happens Now?

The defining statement of the newly formed government – one replenished with Brexiters such as David Davis as 'Brexit Minister' and Liam Fox as Secretary for International Trade – has been avowal made by Teresa May, the Conservative party's newly anointed leader (and lukewarm supporter of the Remain until the outcome) – namely, the mantra

---

[5] Conservative party Conference Birmingham 2nd October 2016.
[6] https://www.ft.com/content/939c7ed0-8e32-11e6-a72e-b428cb934b78.

'Brexit means Brexit'. Her pitch for the future of Britain upon accession to the head of government was the statement that 'We will rise to the challenge. As we leave the European Union we will forge a bold new positive role for ourselves in the world, and we will make Britain a country that works not for a privileged few but for every one of us.'[7]

Her message was both upbeat and recognised the world of English nationalist fervour. It would be very difficult for any English Conservative party to ignore those nativist instincts and their role in the vote – especially from the regions where people have seen a very unequal distribution of the benefits of globalisation in recent decades, notably Wales and the North of England. Attempting to strike a populist chord, the new PM defined the Brexit vote as a notice from people who 'were not prepared to be ignored anymore,' that 'life does not seem fair' for those who believe that they have been made poorer by low-skilled immigration and adding 'Because in June people voted for change, and a change is going to come.'[8]

Such a speech was aimed both to recalibrate the public's increasingly elitist perceptions of the Tories under Cameron and, more broadly, to defuse the anger of those who never felt the benefits of EU membership – thereby stealing ground both from Labour and UKIP. No analysis of the new Prime Minister June Brexit's statement could gauge the direction of travel as no ready plan for 'Brexit' was available – only potential 'options' with impacts not fully examined. It is often forgotten that the government had actually fought its 2015 election campaign on a platform to keep Britain in the Single Market – for which there was both cross-party accord and the sustained support of an average of 59% of the British public both before and after the referendum. But this economic relationship is in jeopardy as the government grapples with the full implications of an EU exit. It is guided in the first instance by the notification procedure laid down in Article 50 of the Lisbon Treaty and, after a long

---

[7] www.reuters.com/article/us-britain-eu-wrapup-idUSKCN0ZR19P.

[8] https://www.theguardian.com/politics/2016/oct/05/theresa-may-conference-interventionist-government-for-workers?.

public procrastination, Theresa May used her opening address on 2 October at the Conservative party conference to announce that formal notification will be given no later than the end of March 2017. Europe is now on notice that notification for withdrawal is coming – almost certainly no later than early 2019. This is a preliminary but important step for each side to draw up their respective battle lines. If May is to hold firm to statements made in Birmingham (Conservative Conference) regarding the imposition of migration controls on EU citizens coming to the UK as being non-negotiable, and also relinquish the jurisdiction of the European Court of Justice (ECJ) it closes any chance of remaining a part of the Single Market – leaving only a 'bespoke' free trade agreement (FTA) for discussion with the EU. The Labour party (with other opposition parties) have galvanised their demands for advanced notice of the negotiating strategy to be deployed by the government. This has been refused as it would give advanced notice to the EU negotiators. One could sympathise with this response if it were not for the PM's statement: 'We are going to be a fully independent, sovereign country – a country that is no longer part of a political union with supranational institutions that can override national parliaments and courts ... So it is not going to a "Norway model". It's not going to be a 'Switzerland model'. It is going to be an agreement between an independent, sovereign United Kingdom and the EU', which already indicates the hard lines around which the negotiations must revolve.[9]

The driving force of the Leave campaigners has rested in their confident belief that Britain can 'can go it alone' economically by establishing new bilateral trade relations with countries around the world; in particular, with India and China, and with the Commonwealth nations, in particular Australia and New Zealand. One of the problems with this approach lies in the timing. Britain is still an EU member and is not in a rightful position to start negotiations never mind that these countries – outside the EU – would want to commit before the ink has dried on the Brexit deal. More disturbing for future negotiations is the state of global

---

[9] https://www.ft.com/content/939c7ed0-8e32-11e6-a72e-b428cb934b78.

trade, with growing evidence of stagnation and a rising tide of protectionism, as evidenced in the anti-free-trade and anti-NAFTA populist policies advocated by President-elect Donald Trump.[10]

The EU Divorce and Article 50 (Lisbon Treaty)

Divorce from the EU is unknown. No precedent exists to guide the parties except as to the form in the Lisbon Treaty for officially starting the process.[11] Under these terms, an agreement must be reached within two years when formal negotiations end with a *decree absolute*.

What must be clear to even the most ardent Brexiteer is the danger of invoking this legal mechanism too soon, without a clear and coherent vision of the alternatives – but all of which requires substantial preparatory work with potential forecasts of the likely success (or failure) of negotiations for the desired result. These will probably be the most complex commercial, economic and political negotiations of any kind ever undertaken by a sovereign state. To help unravel the plethora of treaties with the EU, the UK government has established a dedicated Brexit ministry as well as restructuring many Whitehall departments of state in readiness for the work.

The immediate reaction from UK's main EU partners was sadness and shock, but mingled with a desire for a quick divorce to contain the instability the decision created in stock, bond and currency markets, and to limit the possibility of political or economic contagion.[12] But clearly this could not happen. The British government had to get its act

---

[10] http://www.huffingtonpost.com/dana-geffner/why-stop-the-transpacific_b_11665450.html.

[11] Article 50 Lisbon Treaty, there are other means to leave the EU, but both the UK and the EU have agreed this would be the process for Brexit. To start the process, the UK must make a formal decision to leave the EU and notify the EU Council of member states of this decision. Once triggered, there will be a maximum two-year deadline for exit. At the end of two years, even if no agreement has been reached, the UK will cease to be an EU member state. The deadline can only be extended by unanimous consent. In theory, Britain could leave in less than two years if there is agreement.

[12] http://www.investmentbank.barclays.com/our-insights/brexit-and-europe-the-question-of-contagion2.html.

together and develop its strategy for future negotiations. EU partners without exception – though some with certain caveats – understood this was necessary.[13] The French President Francois Hollande at a press conference with Teresa May on 21 July changed his initial stance on wanting to speed up Brexit negotiations accepting that, 'There could be some preparation for this negotiation... But I repeat, the better, the sooner, in the common interest of Europe, the UK and our economies.'[14]

Legal Aspects

Article 50 of the Treaty on European Union (incorporated into the 2007 Lisbon Treaty)[15] is a far-reaching legal 'known unknown'.[16] Triggering Article 50 provides great uncertainty famously referred to by David Cameron: a vote to leave 'is the gamble of the Century'.[17] Once invoked there is no turning back, at least theoretically – for, in the context of Article 50, very little is 'known'. It was drafted as a framework 'breakaway' clause for any EU member deciding to leave the Union. It entitles any member to withdraw from the EU and establishes how to do it. Art 50(1):

Article 50 states that: In the light of the guidelines provided by the European Council, the Union shall negotiate and conclude

---

[13] Chancellor Merkel at her Berlin meeting with Teresa May 20th July afterwards said in support of the Prime Minister that it was right and necessary for Britain 'to take a moment' to work out what it wants.... We are listening to the UK, we are listening to Britain what it actually wants and then we will give our right response'.

[14] Reported in the FT July 22nd 2016.

[15] Art. 50 of the Lisbon Treaty 1st December 2009.

[16] A phrase famously used by a former US defence secretary Donald Rumsfelt once put it to questions at a NATO press conference before the invasion of Iraq in 2003. *www.nato.int/docu/ speech/2002/s020606g.htm6* Jun 2002 a statement made by Donald Rumsfelt at a NATO press conference in answer to a question as to evidence of weapons of mass destruction held by the Iraqi regime.

[17] http://www.telegraph.co.uk/news/politics/david-cameron/12176325/David-Cameron-Brexit-would-be-gamble-of-the-century.html.

an agreement with that State, setting out the arrangements for its withdrawal, taking account of the framework for its future relationship with the Union.

'1. Any member state may decide to withdraw from the Union in accordance with its own constitutional requirements.' Art 50(2):

'2. A member state which decides to withdraw shall notify the European Council of its intention...'[18]

There is a legal argument that the power to invoke Article 50 of the Treaty on the European Union is a *royal prerogative* – namely, a right that can be exercised by the Crown which, in effect, means that it can be implemented by the government without parliamentary consent. This, however, is a view that has been challenged. Legal action to this could be taken on the grounds that only the sovereign act of Parliament can bring this into effect (mindful of the fact the majority of MPs and the House of Lords supported the Remain campaign in the Referendum). There is a further legal argument that a referendum decision is *only* advisory although the decision to hold the Referendum passed both Houses of Parliament.[19] How the clause is finally interpreted will be the subject of intense and continuing legal discussions.[20] A High Court's ruling on 3 November 2016 in a case brought by private litigants established that the government could *not* trigger Article 50 of the Lisbon Treaty without Parliament's approval. The government appealed to the Supreme Court, and the results of a hearing which commenced on 8 December 2016 are expected in the middle of January 2017. However a non-binding motion in the House of Commons (7 December) backed, by an overwhelming majority, Theresa May's bid to trigger Article 50 and begin Brexit by the end of March 2017.

---

[18] In the light of the guidelines provided by the European Council, the Union shall negotiate and concluded an agreement with that state, to be negotiated in accordance with Article 218(3) of the Treaty on the functioning of the European Union.

[19] In addition the conservative party general election manifesto was to 'let the people decide' ergo not a promise to hold an advisory referendum but stronger closer to representing the 'will of the people'.

[20] There has never been any doubt that a member state could leave the EU in practice under International law.

Exit without Article 50

Article 50 states that 'the Treaties shall cease to apply to the State in question from the date of entry into force of the withdrawal agreement or, failing that, two years after the notification referred to in paragraph 2, unless the European Council, in agreement with the Member State concerned, unanimously decides to extend this period.' This is unchartered territory and relies on the political dynamics at the time. 'It also says that: If a State which has withdrawn from the Union, asks to rejoin, its request shall be subject to the procedure referred to in Article 49.'[21]

Can Britain change its mind once Article 50 is invoked? Can the procedure be stopped or reversed? Article 50 is not clear on this. Lord Kerr, one of the draftees of the European convention in 2003, argues that the absence of explicit guidance is telling. 'There is nothing in the treaty saying it's irreversible. So it isn't. But of course some might want some sort of price to be paid,' he said.[22]

European Commission lawyers take a harder line. To them, a decision to invoke Article 50 is a legal act that cannot be withdrawn. In practical terms, one scenario they want to avoid is a hostile Britain withdrawing and resubmitting its notification, thereby resetting the two-year deadline. 'This cannot be done unilaterally,' says a senior EU official.

It is doubtful, but if this state of affairs arose, then any final deliberation would rest with the member states to adjudicate and come to a collective decision. In a nutshell, to be sure of discontinuing the Brexit process, Britain would need unanimity. Giving notice under Article 50 reinforces only the aim to cease dealing retrospectively with Treaty obligations. The terms of the divorce then need to be hacked out on time regarding any overriding obligations, budget payments, membership rights of EU agencies, liabilities to pensions for EU staff and funding arrangements for UK universities.

The first deadline for discussions expires after two years. Considering the time span for trade deals normally far exceeds this, there is a general

---

[21] https://www.ft.com/content/2f64f006-4dbd-11e6-88c5-db83e98a590a.
[22] www.ft.com › Comment › The Big Read FT 20th July 2016.

consensus that the negotiations are likely to be significantly extended. The way Article 50 is drafted implies that there will be no deal until *everything* is agreed because there are too many moving parts. That suggests a protracted period of uncertainty for businesses and EU citizens.

Britain remains a full member, with full membership rights, until the day it leaves – on present estimates at the end of March 2019. But time on this relationship is in effect running out since the end of the Brexit vote – before even the legalities of formal notification. The UK's influence on Brussels institutions no longer counts as EU leaders now meet in her absence to deliberate on the way forward post-Brexit. Apart from the NATO summit in 8–10 July when all EU (and others) met in Warsaw on security matters, the UK's presence is unlikely to take place at the highest levels in the corridors of power. British bureaucrats will continue to provide a supportive role but otherwise play no part in EU policymaking procedures going forward.

To secure the best arrangements from the UK's 40-year partnership entails an exit deal under Article 50 agreed through EU rules, under the pressure of a two-year deadline which only the EU can prolong. Apart from the business of unravelling from obligations under the treaties, for liabilities such as outstanding budget payments, there are complex negotiations over projects where continued cooperation is seen as mutually desirable – for example, EU university collaborative research such as those in the sciences, health and technology. The appropriate exit deal for these remains unclear.

EU Funding Streams

It is not possible to discuss the potential impact of these funding changes for all sectors of the economy. Focus below is limited to those 'beacons' of success which have attracted substantial EU funding, and which will need special attention in EU negotiations to ensure that the UK's global position and reputation is maintained.

Would the UK continue to make EU budget contributions for these? What about the membership rights of EU agencies and other liabilities and funding arrangements for UK universities? Research and Knowledge Enterprise (RKE) divisions in the Higher Education (HE) sector will be watching closely (and lobbying for) as to whether there interests are sufficiently represented for continued participation and collaboration in EU funding projects, especially those under the Horizon 20/20 programmes, Erasmus Plus and other appropriate funding streams.

Conscious of these feelings of uncertainty – and the potential damage to the flourishing HE sector – the British government has tried to allay such fears. At least in the short term (until 2020), it has signalled a promise to guarantee the continuation of the EU funding that would inevitably halt when the UK leaves the EU. What will replace it remains to be seen and also depends on the climate of negotiations for the sector. UK universities will no doubt find ways of funding and develop parallel arrangements. Representations by the HE sector will force the government to review future funding plans beyond 2020 to sustain the UK's important role and competitive position in research and innovation. In the meantime, the universities may well develop bilateral and parallel negotiations with partners. This will be in the hope that access to EU funding (e.g. Horizon 20/20) will be part of any final UK–EU Brexit terms.

Chancellor Philip Hammond announced that he wants to give people 'reassurance... stability and certainty' by honouring EU funding valued in excess of £4 billion a year. The government would finance it from the savings made from Britain's £8.5 billion net contribution to the European Union, which it would stop paying on exit from the EU.

'The UK will continue to have the all of the rights, obligations and benefits that membership brings, including receiving European funding, up until the point we leave the EU... we recognize that many organizations across the UK, which are in receipt of EU funding, or membership brings, including receiving European funding, up until the point we leave the EU expect to start receiving funding, want reassurance about the flow of funding they will receive...[23] that's why I am confirming

---

[23] He also pledged Government funding to cover the cost of any projects which have secured EU structural funding before the 2016 Autumn Statement, which was worth up to £2.3billion a year including the cost of funds for science parks and research facilities.

that structural and investment funds projects signed before the Autumn Statement and Horizon research funding granted before we leave the EU will be guaranteed by the Treasury after we leave.'[24] It must be noted, however, that this commitment is *only until 2020* – although it is expected that a strategy will be developed in due course. In the meantime, institutions and businesses can continue to bid in the interim while Brexit negotiations take place. This statement gives a measure of very short-term comfort but no clarity on what is to follow, and no assurance for the mid- to long-term future for these sectors ability to tap into EU funding sources.

One of the biggest unsung success stories promoting the 'European ideal' has been the Erasmus Exchange programme for universities now managed in the UK by the British Council. The fear is that Britain could face rejection from this European-wide university study programme.[25] The programme was launched by the European Commission in 1987, and since then more than two million students have benefited from Erasmus-funded awards for studying in other EU destinations. Under the Erasmus scheme, British students have been able to study at European HE institutions for up to a year and European students in the UK. But after Brexit, says the scheme's UK director, Ruth Sinclair-Jones, 'We face a sad moment of uncertainty, after 30 years of this enrichment of so many lives.'[26]

Exclusion from Erasmus would also have a bearing on university student finances, as will those (already noted) for scientific, research and innovation. Since the programme started in 1987, over 200,000 British students have taken part with their grants paid by EU funding. Sinclair-Jones said that those now in the scheme or applying for next year should be unaffected but 'in the long term, it's an unknown situation. We will continue with our plans until 2017 but after that

---

[24] http://www.telegraph.co.uk/news/2016/08/12/britain-will-cover-cost-of-billions-in-eu-subsidies-for-farming/.
[25] The UK could stay in the Erasmus scheme if Brexit accepts a Norway option.
[26] https://www.theguardian.com/education/2016/jul/23/erasmus-scheme-exclude-british-students-brexit.

we have to wait'.[27] 'In Britain, interest has accelerated,' said Sinclair-Jones, who is based at the British Council, which operates the UK end of the programme with an organisation called Ecorys. 'In 2007 we had 7,500 applications to study in Europe. By 2013 that had risen to 15,000.'

Considering the options open to negotiating a way to keep Britain in the scheme, the Universities UK group, which liaises between academic institutions receiving and sending Erasmus students, points out that Norway is a participant but as one of its officers points out that 'Norway has accepted freedom of movement as part of its relationship to the EU, and we don't know if Britain will do that.'[28]

However, he says 'The Swiss had their referendum limiting freedom of movement and were told they are therefore out of Erasmus. Switzerland has now initiated its own scheme but this costs a lot of money – and raises the issue that only better-off families can be part of it. The great thing about Erasmus is that it made the experience and opportunity available to every student, whatever their family means.'

More broadly speaking, the toll from an exit on the HE sector is likely to be substantial. Universities UK calculates that fees paid by EU students totalled £600 million in 2014–2015 and that students from Europe spend £1.49 billion a year in off-campus costs, such as rent and subsistence. The fees alone play a substantial role in grants to poorer British students.

But university income could also suffer from the loss of EU students – and, in a climate less favourable to migration, non-EU students as well – as a recent international student survey showed as much as one third of respondents were less likely to study in UK after Brexit. Of 1014 students surveyed by Hobsons, a careers advisory service, in July 2016[29], 30% said that they were less likely to study in the UK, while 6% said that they would definitely not study in the UK as a result of the vote.

---

[27] Ibid.
[28] www.theguardian.com › Education › Higher education.
[29] Jeremy Cooper, Managing Director of Hobsons in Europe, said: 'Market conditions for international student recruitment look set to toughen and universities need to send a clear message that the UK welcomes international students, as well as providing practical guidance and support.'

Hobsons said that 83% of respondents were from outside the EU. Income from international students is set to reach £4.2 billion in 2016–2017 and £4.6 billion in 2017–2018, and is the biggest source of revenue growth for universities, according to the HE Funding Council for England.[30]

SMEs and Start-Up Post-Brexit

Small and Medium Enterprises (SMEs) are the lifeblood of the economy and the sector which the EU has a mission statement to support. Consequently, Brexit will not be without consequences for them. 'Micro' businesses in the north of England needing a mixture of debt and equity finance are especially at risk after the government stated that it could not yet guarantee a continued flow of cash from the EU similar to the business support provided by ERDF and ESF. These funds, named 'Jeremie' – Joint European Resources for Micro to Medium Enterprises – are vital for growing small- and medium-sized enterprises – they have supported more than 1,700 companies creating more than 10,000 jobs in the past six years.[31] Other regions such as Yorkshire and the North East have been eligible for similar SME funding.

'For many Small and Medium Enterprises losing access to EU funding will create challenges especially as the UK will be even more reliant on the skills of entrepreneurs to grow the UK economy in the uncertain post-Brexit economy environment.' states Amin Amiri, a leading UK Venture Capitalist and Managing Director of a2e Industries Ltd. . . . 'So it is vital that the government ensures that the sector continues to have access to debt and equity finance especially if this is no longer available from the EU.'[32] Amiri is also concerned that 'UK mid-market companies are at a serious disadvantage compared to Germany, France and

---

[30] https://www.ft.com/content/c179cb10-53f3-11e6-9664-e0bdc13c3bef.
[31] Almost half the money in the funds comes from the European Regional Development Fund, with the European Investment Bank matching that with a repayable loan, with the rest from local resources.
[32] Interview on Sept 2016.

USA, when it comes to accessing funds for growth. Successive UK governments have not sufficiently addressed this albeit that sporadic attempts have been made. He went on to say... 'I do hope that EU sources of funds are replicated by the UK Government, in due course,' pointing out that 'the vulnerability of these businesses with the imposition of trade tariffs creating serious complications relating to costs and other factors jeopardising these firms to remain in the supply chains, at least in the medium term. Unless Specific tariff exemptions are negotiated, the UK will effectively surrender its supply chain participation in many sectors (aerospace, automotive, pharmaceutical are example) to the competitors, albeit over a period.'[33]

Venture Capital Funds – The European Investment Fund (EIF)

The EIF was created by the EU in the 1990s as a subsidiary of the older and larger European Investment Bank (EIB). Unlike the EIB, which is wholly owned by the EU's member states, the EIF is a public–private partnership, with commercial banks and other financial institutions amongst its shareholders.

The loss of this kind of funding support for British-based entrepreneurs would be a substantial blow to venture capital if it were not would have substituted with funding from national sources. The EIF's nearest UK equivalent is the British Business Bank, established by the previous coalition government in 2014. As with the EIB, access to the EIF should be a priority in exit negotiations.

For Tim Hames, Director-General of the British Private Equity and Venture Capital Association, what makes the EIF special is not just the scale of its support, but the fact that it is prepared to keep on investing in the same funds again and again. 'It does not regard its role in life as just seed capital. It is a persistent long-term investor,' he said. 'It is a partner

---

[33] Ibid.

rather than just a pump primer. You can perhaps replace the money, but how do you retain that culture?'[34]

Under the EIF's current rules, its lending is limited to EU nations, members of the European Free Trade Association, as well as 'potential' candidates to join the EU. The EIF has been active in Turkey, as it is a candidate country for EU membership, and also has a targeted programme in Israel. The fund sought to strike a reassuring tone in the immediate aftermath of the Brexit vote, saying it 'will not change its approach to operations in the UK' while negotiations on the British exit are under way.[35]

The European Investment Bank (EIB)

The EIB has been an important funding source for larger businesses in the UK. It was established in 1957 with a specific remit to lend to infrastructure projects across the EU. The UK is one of the main shareholders holding over 16% and over the years has benefited enormously from these funds. In 2015, EIB UK investment increased to £7.7 billion by 10.8% in 2014 to finance hospitals, schools, university (€260 million to Swansea and Oxford universities for research and improved teaching facilities) and important transport links. In the past, these included the Channel tunnel, and leading participation with the relevant syndicates in financing projects such as the second Severn Bridge crossing, the Jubilee Line London underground extension, Heathrow Express and fast rail links to Dover.[36] It also finances indirectly through UK banks to SMEs.

Will the UK lose this source of funding post-Brexit – and if so, when? All this, including the continued participation of the UK as a shareholder of the bank, remains an open-ended question. Although Britain

---

[34] https://www.ft.com/content/5a85be66-5d42-11e6-bb77-a121aa8abd95.
[35] Ibid.
[36] https://www.gov.uk/government/news/new-figures-show-record-european-investment-bank-investment-in-uk-in-2015.

has been an important contributor, as a non-EU member, it would *prima facie* not be eligible for EIB loans, so any decision for a loan would be for the EIB Board. The value of these EIB loans to the UK is as follows:

- £200 million to improve Oxford university's research and teaching
- £400 million for social housing in London
- £1 billion for installing electricity smart meters
- £150 million to expand the Port of Liverpool[37]

A recent statement by Werner Hoyer, the president of the EIB, told the Financial Times that recent levels of lending to the UK 'cannot be maintained.' British companies will have difficulties borrowing for infrastructure projects from the European Investment Bank as Brexit draws closer. This has proven a setback for the new Chancellor Philip Hammond and Teresa May, who in abandoning the previous Chancellor's (George Osborne) austerity programme were planning to use this as an opportunity to ramp up infrastructure spending. 'The UK is relying heavily on us and there are many people in the UK who will miss the EIB,' Werner Hoyer said, '[and] I foresee developments in the [Brexit] negotiations that will make it not easier to continue with lending decisions because these will have to be taken . . . by the representatives of the member states . . . Even if we find a way to continue lending in the UK, I am absolutely sure that the enormous volumes we have achieved over the last couple of years cannot be maintained.'[38]

One important casualty following the Brexit decision is the resignation of Jonathan Hill who held – for Britain – one of the most prestigious EU Commissioner portfolios as European Financial Stability, Financial Services and Capital Markets Commissioner since (only) 2015.[39] His work contributed to proposals, which will introduce measures to boost the size of the EU market for venture capital – well

---

[37] http://www.eib.org/projects/regions/european-union/united-kingdom/index.htm.
[38] 'EIB Chief warns UK will struggle without cheap EU loans', https://www.ft.com/content/5494d5ea-8e0d-11e6-8df8-d3778b55a923.
[39] The portfolio included responsibility for the regulation of banks and markets in the EU.

behind that of the Unites States – in a bid to expand access to capital for smaller companies (SMEs) in Europe.

It is well known that venture capital funds invest in riskier, emerging firms that are usually avoided by banks and more cautious investors. The industry is seen as important to foster innovation but remains a small player in Europe with a market of €5 billion (£4.2 billion) – five times smaller than in the United States.

SMEs in Europe obtain 75% percent of their funding from the established retail banks, but lending from these institutions has been less forthcoming in the aftermath of the 2008 financial crisis. This is due both to the need to maintain higher capital requirements and growing aversion to risk influenced by the increase of non-performing loans (NPLs) that plague the balance sheets of most European banks. The EU Commission has recognised the advantages of opening up the venture capital markets and permit larger funds to invest in riskier start-ups without facing higher requirements. The Commission has also sought to expand the assets in which venture capital funds can invest to include smaller firms. Red tape and fees will therefore be lowered. The fund industry supported the Commission proposal, though EU states and the European Parliament will have to approve the proposals before they can take effect.[40]

Reactions in Europe

Across Europe, the reaction to the British referendum result goes beyond the simple shock and sadness that, for the first time since the EU's founding 1957 Treaty of Rome, a member will be leaving the union. In Spain, for example, it is stimulating apprehension that Scotland's reinvigorated push for independence after the English-driven Leave vote in Britain will inspire barely dormant separatist currents in the region of Catalonia. In Ireland, the British result is stirring concern about the resilience of Northern Ireland's Good Friday peace settlement – founded

---

[40] http://uk.reuters.com/article/uk-eu-funds-venturecapital-idUKKCN0ZU14F.

as it is on a common border between north and south through the infrastructure of EU free movements laws. Even the status of Gibraltar could also be a concern in that the Remain vote was 98% in favour of remaining in the EU. The Gibraltarians have a dichotomy in that they want to remain in the United Kingdom but not at the expense of losing their sovereignty. This, to some extent, mirrors the dilemma facing the countries of Britain.

The Bratislava Summit 16 September 2016 hosted by Slovakia was held in the shadow of Britain leaving the EU, continuing debates about immigration, which also dominated the Brexit campaign, and the weak and uncoordinated response to the refugee crisis. It followed also the NATO security summit in Warsaw 9 July, dedicated to security and terrorism.

The summit was an attempt to set the stage for addressing outstanding challenges for the European project, to create the mindset for correcting what was wrong and to agree a roadmap for progress on a number of fronts. Donald Tusk, the European Council president asked EU leaders to take a ' brutally honest' look at the bloc's problems ... 'We must not let this crisis go to waste.' 'We haven't come to Bratislava to comfort each other or even worse to deny the real challenges we face in this particular moment in the history of our community after the vote in the UK,' He went on to stress:

'We can't start our discussion ... with this kind of blissful conviction that nothing is wrong, that everything was and is OK,' he added. 'We have to assure ... our citizens that we have learned the lesson from Brexit and we are able to bring back stability and a sense of security and effective protection.'[41]

Even before the Referendum took place, Donald Tusk had warned EU leaders of the centre-right at a meeting in Luxembourg ... ' that ordinary European citizens did not share the enthusiasm of some of their leaders for 'a utopia of Europe without nation states, a utopia of Europe without conflicting interests and ambitions, a utopia of

---

[41] https://www.theguardian.com/world/2016/sep/16/bratislava-summit-donald-tusk-urges-eu-leaders-not-to-waste-brexit-crisis?CMP=Share_iOSApp_Other.

Europe imposing its own values on the external world, a utopia of Euro-Asian unity'. It followed that EU politicians and policymakers should scale back their ambitions in this regard. He went on to warn that 'Increasingly loud are those who question the very principle of a united Europe. The spectre of a break-up is haunting Europe and a vision of a federation doesn't seem to me to be the best answer to it.'

Echoing these remarks, Jeroen Dijsselbloem, the Dutch finance minister, who chairs the Eurogroup (the finance committee of the Eurozone), told a meeting on 21 June at the Wirtschaftstag in Berlin: 'In the eurozone some are pushing for a completion of the monetary union by creating a full political union, a euro area economic government or even a euro budget ... To me it is obvious: we need to strengthen what we have and finish it, but let's not build more extensions to the European house while it is so unstable.'[42]

Dijsselbloem has been a central figure in Eurozone bailout programs and is a keen advocate of completing the implementation of the EU's banking union, establishing a capital markets union (CMU) and deepening the bloc's Single Market. However, the plan for banking union is sowing rising discord amongst member nations. Germany's reluctance to approve a common deposit insurance scheme, on the grounds that the Eurozone has not done enough to curb excessive risk-taking in the financial sector, means that one pillar of banking union is blocked.

For some time now, observers of the EU political experiment could be forgiven for detecting a certain assertiveness by the leaders of the Visegrad group. Apart from vocally voicing their views against imposed refugee quotas, they have been in the vanguard in challenging the hegemony and centralization of EU power in Brussels. However, both Hungary and Poland have been under the Commission's scrutiny for the attempts by their governments to interfere with their judicial systems and the Rule of Law. In Poland it relates to the on-going Venice

---

[42] www.consilium.europa.eu > council-eu.

Tribunal investigation into breaches of the principles of democracy and the Rule of Law.[43] The ruling Law and Justice Party (PIS) has tried to strip the power of the Constitutional Court, and therefore the independence of the judiciary of the highest court in the land. The government's reforms aim to change how the Constitutional Court works as well as blocking the appointment of judges which in effect goes against the principle of separation of powers and therefore comes into conflict with EU principles which Poland has signed up. Michael Kobosko, Director of Poland Office at the Atlantic Council on international affairs, says, 'This means in effect the review process of legislation will actually no longer be in the hands of the Constitutional Court. This is probably the biggest dispute between Poland and the EU at present.'[44]

This dispute with Brussels is on-going and will not end anytime soon. In the case of the Orbans government in Hungary, it concerns changes to the Constitution, eroding the legal framework consistent with democratic principles and EU treaties.[45]

A number of points need to be stated about the appointees to the EU Commission. Strictly speaking, it is wrong to speak of the EU Commission as unelected – as its appointment is made by those who *are* directly elected. So in the case of the 28 Commissioners their 'appointment' is made by *directly* elected national governments, many candidates of whom served in previous administrations such as the present Commissioner for the Internal Market (Elzbieta Bienkowska) who was formerly a minister in Donald Tusk's government in Poland. Each commissioner is vetted by the European Parliament who must give their approval. The next step is to be taken formally by the European Council.[46] With the appointment of the President of the Commission, the selection process is by the national Heads of State and Government,

---

[43] http://www.liberties.eu/en/news/rule-of-law-framework-poland.
[44] Interview held on 11th July 2016 with Michael Kobosko Director Atlantic Council; Wroclaw Global Forum.
[45] https://www.ft.com/content/e99d3b12-6b96-11e6-a0b1-d87a9fea034f.
[46] Treaty on the European Union 2009 Art: 17.7.

taking into consideration the outcome of the EU Parliamentary elections and so based on the party with the most seats. Nomination of the President must be further approved by a majority of those elected Members of the European Parliament.[47] Member states maintain their democratic control over the EU's decision-making procedure at the national level. Democracy works at the EU level through the reinforcement of the legislative, budgetary and supervisory functions of the Parliament acting as a 'co-legislator', with the European Council. Democracy, in the context of the EU, is made more difficult by the complexities of juggling as a whole the national interests of the 28 member states. This is best done through an *independent* Commission that serves the interests of *all* the member states. It is simply incorrect to assert that the EU's system is undemocratic. The EU's operation is precisely aimed to function on a consensual basis where agreement has to be reached with the joint consent of the Commission, Parliament and member states' governments in the Council.

Adoption of legislation is according to the EU treaties but left to the member states to implement regulations and directives (subject to different timescales). There are opponents of the legitimacy argument as the Commission is still responsible for initiating legislation. Though it is re-appointed every five years.[48] Individual Commissioners (one appointed by each member state) have to be approved jointly and severally by the Council of the European Union and the European Parliament which has the power to dismiss before the full term.[49] The extension of qualified majority voting (QMV) is a major criticism of Eurosceptics, which means that the British government can

---

[47] The President must be further approved by a majority of those elected Members of the European Parliament.

[48] In a domestic parliament such as in the UK, proposals are made into 'bills' which are then debated by each House. Bills in most cases are in fact introduced by the government and in the case of taxation by the House of Commons.

[49] https://www.theguardian.com/world/2016/jun/13/is-the-eu-undemocratic-referendum-reality-check.

be outvoted.[50] Between 2009 and 2015, however, this has *not* been a major problem as Britain has voted, e.g. in such matters as environment. The UK voted with the majority more frequently on international trade, industry, environment, transport, legal affairs, economic and monetary union, and Internal Market policies in nearly 90% of the cases. In matters of taxation, defence and foreign policy decisions have to unanimous. In reality, taxation as with national defence is the prerogative of national governments only.

Furthermore, criticism has frequently been levied that judges of the European Court of Justice are 'unelected'. Yes they are appointed and described as 'unelected' but on that basis so are judges in the UK and other EU countries (one judge is appointed for each member state). What is absolutely clear is a member state's power of veto over the appointment of EU judges. Each judge and advocate general is appointed for a renewable term, jointly by national governments. So none of them can take up their jobs in the first place or keep their jobs (appointments are reviewed every six years) without, for example, the UK government's approval. Election to the office of Prime Minister, even in national governments, is not by universal suffrage or indeed by the *voters* of the winning party in government. The leader of the Conservative party in the UK is elected by its party MPs not by its supporters in the country. Similarly, government ministers are not always elected members of domestic parliaments and may be appointees with no 'legitimacy'. Furthermore, examples exist in the French and UK cabinet that have ministers unelected – in the case of the UK normally with a seat in the House of Lords.

Clearly, however, the European project has been under threat from mounting criticism across Europe and a growing antipathy towards governing elites – whether perceived as leftist bureaucrats or neoliberals. Euroscepticism in all its guises is not just the preserve of

---

[50] In QMV, a law passes if it is backed by 16 out of 28 countries that make up at least 65% of the EU population. The UK has 13% of the EU population, ergo gets a 13% vote share.

Britain – historically, it has always been linked to the notion that ever increasing powers within the EU reduce the powers of the nation state.[51] A level of Euroscepticism has been present in most western political parties in western Europe – particularly France, Spain, Holland and Europe – but the concept has intensified more recently in central and eastern EU members too – the very countries benefiting most from the structural funds to develop their economies post-EU accession. Every attempt by the Brussels establishment to move in that direction has been met with a wall of opposition from predominantly right-wing governments – especially in Hungary and Poland.[52]

From consultations in Brussels with politicians in the Committee of the Regions, a number of concerns were expressed about problems they face domestically on dealing with internal integration issues before even addressing any further 'closer union' on the broader EU front. Prioritizing the concerns of border security against migrant inflows and perceptions of increased hostility by Russia were far more on the minds of the Baltic and Visegrad States.[53]

Professor Jan Gorecki, a former Polish ambassador to Denmark, suggested that Brexit meant a loss of a kindred partner aligned to Poland's own views on Europe and one of a naturally moderate scepticism, where Britain served a role to counterbalance the Franco–German axis. Euroscepticism is on the rise in several EU countries and exacerbated by internal political conflicts and a Catholic conservative reaction against what they see as a liberal European consensus on a range of matters including immigration and social issues. Poland has a lot of baggage with other countries so it is difficult to accommodate this in an EU setting when these previous issues come to the surface. However,

---

[51] This is not just a British problem', says Professor Jan Gorecki, a former ambassador to Denmark in an interview held on 13th July 2016 at SGGW Warsaw University of Applied Sciences.
[52] JG went to explain in 'Poland needs integration in the country' now divided into liberal and conservative JG advocating a process of individualism – 'no collective discussion of political issues' – a notion of 'political correctness' is coming very much in Poland.
[53] Interviews held on the 14 and 15th of June during the Plenary Sessions with members of the Committee of the Regions (CoR).

Poland is a very EU positive country seeing great opportunities in development of the European Union in the process of moderating not ruling.[54]

Bratislava

At a crisis summit in Bratislava in September 2016, Europeans attempted to put up a united front, despite the open disagreements over immigration and austerity so heated that many leaders simply refused to share a platform together.[55] In an open appeal to the EU leadership, Donald Tusk made it clear that it would be 'a fatal error' to assume that the UK vote was a specifically British issue, describing it as 'a desperate attempt to answer the questions that millions of Europeans are asking themselves daily' about security, cultural heritage and way of life. In essence, it was a wakeup call to which Brussels and the neoliberal elite had to respond to counter the forces of populism. This would let national governments to coordinate with each other and take responsibility for their actions, rather than simply blaming Brussels when problems arise. The refugee crisis, for example, needed such cooperation to secure the EU's external border and manage the inward flows of migrants. This, of course, they wholly failed to do. Other points raised at the summit had a more constructive tone, and included support for Greece with EU supervision at the border control points – particularly in separating asylum-seekers from 'economic migrants' before they reach the passport-free Schengen zone (Fig 5.1).

As for a capital markets union, it remains to be seen how much progress will be made after the withdrawal of Britain, home to Europe's pre-eminent financial centre in London: Lord Hill, the British EU Commissioner responsible for the project, resigned almost immediately on this matter.[56]

---

[54] Interview held on 13th July 2016 with Professor Jan Gorecki at SGGW Warsaw University of Applied Sciences, a former ambassador to Denmark.
[55] http://www.telegraph.co.uk/news/2016/09/16/eu-bratislava-summit-donald-tusk-calls-for-sober-and-brutally-ho1/.
[56] https://www.ft.com/content/2b84027e-3b93-11e6-9f2c-36b487ebd80a.

Circle 1 - Eurozone/European Union countries – **19 EU countries;**

Circle 2 - Non-Eurozone/European Union countries – **9 EU countries;**

Circle 1 + 2 - European Union **(28 EU countries);**

Circle 1 + 2 + 3 - European Economic Area (EEA) – **31 countries;**

Circle 1 + 2 + 4 - Customs Union – **32 countries;**

Circle 3 + **Switzerland** - European Free Trade Association (EFTA) – **4 countries.**

Fig. 5.1 EU Countries – Total 28: Relationship and ties between EU countries

The Models for Exiting the EU

Economists from both sides – and all shades – of the argument have expressed their varying views on the options for the UK's preferred exit from the European Union. But one cardinal principle underlines these negotiations and functions as its biggest stumbling block – namely that the EU will not budge on the four freedoms of customs, capital, services and movement. To do so would be the death knell of the EU. put it, One immovable thing is control of migration – everything will pivot on that and if they will not allow Freedom of Movement from the 27 to the UK them they will not get full access. What are the available options? You either go for the 'bespoke' arrangement as it is believed that Theresa May would seem to have ruled out EEA membership as with Norway or Switzerland. Or the decision tilts towards a hard Brexit and go for the WTO that we have to join as we are not an *independent* member of the WTO. The UK is already a member of the EU, but it would have to re-establish itself in its own right.

Hard and Soft Brexit? The Options

Simply putting, the colloquially 'Soft' option means giving priority to participation (or possibly full membership of) the Single Market, at the cost of accepting some limitations on control over borders and laws – as well as contributing to the EU budget. Hard means taking back border and immigration controls, and sovereignty over laws – and therefore necessarily and leaving the Single Market and customs union. Staying in the Customs Union would still mean continuing to let the EU Commission negotiate international trade deals on Britain's behalf as opposed to bilateral free trade agreements with other countries.

With the 2016 Conservative Conference articulating a firm desire to trigger Article 50 by the end of March 2017, the government has the task of considering its negotiating strategy.

If a viable model for UK's exit is found, the danger for the EU is that it may be become a template for other members wishing to change their 'arrangements' – and so is a motivation from the Brussels perspective for tough, possibly punitive negotiations. The government may not reveal its cards so early in the preparatory phase as it tries to gauge potential change(s) in policy in Brussels because political and economic events unfold in the coming months. The accusation that the UK may play a cat-and-mouse game could equally apply to the other side. A summary of the various options below will help to identify possible scenarios. Economists are not in agreement on the best model. A few – admittedly a minority – advocate a complete break with the Single Market acknowledging that it started as a good idea seemingly; however, so many things have gone wrong with the Single Market . . . ' to turn it into such a large project without any of the usual democratic safeguards was asking for trouble.'[57]

Professor Minford suggests looking at the options rather starkly: 'Joining the European Economic Area (EEA) would mean free movement of people, EU regulation and a big annual contribution to Brussels – a complete denial of the Brexit vote,' he says. 'So I'm glad people are starting to realise that declaring unilateral free trade is not only the best strategy for Britain economically, but the only one that can fly.'[58]

Minford is hoping there will not be too much of a compromise on this. He suggests in line with those advocating a *clean break* that the process must happen quickly. . . . 'Essentially (you see) what these deals would be is a continuation of the status quo on a micro level therefore quick to arrange actually with some tailing off over time which could be talked about. What happens with this set of policies is that prices come down. We get rid of the common agricultural policy and food prices come down we get rid of the single market customs union, manufactured good prices come down and then we have these deals that modifies that in the short run to some degree. As far as the Common Agricultural Policy (CAP) we have very little stake in it. He went on to argue that . . . "To deliver anything than what Brexit wanted is going to be a very dangerous thing to do" so micro deals for particular industries for a

---

[57] Interview with Professor Patrick Minford, 4th July 2016. Chair of 'Economists for Brexit' campaign group.
[58] http://www.spectator.co.uk/2016/10/the-man-who-triumphed-over-project-fear/.

finite time (transitional arrangements) to allow for general free trade at the end of this period.'[59]

A hard Brexit – now euphemistically referred to as a 'clean Brexit' by its proponents – would entail a clean break from the Single Market, and thereby a default to the WTO model of conducting international trade, to be built around a tariff structure. It would mean selling goods and services to the EU on similar terms as the United States and Canada, and the EU would reciprocate on the same basis. The UK would be free in this model to negotiate other trade deals with the rest of the world once it had formally exited the EU. A clean/hard Brexit suggests much more austere changes, such as limited access to the Single Market, in which the pound could remain weak. Furthermore, the process may take years and continue to provide uncertainty for the markets. Nevertheless, this would seem to be the preferred approach of Eurosceptic diehards believing that the UK can 'go it alone'.

If the UK leaves the tariff-free customs union and enters a free-trade agreement with the EU, rules of origin would apply to exports of goods from the UK to the EU. Bureaucratic processes would still be required to guarantee that imports into the UK did not become a route to bypass the EU's external tariff barriers. Rules of origin would put UK-based exporters at a disadvantage vis-à-vis those based in the EU.[60]

Attitudes towards these options have crystalised along a wide front on this option, with politicians, economists and industrialists all ready to offer their views preferences and caveats to the models on offer. From the EU establishment, the official message delivered by the President of the Council, Donald Tusk (a former Polish Prime Minister) contains a stern warning that 'hard Brexit' is the only offer on the table, unless the UK changes its mind and decides to stay in the EU. He reiterated what has been constantly voiced, with renewed emphasis that the UK should

---

[59] Interview with Professor Patrick Minford, 4th July 2016. Chair of 'Economists for Brexit' campaign group.

[60] By remaining in the customs Union industrial manufactured goods exported to and from the UK would not be subject to EU customs duties and custom border checks that would increase their cost and risk the value chains between the UK manufacturing sector and the European Union.

dispel any hope of retaining the benefits of the EU club while acting in flagrant breach of fundamental treaty obligations to allow free movement of people – while also avoiding contributions to the EU budget. He further stated it was 'useless to speculate about soft Brexit', which would enable the UK to retain the closest possible ties to the bloc after leaving.[61]

Much of the foreign direct investment (FDI) that has taken place over the last 20–30 years, particularly by Japanese companies, was made in the firm belief that Britain provided a stable launch pad or 'gateway' for trading with the rest of the EU. Japanese and other east Asian investors (notably also South Korea and Singapore) were attracted by the UK's flexible employment laws and a spirit of entrepreneurship that manifested into a desire to be perceived as 'being open for business'. The Japanese government's reaction to a hard Brexit is understandable when they gave a clear, though largely ignored, warning that major companies such as Hitachi, Fujitsu and Renault-Nissan could move their European headquarters elsewhere – with serious implications for the 140,000 people employed by Japanese businesses in the UK.[62] Their demands have been explicit and include the following:

- Maintenance of trade in goods with no burdens of customs duties and procedures[63]
- Unrestricted investment
- Maintenance of an environment in which services and financial transactions across Europe can be provided and carried out smoothly
- Access to workforces with the necessary skills
- Harmonized regulations and standards between the UK and the EU

---

[61] http://news.sky.com/story/hard-brexit-is-the-only-brexit-warns-eu-president-donald-tusk-10616074.
[62] http://www.independent.co.uk/news/uk/politics/japan-brexit-letter-eu-uk-g20-europe-great-turmoil-economy-a7224841.html.
[63] Leaving the customs union (and single market) to trade under the WTO from 2019 would not only involve companies such as Nissan Toyota and Kia paying a 10% tariff to sell cars into Europe (and the other 53 markets with which the EU has trade deals) but it would also put supply chains at risk as most of the parts have to be imported and will then have to abide by the rules of origin. £12bn of the £15bn materials needed to build cars are imported to the UK (annually).

The same applies to other multinationals whose plans to originally invest were made on the assumption that the UK had a settled policy of staying inside the EU.[64]

Northern Ireland and Scotland

Scotland and Northern Ireland voted to the Remain in the EU so the government led by Teresa May needs to carry the support of at least some of the Remain vote (48%). A soft Brexit was, by far, the position they advocated the strongest. Her act on becoming Prime Minister to meet with Nicola Sturgeon, the leader of the SNP and Scotland's first minister, as well as Belfast politicians and Enda Kenny, the Irish Taoiseach,[65] suggested a strong desire that reinforced in her Birmingham conference speech to develop a consensual approach that would maintain the integrity of the United Kingdom. This includes maintaining a relatively open border between Northern Ireland and the Republic of Ireland. At the London meeting, Enda Kenny stated: 'We reiterated the importance of the partnership between our two governments in supporting the peace process and in contributing to stability and continued progress in Northern Ireland'.[66]

What does this mean? At present, the EU has this kind of deal with six of its ten largest trading partners,[67] as well as former Commonwealth nations Canada, Australia and New Zealand. The UK would be able to take back control of its own customs union, setting its own external tariff.

The downside of this approach is that such tariffs could adversely impact industries heavily tied to European trade: in particular, agriculture,

---

[64] http://www.independent.co.uk/news/uk/politics/japan-brexit-letter-eu-uk-g20-europe-great-turmoil-economy-a7224841.html.

[65] July 27th 2016 irishpost.co.uk/prime-minister-theresa-may-taoiseach-enda-kenny-promise-close-relati....

[66] http://irishpost.co.uk/prime-minister-theresa-may-taoiseach-enda-kenny-promise-close-relationship-britain-ireland-post-brexit/.

[67] The EU has this deal with six of its largest trading partners: USA, Japan, and the Brics: Brazil, China, India and Russia.

cars and chemicals. However, the same is true for EU members trading with the UK to sell cars, food and luxury and goods. A business for Britain's 'Change or Go' report found that the UK would lose around £7 billion income from tariffs levied on imports and EU savings, so compensation may have to be paid out annually to farmers and manufacturers.[68] Conversely, consumer prices could fall from cutting EU tariffs on incoming goods such as Australian or New Zealand wine and Caribbean sugar cane, developing nations' textiles.

The Norwegian Model

As a European Economic Area country, Norway is part of the EU Single Market but pays budget contributions for access to the Single Market. In 2016, Norway's payments in relation to its membership of the Single Market and other EU programmes which it participated in came to about £623 million, or around £119 per head, according to an analysis by InFacts. This is comparable to the payment per person of Britain at the same time.[69] Unfortunately, there are no public or published figures on the money Norway receives from these programmes. Crucially, it also has to accept the rules regarding free movement. Norway has established freedom over the rules relating to fisheries and farming policy but is still substantially linked to EU regulations on them.

Norway is in the position where it adopts EU Single Market laws without having much power to influence them. It can negotiate its own trade deals, though this is subject to restrictions on what can be sold to the EU. It agrees to take decisions of an EEA court, which often follows decisions by the European Court of Justice. Those who have advocated the Norway option of belonging to the Single Market institutions, without membership of the EU, have also suggested that the UK can simply maintain free trading relations with the bloc it has just left by signing a bilateral trade agreement. But the downside would be that

---

[68] *uk.businessinsider.com/eu-referendum-change-or-go-report-brexit-if-uk-renegotiatio*...

[69] https://infacts.org/norwegians-pay-same-brits-eu-access/.

Britain would have to adopt relevant EU legislation – with no power to influence it – and it would have to accept the free movement of people from the EU – something now highly political undesirable, considering the role the immigration issue that played a key role in the Brexit campaign. These scenarios have now been firmly rejected by the UK government.

Switzerland, by contrast, has a more complicated relationship with the EU than Norway. It is framed by a series of bilateral treaties in which nation has adopted various provisions of European Union law to participate in the Single Market – in effect, it negotiates access to the market on a sector-by-sector basis. Instead of following Norway's EEA model, Switzerland agreed to a thicket of bilateral trade accords over the past 30 years. While it accepts free movement and pays some fees towards the EU, its courts are largely not bound by EU rulings. But the model has been in trouble, and the EU would be reluctant to offer a similar relationship to the UK; indeed, the bloc threatened to cut off market access after Switzerland prepared to Cap EU immigration, and it is pressuring the Swiss to acquiesce to the supremacy of EU courts. At the time of writing, they have begun to back down on these issues.[70]

Turkey is part of the EUs' customs union. It is also at a very early stage of satisfying the requirements of the *Acqui Communitaire* (the accumulated legislation, legal acts and court decisions which constitute the body of European Union law) as part of an eventual entry to the EU. Ongoing political events in Turkey – the democratic process is under EU scrutiny, especially post-coup attempt – may well stall its ongoing application process. In addition, the whole issue of future enlargement to incorporate Bosnia and Serbia appears to be on hold to give Brussels time to deal with the mass immigration and security problems that Europe is currently facing. In the meantime, Turkey can at best maintain the current customs union, without enjoying the benefits of Freedom of Movement, but while playing a pivotal role in helping to

---

[70] https://www.theguardian.com/world/2016/sep/06/swiss-eu-standoff-striking-similarities-uk-predicament.

ameliorate the EU's external refugee problem (as discussed in the migration chapter). Turkey's external tariff is set by the EU and Turkish exports to the EU are tariff free, giving Ankara access to the bloc's Single Market for goods. But the deal excludes areas such as services (vitally important to the UK), agriculture and public procurement – for Britain, this model would simply not be attractive. Under such an accord, the UK would lose trade sovereignty. It would not influence or directly benefit from free trade deals between the bloc and other countries, while being presented with a far inferior arrangement to the Single Market.

By contrast, with the very limited arrangement with Turkey, the EU's trade deal with Canada is the most ambitious to date. The Comprehensive Economic and Trade Agreement (CETA), which took a number of years in the making, between the EU and Canada was finally approved on the 30 October 2016. As a model, it could provide a frame of reference for the UK going forward. The agreement eliminates tariffs on all industrial and most agricultural products. It will remove customs duties and offer EU firms, access to Canadian markets opportunities in Canada and support jobs in Europe.[71]

Ultimately, the preferred option of a 'clean' Brexit is a comprehensive free-trade agreement with the EU – one that would give the UK access to the Single Market without formal membership. But this does not mean that it escapes all the unwanted rules and regulations, as these depend on any new terms and conditions applied in the new FTA. Negotiations may not in fact lean towards any of the existing 'known' options described. Professor Minford, one of the few economists who advocated for Brexit, anticipates that 'there is definitely going to be transitional adjustments for example for the car industry – where we in the UK will be open to the world market and others in the EU will not be happy because their prices will fall'. 'What I envisage is micro deals and over time it would be hoped the EU would move to a less protectionist position.'[72] Notions that Britain could achieve a trade deal like

---

[71] http://ec.europa.eu/trade/policy/in-focus/ceta/index_en.htm.
[72] Interview with Professor Minford on 4th July 2016.

Albania or Moldova, as with the 'Leichenstein model' (a micro state with only 37,000 citizens) appear fanciful. The former are small undeveloped economies whose fledging industrial sectors provide little threat or competition to EU companies – unlike those of the highly developed British economy, the second largest in the EU.[73]

A bespoke, sector-by-sector approach may prevail in terms of the 'exit' options being most prominently discussed. A unique, crafted formula could be sold more easily at home – one that keeps the chord of the national mood, that can minimize the damage to British business and finance and which provides the desired immigration controls and exit from compliance with the European Justice Court decisions. This is of course a 'best case scenario' that will involve tortuous compromises and complex agreements for companies to effectively function outside the formal boundaries of the Single Market. It is also all hypothetical until the finalisation of the negotiations, which are very likely to stretch on to at least early 2019. Political observers and economic experts alike continue to reinforce the view that control of immigration is a 'red line'. Everything pivots on that and if the UK Government will not allow Freedom of Movement from the EU27 to the UK then the UK will simply not be accorded full access. For the EU, which is still formally in the business of creating a single political entity of 'ever closer union', the four freedoms remain precious and inviable.

There is a confident desire (not unjustified) in UK government circles to expedite key priority sector arrangements in the interest of maintaining trade flowing. This includes a special regime for the car industry (and pharmaceuticals) where the UK is a key market for EU goods. But in the case of London-based financial services what is the *quid pro quo* if the E27 gives the UK full access for the City – namely, what form of 'full access' will be given to them in return? Such arrangements will have their drawbacks as under what are termed

---

[73] In terms of GDP, the drop in the value of the £ sterling against the Euro may challenge the ongoing veracity of that claim. Below £1/ 1.16 the UK takes up third place behind France.

'equivalence' deals, companies can trade provided domestic regulation is 'equivalent' – and as rigorous – as that in the EU *and* where the terms of any such agreement incorporate ongoing compliance, assessment processes and permit rule changes.

Chancellor Merkel, hardening her stance in response to the signals given at the Birmingham Conservative party conference, has pressed companies in sectoral talks to resist 'pressure from European industry associations' and avoid the temptation to set aside EU principles – especially Freedom of Movement – because it was 'comfortable' or convenient to do so. Justified concern is that if the UK achieves a special status (for example, an enhanced version of the Canadian deal), other EU members or non-EU countries may ask for equivalent treatment. Consequently, the naked self-interest of member states could surface to 'rock the boat' and potentially trigger an unwinding of the whole EU project.

Merkel delivered this message to the annual conference of the BDI, the German industry association: 'If we don't insist that full access to the single market is tied to complete acceptance of the four basic freedoms, then a process will spread across Europe whereby everyone does and is allowed what they want.' She voiced the question, 'How much access to the single market does Great Britain get, and in a reciprocal way, how much access to the British market do we get? . . . and how ready are we to link this access politically so that the four freedoms are defended.'[74]

The irreconcilable difference turns on understanding the difference between *access* to Europe's Single Market and *participation* in it. Participation has a deeper significance than mere access – technically, to offer an extreme example, even North Korea has 'access' in some form. The deepest example is Norway's association as a member of the Single Market – accepting all its regulations and court jurisdictions – in contrast to Switzerland, which while retaining sovereignty has merely open 'access' to the EU but no formal 'participation'.

---

[74] Financial Times Friday 7th of October 2016.

The Financial Services Sector-What about the Banks?

The UK Financial services industry is the single biggest driver of the British economy. It adds over £60 billion to UK GDP and around 12% of total tax revenues. Consequently, conventional wisdom has it that any deal with Brussels *must* ensure comprehensive access to the Single Market for it to maintain supremacy as Europe's financial capital. London has lead the way in key investment areas such as fixed income securities, currencies and commodities, and is also highly active in Fintech, private equity, hedge funds and asset management.

In response to the Referendum result, the sector's banks, insurance companies, myriad international accountancy and legal firms are planning their moves to establish offices in the EU in the event of an (increasingly likely) hard Brexit.[75] Currently, they can operate relatively freely across the EU – a practice known as 'passporting', which means that they can provide services across the EU from a holding base in Britain. Non-EU banks can do the same if they set up a subsidiary in the UK. Consequently, the US and other non-EU banks have a strong presence in London – seen as the financial services capital of the EU, if not the globe – and are anxious that the UK maintains its ability to provide a base from which they can 'passport' – without having to be separately authorized by each EU state – across the EU.

Financial and legal experts agree that in order to get a passport, financial institutions will have to create a licensed bank and conduct business operations there. With data provided by the Financial Conduct Authority (FCA), the Chairman of the Treasury Select Committee, Andrew Tyrie reported the figures on the Treasury Committees website saying: 'These figures give us an initial idea of the effects of losing full access to the Single Market in financial services. The business put at risk could be significant.[76]

---

[75] City law firms have been registering solicitors in the Republic of Ireland to continue in practicing in EU law following Brexit.
[76] http://www.bbc.co.uk/news/business-37416280.

'None of the current off-the-shelf arrangements can preserve existing passporting arrangements, while giving the UK the influence and control it needs over financial services regulation as it develops.

'Efforts to secure an appropriate arrangement for UK-based firms will be one of the most challenging aspects of the negotiations about the UK's future relationship with the EU.'[77]

Even banks that already have licenses in other EU countries are not guaranteed an easy ride because licences are business-specific. 'Whenever a regulated entity wants to change materially its business plan that will generally involve regulatory engagement,' said Damian Carolan, a banking lawyer with Allen & Overy. 'You don't just have this magic box into which you can drop new bits of business into and carry on as usual.'[78]

Passporting from the UK into the EU will not be possible unless the UK remains part of the Single Market and accepts the conditions that apply to that. Investment banks are therefore quickly preparing contingencies to transfer work and workers to cities such as Frankfurt, Paris and Dublin, and are approaching their regulators to secure licenses to enable them to passport into the rest of the EU. Additionally, there may be pressure on EU banks such as Deutche and Societe General, which conduct investment banking in London, to relocate back home after Brexit takes effect. But France's central bank Governor François Villeroy de Galhau made clear as early as 25 June, the day before the Referendum, that this is no longer going to work. 'If tomorrow Britain is not part of the Single Market, the City [of London] cannot keep this European passport, and clearing houses cannot be located in London either', he said.[79]

London-based investment banks have not been slow to voice their preferred views suggesting that comprehensive access – ideally, continued membership – to the Single Market would help the UK to secure a 'civilised divorce' from the EUMorgan Stanley's chief economist, Jacob

---

[77] http://www.bbc.co.uk/news/business-37416280.

[78] https://www.ft.com/content/52d968b0-3a52-11e6-9a05-82a9b15a8ee7.

[79] https://app.ft.com/cms/s/52d968b0-3a52-11e6-9a05-82a9b15a8ee7.html?sectionid=companies.

Nell said such a deal would be 'less disruptive' for the economy...negotiating membership of the European Economic Area and retaining access to the Single Market would help the UK to secure a 'civilised divorce' from the EU. He added...'A nice divorce might be that the UK accepts some level of free movement and EU regulations and has fairly full access to the single market – a Norwegian model (not favoured by Brexit campaigners) which would be less disrupting economically.'[80] Both JP Morgan and HSBC played their part in so-called Project Fear with dire warnings that Brexit would cause the loss or transfer of thousands of EU jobs, but as with other notes of 'expert' caution, particularly from bankers and financiers, there is no evidence it helped the 'Remain' cause: and at least some that it harmed it. Leave voters were told by the Brexit campaigners, lead in this respect by Michael Gove on Question Time, to snub the 'experts'. Such a message, as discussed elsewhere in this book, has a powerful resonance in the wake of the financial crisis. Their vote protested not just against the ruling elite in Brussels, but those in power at home.

What could the UK do to retain the banks? In theory, they could still negotiate for the so-called Norwegian option, which entails becoming a member of the European Economic Area and so gaining unfettered to the Single Market - but without being a full member of the EU. This scenario is now highly unlikely. Brussels is in no mood to accommodate a breach of the Treaty rules by giving Britain special exemptions from continuing to adopt relevant EU legislation – with no power to influence it – and abiding by the principle of free movement of people from the EU. What final compromises can be achieved will only be seen once divorce talks have fully commenced after March 2017, and when both sides have examined the impact of decisions resulting from them.

Indeed, research published by OpenEurope in October 2016 suggests that the negotiations are very likely to be complex, on the grounds that there is not one single 'passport', but rather several sector-specific ones based on a number of different EU regulations. This means the UK is

---

[80] http://www.telegraph.co.uk/business/2016/06/27/brexit-norway-style-deal-with-eu-would-help-uk-avoid-damaging-re/.

not faced with a simple black-and-white choice, but a range of graded options.[81]

Apart from financial institutions, all businesses that trade with the EU will be affected by the 'divorce': whether they are exporting (supplier) or importing goods (purchaser) and services. This is the effect of the UK legal system being involved with the development and implementation of EU law. How this will be untangled remains to be seen, but in practical terms, questions begin to arise on a range of issues – how, for example, will contract compliance work vis-a-vis EU law after Brexit? What principles of EU Law will have an impact on the English courts? What are the practical implications on jurisdiction for contracts and how they will be enforced (i.e. from another EU state) judgements in the UK? But EU laws and regulations will still be applicable in the UK after Article 50 has been invoked, and until the Brexit negotiations and settlement terms are complete.

The Airline Industry

The industry has played a crucial role in the growth and development of tourism in Europe's regions. As such it remains a vital instrument for EU and the Eurozone recovery. The impact and shape of the final Brexit negotiations will be important on this sector for UK business and tourism.[82]

Generally, the reaction from the industry as a whole was one of surprise and disappointment; many of the big players, particularly Ryanair, had campaigned strongly for the Remain. EasyJet, which had also identified strongly with the campaign to remain, issued a statement saying it is confident the vote 'will not have a material impact on its strategy or its ability to deliver long-term sustainable earnings growth and returns to shareholders.' British Airways' parent IAG said the same but also downgraded its profits forecast for the year: its share price

---

[81] http://openeurope.org.uk/intelligence/britain-and-the-eu/how-the-uks-financial-services-sector-can-continue-thriving-after-brexit/.

[82] http://www.travelweekly.co.uk/articles/62110/industry-reaction-after-uk-votes-to-leave-the-eu.

immediately dropped 22% (Ryanair also fell by 14%). In a statement on the result, IAG said: 'IAG believes the vote to leave the EU will not have a long-term material impact on its business. However, in the run up to the UK referendum during June, IAG experienced a weaker than expected trading environment. An important concern for British registered airlines – which includes IAG, owner of British Airways, and the budget airline, Easyjet – is the *UK's access after Brexit* to the *European Common Aviation Area*, which *allows carriers* to *fly freely in Europe*.[83]

If the UK were to leave the EU, its airlines lose their automatic access to the market, although the UK would be expected to negotiate continued access. The most obvious way for the UK to do this would be to participate in the ECAA Agreement in the same way as countries such as Norway currently do.[84]

'While IAG continues to expect a significant increase in operating profit this year, it no longer expects to generate an absolute operating profit increase similar to 2015.'[85] Michael O'Leary, a staunch supporter of the Remain, made it clear that he would cut investment in Britain if the Leave vote succeeded: 'We will pivot all of our growth into the European Union,' a positon cited in an interview published on the 28 June, adding that the airline's overall growth targets remained unchanged.[86] The expectation of the airline was that Brexit uncertainty would lead to weaker sterling,[87] slower growth in the UK and EU economies, and downward pressure on fares until the end of 2017 at the least. Over the longer term, if the UK proved unable to negotiate access to the Single Market and thereby guarantee 'open skies', this would have potentially substantial implications for UK domestic routes and UK nationals, though the risks were expected to be manageable. There may also be some opportunities if UK registered competitors are

---

[83] http://centreforaviation.com/analysis/brexit-up-in-the-air-implications-for-aviation-if-the-uk-votes-to-leave-the-european-union-262860.
[84] http://www.telegraph.co.uk/business/2016/06/24/british-airways-owner-sounds-profit-warning-within-hours-of-brex/.
[85] www.travelweekly.co.uk/articles/ . . . /industry-reaction-after-uk-votes-to-leave-the-eu.
[86] www.rte.ie/news/business/2016/0628/798618-ryanair-and-brexit/.
[87] The fall in Sterling will affect Ryanair, which reports in Euro.

no longer permitted to operate intra EU routes, or must divest their majority ownership of EU registered airlines.[88]

O'Leary said that he expected Britain to negotiate some sort of access to the EU market, but, if that failed, Irish-registered Ryanair could seek a UK operating licence.[89] As with other business leaders he expected months of 'considerable uncertainty'. This point was echoed by David O'Brien Ryanair's Chief Commercial Officer, in an interview with the authors, when he said: 'We were disappointed with the result but the implications and outcome are not yet particularly clear to have a contingency plan, also it is too early to say has it suppressed demand, customer demand in the UK because most of the bookings for this period (June, July and August) were made prior to the Brexit vote.'[90] He pointed out that, depending on the outcome of negotiations, there may be issues for the UK for if not being a member of the EU it would need an air operating licence (AOC) across Europe[91] – required by UK airlines to operate in the EU if there was a hard Brexit. Added to this was the fact that 'a UK airline having an AOC may be simply not enough as the real issue relates to ownership as non-European parties are not allowed to own a majority share in European airlines and vice versa'.[92]

Brexit poses a far greater concern for EasyJet. With its home base in the UK, it reports its earnings in pound sterling – meaning it is heavily exposed to the pound's fall in recent months, which has added over £100 million to its annual costs. As the second-biggest carrier in France, business there has been significantly affected by the Paris and Nice terror attacks, leading to the cancellation of over a thousand flights in the three months to the end of June 2016, with a loss of £20 million. As a result, the Brexit negotiations are crucial for the company, which is ready to

---

[88] http://investor.ryanair.com/results/q1-results-fy17/.

[89] A Norway solution would avoid all this but then the UK would be accepting freedom of movement (and budget contributions) the very concerns that the Leave group campaigned against in the Referendum.

[90] Interview with the authors 5th August 2016.

[91] An AOC would require the airline to have a subsidiary in that country, but that would not be an obstacle as EasyJet already has bases and operations across Europe. The holding company would have to be 51% owned by local investors and would have to comply with local regulations.

[92] Interview with the authors on the 5th August 2016.

move its legal headquarters back within the EU if necessary. As a further precaution, the airline is applying for an air operator certificate (AOC) in an EU member state in the same way as Ryanair (HQ based in Dublin) would require in the UK when a departure from the EU takes effect.

The EU Commission is under pressure to reconsider the ownership rules and relax its requirements on foreign investment for European airlines which have a limit of 49% on non-European ownership of EU airlines. As a quid pro quo, there would be tighter rules regarding state aid for airlines of non-EU countries (rules which EU members already carry for their airlines). Behind this is the desire to increase the competitiveness of the European aviation industry, which has been affected by the challenge of lower-cost rivals such as Emirates, Etihad and Qatar airlines, together with rise of rival airport hubs in Asia and Dubai. Both Lufthansa and Air France-KLM have expressed concern about whether they are competing on a level playing field with the Gulf airlines. They have both joined with IAG, Ryanair and Easyjet to form a group to lobby for amendments in public policy and regulation – ultimately with the intention of reducing taxes and the effect of (air traffic control) strikes. These and other issues draw together erstwhile rivals in speaking with one voice to EU transport commissioner, Vioelta Bulc. They have also pushed for her support on possible action regarding cutting costs at large airports and air traffic control providers. Bulc called the shift 'economic diplomacy', but she refused to say whether Gulf carriers benefited from 'unfair' subsidies from their home states. 'There has been lots of hype about that, but strong fair negotiation is a good answer to that,' she said. The European Commission will rip up its current rules on state subsidies within the airline industry, arguing that they are 'not considered effective'.

The Commission will propose that it leads EU-wide negotiations with countries such as China and the United Arab Emirates. 'Part of the negotiation – a strong component – will be an equal playing field and reciprocity,' said Ms Bulc. 'If someone wants to play a role in the EU markets, they have to play by European rules.' Etihad, which owns stakes in the European airlines Alitalia and Air Berlin, said it looked forward to a 'pro-aviation' EU strategy that would enhance the competitiveness of European carriers.[93]

---

[93] https://www.ft.com/content/246e2500-9c0b-11e5-b45d-4812f209f861.

Impact on Tourism

Tourism is one sector where the success of the Leave vote had an immediate impact for UK outbound tourism.[94] But as TUI group chief executive – one of the biggest stakeholders in the Tourism industry – Fritz Joussen, said: 'The EU without the UK is barely conceivable but we respect the democratic decision of the British people and trust the UK government will take all steps necessary to ensure economic and political stability. 'UK airlines seem unanimous in the opinion that a Brexit will lead to reduced competition, reduced routes and higher travel prices. A concern shared by UK consumers with over a quarter (28%) saying they're worried a Brexit will lead to more expensive holidays.[95]

His remarks were echoed by Andrew Shelton, Managing Director of global flight search and travel deals website, Cheapflights.co.uk... 'Holidaymakers shouldn't assume that Brexit means all that will be lost. The UK travel market is vital to the economy of many European countries and regions. It will be in their interests to seek ways to maintain the status quo...'[96]

Travelzoo UK Managing Director, Joel Brandon-Bravo, has said that 'Other factors now also up for negotiation, that could lead to a price hike for British tourists include the loss of the EHIC card – which gives EU members the right to health treatment in any EU country, a potential increase in roaming charges following a recent EU initiative cap on charges, and, inevitable changes to visa regulations for Britons travelling to the EU.'[97]

---

[94] Inbound tourism from the EU and globally will profit from a weaker pound following the Referendum.
[95] http://www.travelweekly.co.uk/articles/62110/industry-reaction-after-uk-votes-to-leave-the-eu.
[96] http://www.traveldailymedia.com/238075/uk-travel-sector-deserves-respect-industry-stake holders-have-their-say-on-brexit/.
[97] http://www.travelweekly.co.uk/articles/62110/industry-reaction-after-uk-votes-to-leave-the-eu.

6

Brexit and the Economy

The instability and uncertainty following the Referendum outcome will set to continue up to at least 2019 – the earliest possible date for a full formal exit from the EU. The outcome has already set in motion processes that have led to a decline in the value of the £ Sterling equivalent to around 20% at the time of writing. Its depreciation in relation to the Euro and the US dollar will continue apace before the prospects of a viable UK–EU trade arrangement become apparent. A downward trajectory in the value of the pound could have a minor positive impact on growth rates, as long as the UK remains and has access to EU markets. It could also help alleviate the pressures from the record current account deficits of 6.9% for 2016 Q1.[1] However, this would not suffice to counterbalance the losses emanating from the deteriorating macroeconomic environment. Further, substantial volatility and depreciation in the value of the pound cannot be ruled out, with some analysts convinced it will reach parity with the Euro or fall as low as <$1.10 against the dollar.

---

[1] Bank of England, 'Inflation Report' (2016). http://www.bankofengland.co.uk/publications/Documents/inflationreport/2016/aug.pdf downloaded 11/11/2016.

© The Author(s) 2017
J. Theodore et al., *The European Union and the Eurozone under Stress*, DOI 10.1007/978-3-319-52292-0_6

One of the immediate consequences of the fall in pound sterling is that UK budget contributions to the EU (while it remains a member) will increase, as will future liabilities, e.g. the UK's share of pension obligations for all those employed by the EU over the period of membership. A conservative estimate for this is 20 billion Euros. At the present rate of exchange, the latter would increase by at least two billion.[2]

Exchange rate volatilities are likely to have implications for the UK debt market. Weathering the 2008–2010 financial storm very well as a 'safe haven' investment – comparable in this regard to US treasuries – UK gilts are very attractive to capital markets, enjoying historically low interest rates since 2011. Capital markets' perception of the pounds depreciation – and whether it is permanent or not – is vital in determining whether they will keep purchasing UK debt. In the case of very significant depreciation, that could drive inflation above the 2% Bank of England target.[3] In this case, a credit crunch could materialise, 'forcing' the BE to engage in further rounds of Quantitative Easing (QE). This could exacerbate exchange rate volatility and increase the cost of borrowing to firms and mortgages. However, the analysis above is based on the assumption that the UK will retain access to the Single Market, while curbing immigration, which, without a change of mind by one or both parties, is unlikely. Under the existing arrangements, the Bank of England can devalue in order to export more to and import less from France: although this reduces unemployment here, at the expense of potentially higher unemployment in France. Following the financial crisis, the Bank of England engaged in four rounds of QE from 2009 to 2012, pumping $375 billion into the financial system. This led to a considerable depreciation in the pound.

QE, inspired by the policies of the US Federal Reserve under Chairman Ben Bernanke, was conducive in reducing unit labour costs and making UK exports more competitive in international markets – thereby helping decrease unemployment rates from 8.5% in 2010 to 5.6% in 2015. However, Eurozone countries such as France were unable

---

[2] researchbriefings.files.parliament.uk/documents/RP13-42/RP13-42.pdf.

[3] http://www.bankofengland.co.uk/monetarypolicy/Pages/framework/framework.aspx.

to pursue the same policy, due to the monetarist position held by the European Central Bank (ECB) towards QE until 2015; the institution's scope of monetary policy is defined almost exclusively as 'maintaining an environment of stable prices'.[4] This contributed to the fact that after the 2008–2009 recession, Eurozone countries experienced a substantial increase in unemployment rates, in particular youth unemployment (which reached 50% in Spain). By contrast, the UK has, in part, effectively exported its unemployment to Eurozone countries. As Britain enjoys low unemployment and the Eurozone experiences exceptionally high youth unemployment, this creates very strong incentives for unemployed workers in other EU countries to relocate to the UK. This is especially the case for the younger and more mobile elements of the workforce.

The Bank of England, with its ability to engage in QE,[5] helps one to create jobs in the UK that are potentially available to all EU citizens. But creating jobs in the UK, for its citizens only, clearly violates EU's free movement of labour and risks the free movements of capital and trade. Requesting access to the Common Market and the preservation of free capital movements, while preventing people to move to the UK freely, asks the best of both worlds and is clearly not achievable. This lies at the core of the ongoing debate.

Given that monetary autonomy is branded as 'unfair competition' in the Single Market, it is not inconceivable for the French Parliament to legislate tariffs and quotas on UK exports (e.g. agricultural products, automobile industry) in the second half of 2018 – in particular given the widespread strikes due to low prices for French agricultural exports that escalated in the summer of 2016.[6] The French Parliament may not do that in good spirit. This set of affairs has led many economists (including

---

[4] 'The Scope of monetary policy' as defined by the ECB, available online at http://www.ecb.europa.eu/mopo/intro/role/html/index.en.html.
[5] A form of monetary policy used by Central banks (in this case the B of E) creates money electronically to purchase financial assets like government bonds – to increase private sector spending in the economy.
[6] http://www.telegraph.co.uk/news/2016/06/09/french-strike-chaos-deepens-24-hours-ahead-of-euro-2016-as-union/.

Robert Mundell, the 'father' of the Euro) to predict that EU countries not joining the Euro will find themselves increasingly isolated or marginalised in the Single Market. The eventual outcome of this collision was the British Referendum.

Overall, Brexit is potentially damaging to all parties. To start with, most European capital markets are located in London. Thus, raising capital in London for European countries is subject to Pound–Euro exchange rate volatility. As a result, financial integration in the EU is far from complete. Sterling also depreciated by 30% in 1931 and in 1947–1949, 14.7% in 1967, 25% in 1975–1976, 15% in 1992–1993 and 30% in 2008–2009. The latter improved markedly the UK economy's competitive position against the Eurozone nations. That is not to say, of course, that exchange rate fluctuations in the Pound-to-Euro exchange rate are the only reason to explain the number of EU workers to the UK – rigid labour markets in many Eurozone countries, especially France, and differences in tax systems are also exerting major influences. But the exchange rate plays a central role. For example, in the extreme case the value of the pound drops below 1 Euro; this will provide a major disincentive to European workers to move to the UK. On the other hand, the substantial appreciation in the value of the pound during 2014 and 2015, leading to a ratio of 1:1.4 Euros per pound by December 2015, has had adverse effects on UK exports to the Eurozone. As a consequence of all this, the absence of exchange rate arrangements between the UK and the Eurozone reflects the incomplete nature of both the Euro currency and the Customs Union.[7]

A Review of the UK Economy, June 2010 to June 2016

Before assessing the impact of the Referendum on the UK economy, it is important to review the UK economic performance from July 2010 to July 2016. This is vital in order to identify the trends established in

---

[7] The Customs Union Market accounts still for less than 40% of all economic activity in the EU.

the UK economy before the Referendum and to evaluate the extent to which these have been reversed – or not – as a consequence of the widely unanticipated of the unanticipated outcome. The question must be whether the prior economic recovery was balanced, *regardless* of the outcome of the Referendum. That is, would the recovery be sustained had the Referendum result gone the other way? We return to the issue of productivity later on.

The UK economy registered the strongest growth performance among the G7 countries during 2013–2015 – peaking at 2.6% in 2014.[8] However, this did not render it a necessarily sustainable trend. There were significant challenges facing the UK economy prior to the Referendum that may mistakenly be attributed to its outcome unless recognised. One such issue relates to the successful performance of the UK economy since 2013 against its major peers in light of its weak productivity rates.

How could sluggish productivity coincide with (relatively) high economic growth? Identifying the key drivers of the UK economic recovery since 2013 is vital. The UK economy performed quite satisfactorily from mid-2013 to June 2016. This performance provided evidence which, according to the former Chancellor George Osborne and the election campaign of early 2015, vindicated the policies put forward in 2010, with priority given to deficit reduction and restoration of confidence in capital markets. However, it has to be borne in mind that this strong growth performance took place against the background of a deeper (in some cases far deeper) recession in the UK than the other G7 economies during the Great Recession – reaching 6.0% of GDP in real terms from the first quarter of 2008 to the third quarter of 2009 (The disproportionate importance of financial services to the UK economy can be attributed to much of this.) The only country that experienced a harsher recession was Germany – with a loss of output equal to 7.1%. The USA and France faced a loss of output equal to 4%, with the USA experiencing strong growth from the first quarter of 2008 to 2015 reaching a

---

[8] https://www.ft.com/content/0260242c-370b-11e6-9a05-82a9b15a8ee7, http://www.bbc.co.uk/news/10613201.

cumulative 10%, whereas France has registered a modest growth of 2%. In addition, the structure of the economy and the nature of the recession were quite different in the UK, from, e.g. France or Germany.

In addition, the UK experienced the slowest recovery in relation to France, Germany and the USA – and the very slowest on record, including that of the Great Depression. The loss of output incurred by the Great Recession was recovered only after 22 quarters, in autumn 2013.[9] Indeed, this made it the worst economic recovery in the last 150 years.[10] In other words, the UK economy exhibited strong growth potential, partly because it started from a very low basis in the second half of 2009, and because it took six and half years to reach its 2016 level. Furthermore, UK GDP *per head* remained below its 2008 peak up to the second quarter of 2015.[11] Overall, low growth during 2010–2012 was followed by strong economic performance during 2013–2016.

The sustainability of the UK's economic recovery had been questioned well before the July Referendum. Overall, an economy can recover in three ways: Firstly, by a rise in *consumer expenditure,* second by increases in *investment* – either public sector or private sector – and finally by an increase in the *volume of exports*. Overall consumption registered a significant increase since 2013, as consumer confidence was restored. However, as wages lagged behind increases in prices up to the end of 2014, the increase in consumption was financed by savings and the continued expansion of credit. This is clearly not sustainable in the medium to the long run. The decrease in savings and credit expansion could not continue indefinitely and beyond a point, savings could no

---

[9] Giles and Fray, 'Eight Charts Showing State of UK Economy before Bank of England Rate Decision', *FT* (2016). http://www.ft.com/cms/s/0/fd522642-5596-11e6-9664-e0bdc13c3bef.html#axzz4GQotgOYv downloaded on 07/08/16.

[10] Hughes and Saleheen, 'UK Labour Productivity since the Onset of the Crisis – An International and Historical Perspective' International Economic Analysis Division, Bank of England Quarterly Bulletin, Q2 (2012). http://www.bloomberg.com/news/articles/2016-07-29/monte-paschi-capital-wiped-out-in-european-bank-stress-test.

[11] Stiglitz, 'GDP Per Capita in the UK is Lower than it was Before the Crisis. That is not a Success' *Guardian* (2015). http://www.theguardian.com/books/2015/may/24/joseph-stiglitz-interview-uk-economy-lost-decade-zero-growth 25/05/16.

longer be depleted. The only alternative for maintaining consumption is expanding access to credit. This process was facilitated by households taking on more credit – and more specifically mortgages – in their efforts to take advantage of an early entry to a booming housing market.

What is striking is that different sectors' contributions to growth resemble the features and processes under way from 2003 to 2007 and subsequently led to the 2008–2009 credit crisis.[12] It can then be concluded that the 2008–2009 Great Recession was overcome by creating another, potentially more damaging, cycle of credit expansion. The only way to avert such a development is for the Bank of England to increase interest rates as a means of increasing the rate of return on savings, and thus providing incentives for higher saving ratios and disincentives for households against taking on more credit. But the retort to this is that if interest rate increases took place prematurely, they could damage the recovery (as has driven the logic behind the US Federal Reserve keeping rates so low since 2009). That best explains why the Governor of the Bank of England was so eager to point out that, when the rate of interest will finally go up, it will increase gradually and would not return to its pre-crisis levels.[13]

Regardless of the debate on interest rate policy, a more balanced growth approach requires an increase in investment and the volume of exports to accompany a rise in domestic (private) demand in the medium to long run.[14] As companies increased sales, they responded by increasing investment (in particular inventories). However, the rise in the volume of investment did not reach its 2008 level. In addition, export growth did not materialise. Rather the rate of decline in exports was reversed. On the other hand, the increase in private sector investment reflected a return of confidence.

---

[12] Guest, 'The Global Financial Crisis and Undergraduate Macroeconomics' *The Australian Economic Review*, 44:1, pp. 113–120 (2011).
[13] Bank of England, 'Official Bank Rate History' (2015) http://www.bankofengland.co.uk/boeapps/iadb/Repo.asp.
[14] King, 'The UK's Balance of Payments Conundrum' *FT* (2016).
 http://blogs.ft.com/the-exchange/2016/07/20/the-uks-balance-of-payments-conundrum/?sitee dition=intl#recommended-h-504491470546859260 downloaded on 07/08/16.

Export growth, however, depends on a number of factors – such as events in the Eurozone, the value of the pound and political developments that determine the exporting framework, e.g. trade agreements. With a bit less than 50% of UK exports sold to EU member countries, it becomes clear that the UK cannot insulate its economy from events in EU.[15] Indeed, the referendum's outcome has set in motion processes leading ultimately to the country's departure.

The protracted negotiations leading to Brexit would have a detrimental effect on UK exports to EU that is almost impossible to estimate – as it depends both on the new trade agreement between the UK and the EU and volatility and ongoing depreciation of the pound. What is more likely, however, is that the right to apply tariffs and quotas on UK exports by the remaining EU countries will act in favour of EU's domestically produced goods and services and would reduce UK exports to the EU countries, as it would distort price competition and thus discriminate against UK products.

Exchange Rate Volatility

UK exports to the EU are sensitive to the pound/Euro exchange rate. The value of sterling has undergone significant fluctuations since 2007 when it traded between 1.40 and 1.45 Euros. The decrease in its value during the second half of 2008, by almost 30% in relation to the Euro, led briefly to a one-to-one exchange rate between the two currencies in December 2008. This was followed by the pound fluctuating from 1.10 to 1.25 Euros from the second half of 2009 up to the end of 2013. During 2014–2015, the pound recovered considerably reaching its pre-crisis levels of 1.4 Euros from May to November 2015. This trend followed the momentum of the UK economy reflecting in its strong growth performance.

---

[15] King, 'The UK's Balance of Payments Conundrum' *FT* (2016). http://blogs.ft.com/the-exchange/2016/07/20/the-uks-balance-of-payments-conundrum/?siteedition=intl#recommended-h-504491470546859260 downloaded on 07/08/16.

Increases in the value of the pound are encouraging in terms of reflecting a strengthening UK economy, absorbing inflationary pressures and increasing the purchasing power for the UK consumer. However, excessive increases are not desirable as they have a negative impact on export growth and firm's short-term profitability. Together with reflecting a strengthening UK economy, the pound's appreciation during 2014–2015 also reflected speculation regarding increases in the base rate by the Bank of England. Similar speculation for the Federal Reserve in the United States led to the pound depreciating in relation to the US dollar but has led, as mentioned, to appreciation in relation to the Euro. However, the potential of monetary policy divergence following different growth patterns added to the pound's volatility causing further problems for UK exporting companies to EU markets. QE, the pound's depreciation and higher inflation will lead once again to negative real interest rates.

Negative Real Interest Rates

Whether real interest rates are negative or positive is vital for the performance of the UK economy. Defined as *the base interest rate minus inflation,* real interest rates determine saving and investment decisions. Negative real interest rates, e.g. considerably increase the 'opportunity cost' of savings. With negative interest rates, households are better off investing in alternative assets, such as bonds, stocks and shares, or purchasing foreign currencies. However, with lower savings, banks' profitability is reduced. Negative real interest rates are the main implication of expansionary monetary policy, which includes reducing the base rate and increasing the money supply. They change the macroeconomic framework within which economies operate as they have a major impact on households' economic decision-making.[16]

---

[16] Blanchard, et al., 'A Prolonged Period of Low Real Interest Rates?' In Teuling, C. and Baldwin, R. (eds). *Secular Stagnation: Facts, Causes and Cures.* London: Centre for Economic Policy Research (2014).

In the UK, real interest rates remained negative for a prolonged period, as the rate of inflation has exceeded the nominal interest rate of 0.5% from 2010 to 2014. Only in the beginning of 2015, with inflation reduced to 0.3% (at least partly due to the 60% drop in oil prices), the real rate of interest turned marginally positive. Negative real interest rates are contributing to the reduction of the real value of national debt (total savings for the UK government exceed £100 billion since 2009). The reduction in the real value of national debt is occurring in the same way as the real value of mortgage repayments is reduced, when inflation accelerates to levels exceeding the rate charged on mortgages. However, negative real interest rates provide strong disincentives for households to save. As a result, the longer the UK experiences negative real interest rates combined with modest growth, the easier would find it to service maturing debt, but the more difficult to raise capital for investment.[17]

However, given the reduction in the rate of interest in August to 0.25% and the impeding increase in inflation during 2016 and 2017, the depreciation of the pound would ensure low or even negative real interest rates for some time, perhaps up to the end of the decade. This would help the government making additional savings when paying maturing debt but add to the lack of available capital for investment. Reductions in inward Foreign Direct Investment (FDI) will be the main consequence. Reducing FDI will contribute to deteriorating productivity and hence lower the long-term growth trajectory. The only way to avert lowering productivity can be provided by investment programmes by the UK government.[18]

A short-term stimulus is provided by the Bank of England and its QE programme, which has led to an injection of an additional £60 billion, on top of the £375 billion injected in the UK's financial institutions from 2009 to 2012. An extra £10 billion would be injected by

---

[17] Blanchard, et al., 'A Prolonged Period of Low Real Interest Rates?' In Teuling, C. and Baldwin, R. (eds). *Secular Stagnation: Facts, Causes and Cures*. London: Centre for Economic Policy Research (2014).

[18] Cadman, 'Carney Issues Stark Warning with Package to Ease Brexit Downturn' *FT* (2016). http://www.ft.com/cms/s/0/0d729692-5a1a-11e6-9f70-badea1b336d4.html#axzz4GQotgOYv downloaded 05/08/2016.

purchasing corporate bonds of companies that support investment programmes and a new £100 billion funding scheme for banks to be put in place.[19] These measures follow the £150 billion that would become available by the UK banks after relaxing their capital ratios. This would bring the total injection to the UK financial institutions to date to £320 billion. To put this into perspective, the volume of injection is equal to 17.1% of the 2015 UK GDP, and it compares to the 20% addition that took place during 2009–2012. The objective is to stimulate economic activity by increasing the supply of credit at an even lower cost. However, for sustainable increases in investment the private sector needs to come along. With negative (or marginally positive) real interest rates in the years to come, it is not surprising that business is loath to input such investment, *regardless* of the new trade agreement between the UK and the EU.

A resolution of EU's economic and political obstacles, facilitated by the ECB's QE programme and a 'good' trade agreement with the EU, could create favourable macroeconomic conditions for the UK economy to recover beyond 2017 and register modest growth up to 2020. Under these circumstances, the pound's depreciation could boost export activity and short-term profitability. Sustainable macroeconomic fundamentals, however, will require improving productivity rates and closing the productivity gap with other countries such as the USA, France and Germany. Until this occurs, inflating UK asset prices via money expansion – while desirable in the short-run, as it prevents deflation and ensures households do not postpone consumption to take advantage of lower prices in the future – can only lead to short-run improvements in the economy that are prone to cyclical fluctuations.[20] For a self-sustained recovery, increases in real domestic asset prices and the value of pound sterling will follow the economic fundamentals of the economy.[21]

---

[19] http://www.economicissues.org.uk/Files/2013/213Sharpe.pdf.
[20] De Grauwe, 'Should We Worry about Deflation?' *The Economist* (2014). http://www.economist.com/blogs/freeexchange/2014/01/deflation-euro-zone-1, downloaded 24/04/2014.
[21] Minsky, 'The Financial Instability Hypothesis' Levy Economics Institute, Working Paper No. 74 (1992).

The Economic Impact of Brexit – Early Indications

The impact of the Referendum's outcome on the UK economy with the decision to leave the EU is yet to be determined. Even the evaluation of the costs and benefits of being an EU member state is a challenging task. When the potential for a Referendum on the EU membership was first conceived in 2013, the House of Commons summarised the difficulties that could be encountered in doing so, by stating:

> There is no definite study of the economic impact of the UK's EU membership, or equivalently, the costs and benefits of withdrawal. Framing the aggregate impact in terms of a single number, or even irrefutably demonstrating that the net effects are positive or negative, is a formidably difficult exercise. This is partly because many of the costs and benefits are, in certain respects, subjective, diffuse of intangible; and partly because a host of assumptions must be made about the terms on which the UK would depart the EU, and how the Government would fill the policy vacuum let in areas where the EU currently has competences. (House of Commons Library, 2013, reproduced in Eichengreen 2016e).

Brexit proponents have frequently asserted their case by resorting to pointing out the UK's relative economic strength as the world's fifth largest economy (now, ironically, sixth with the plunge in the pound), thereby providing, with the substantial and widening British trade deficit,[22] an apparent motive for the EU in maintaining the current status quo – that is keeping in place the UK's position in the Common Market, without resorting to tariffs and quotas on UK exports to EU. Indeed, the volume of German exports to the UK, standing in excess of £50 billion in 2015, makes a seemingly compelling case for that argument. However, whether or not the EU will come to agree on a deal that is satisfactory to the UK is far from certain. For example, for how long

---

[22] http://www.tradingeconomics.com/united-kingdom/balance-of-trade.

would the UK consumer be able to sustain purchasing the same volumes of German or other EU exports to the UK? The ability of the UK households to purchase EU products depends on their purchasing power. This power is inextricably linked to the value of the pound and domestic inflation in relation to other competitors' inflation. Depreciation of the pound sterling in relation to the Euro implies an equal erosion in the UK households' capacity to purchase Eurozone products. Brexit proponents have drawn on the positives of the sharp devaluation in the pound over 2015–2016: namely, the reduction in the cost of production and the increase in the volume of UK exports that this will bring. However, little has been said on the limitations of the depreciation's effectiveness and its negative effects. While making domestic products more competitive in international markets, declines in the value of the pound reduce UK assets worth, and as such render easier their sale to foreign companies – most notably, the sale of ARM Holdings on 18 July 2016 to Japanese firm Softbank, three weeks after the Brexit vote and with the pound down 10% on the result.[23] Furthermore, with the reduction in the volumes of foreign products purchased, these will likely become more expensive as import push inflation will increase – creating the danger of a negative spiral of inflation–depreciation that can only be broken by the Bank of England. To counter the new inflationary pressures, the Bank of England could increase the rate of interest. However, given the slow-down in growth, the reverse policy has been in place. However, given a sharp increase in the rate of inflation, the BE could be caught in a dilemma over output versus inflation targeting. Based on the Governors and other Monetary Policy Committee' members, it would seem that the Bank would prioritise stimulating growth, subject to modest deviations from the 2% inflation target.

The depreciation in the pound not only erodes the UK households' purchasing power, it reduces the UK assets net value and makes UK companies easier to purchase, it also puts in question the strength of

---

[23] https://www.theguardian.com/politics/2016/jul/18/tech-giant-arm-holdings-sold-to-japanese-firm-for-24bn.

Table 6.1 UK's GDP in $ and £ terms (trillions)

Year	GDP measured (in $)	GDP measured (in £)	£/$
2016	2454.8	1888.296	1.3
2015	2848.8	1869.6	1.5237484
2014	2990	1822.5	1.6406036
2013	2712.3	1739.6	1.5591515
2012	2630.5	1675	1.5704478
2011	2595	1628.3	1.5936867
2010	2403.5	1572.4	1.5285551

the UK's economy. International comparisons of countries' relative economic strength are made based on GDP expressed in *US dollar terms*. As a result, the UK's GDP in 2014 reached its peak with $2990 billion and then was reduced to $2850 billion in 2015, as can be seen in Table 6.1. The reduction in the UK's GDP in dollar terms took place despite the UK's strong economic performance in 2015. This reduction is attributed to the reduction in the value of the pound from $1.64 per pound in 2014 to $1.52 in 2015. The reduction in the value of the pound following the June Referendum to $1.22 per pound by October 2016 undermines the UK's relative economic strength. Let us assume the first two quarters' economic growth of 0.4% and 0.6% are confirmed and zero growth is registered in the second half of 2016 – projections that are in line with the BE's forecasts. Therefore, unless growth recovers substantially in the second half of the year, or the pound strengthens considerably in relation to the US dollar, the UK's economic weight in dollar terms for 2016 will be reduced to $2454.8 (Table 6.1). This actually corresponds to a reduction on 13.8% from its 2015 level.

With French GDP at $2421.7 for 2015, and India forecasted to overtake the UK in 2018 prior to the Referendum, these two countries are expected to overtake the UK in the world's largest economies' rankings by early 2017, if not earlier. Things are even worst when the Purchasing Power Parity (PPP) measurements are taken into consideration. This includes the impact of domestic inflation when making cross-country comparisons, and it reflects household's purchasing power. It compares what £1 can buy in the UK with what the equivalent of £1 (=1.15 €) can purchase in e.g. France (i.e. instead of nominal comparisons, these rankings are based on real comparisons). The UK prior to the Referendum stood ninth internationally. The combination of the depreciating pound and higher domestic inflation will cause a drop in the international PPP comparisons.

In addition, the BE's growth forecasts point to a cumulative loss of output of 2.5% during 2016–2019, as a result of the regime change brought about by the Referendum's outcome.[24] The BE forecasts assume a return to its long-run growth trajectory of 2.2% towards the end of 2019. In the meantime, according to the BE's forecasts, growth will be reduced from 2.3% to 0.8% in 2017 and 1.8% from 2.3% in 2018.

Thus, assuming return to long run growth at the end of 2019, the Referendum outcome's impact on the UK economy is likely threefold. Firstly, it downgrades the UK economy from the fifth to sixth or seventh biggest in the world. Second, it causes an output loss of 2.5% in the next 3.5 years. Thirdly, it reduces the UK economy from one of the best performing among its G7 peers, second only to the USA, to one of the worst performing for 2016–2019, above Japan. The downgrade in international rankings could take place, even before Brexit finally materialises. These forecasts are in line with the late-July IMF's revisions over the UK's GDP trajectory in 2016 and 2017.[25] According to these, the UK economy is set to grow by 1.7% in 2016, instead of 1.9% and 1.3% in 2017, down from a previous estimate of 2.2%. This revision was the greatest among G7 economies for 2017.

However, one crucial element relating to both the BE's and the IMF forecasts is the treatment of the Referendum outcome and its impact as only temporary in nature. This assumes a resumption of normal trade patterns with the EU post Brexit. Even more worryingly for the economy's international standing. If the impact is permanent, Brexit would reduce potential growth. In this case, output loss will be far greater than

---

[24] Bank of England, 'Inflation Report' (2016) http://www.bankofengland.co.uk/publications/Documents/inflationreport/2016/aug.pdf downloaded 11/11/2016.

[25] https://www.imf.org/external/pubs/ft/weo/2016/update/02/.

2.5%. Indeed, as acknowledged by the BE Deputy Governor, Ben Broadbent:

> We would *need [the PMI] to recover over the coming months to meet the forecast we have*, which is for a little bit of growth during the second half of the year. (Eichengreen 2016e)

As a result, the analysis conducted so far by the BE and the IMF is implicitly based on the assumption of a 'soft' landing of the UK economy, as a result of the Referendum and final exit from the EU and Single Market. For example, the IMF's forecasts are based on the assumption that the UK and the EU will maintain good trade relations and eventually accede to a trade agreement similar to that of Norway – i.e. one retaining almost complete access to the Common Market. By contrast, the National Institute of Economics and Social Research revised downwards its growth forecasts for 2017 by 1.7%. It also forecasted that slower growth will increase national debt by approximately £50 billion by 2020 and will lead to an increase of the debt-to-GDP ratio to 90%. These forecasts assumed no increase in government expenditure. The IFS puts the additional debt bill to £39 billion.[26] Bloomberg's survey of economists also points to a reduction in GDP to 1.6% in 2016 and 0.6% in 2017.[27] Overall, there is a consensus reached over a severe slowdown in growth as a result of the Referendum's outcome for the period during 2016–2019, with the debate focusing on whether this would lead to a recession in 2017. Early indications for the impact of the Referendum pointed to a significant decline in London's residential property market. Projections based on the Purchasing Managers' Index (PMI) survey that registers activity in manufacturing, construction and services pointed to a sharp slowdown in the country's GDP, at least in the short term.

---

[26] Institute of Fiscal Studies, 'Brexit and the UK's Public Finances' *IFS Report* 116 (2016). https://www.ifs.org.uk/uploads/publications/comms/r116.pdf downloaded 11/11/2016.

[27] Meakin, *Carney to Ignore Inflation Overshoot as Economists See Rate Cut*. Bloomberg (2016). http://www.bloomberg.com/news/articles/2016-08-12/carney-to-ignore-inflation-overshoot-as-economists-see-rate-cut downloaded on 13/08/16.

Brexit advocates have long argued that the UK will manage to get a very good trade deal with the EU, as it consists one of the EU's biggest exporting markets. However, in order for the UK to maintain its status as the biggest EU's market, the post-Brexit period requires a relatively strong pound, with which UK customers can continue purchasing EU products. With the pound's slide likely to continue – or at the very least not see a dramatic recovery back to pre-Referendum levels – the UK customers' purchasing power would be further eroded, leading to purchasing less EU products. This will reduce the significance on the UK as an EU trade partner. As such, it will also reduce the likelihood of a 'good' trade agreement for the UK.

Further, as GDP and real GDP per person are measured in domestic prices, cross-country comparisons are also made based on purchasing power parities. A decline in the value of the pound means that the UK becomes less wealthy in international terms, as discussed above – the effects of which tourists experience when travelling in Europe. Despite, therefore, the economic performance of the period leading to the Referendum, the recent BE forecasts point to a severe slowdown for the year ahead.[28] The UK hiring on permanent posts declined to a 7-year low, as indicated by the drop of the Index of Permanent Positions that dropped from 49.3 in June to 45.4 in July, while the BE's forecast for unemployment suggest an increase from 4.8% to 5.6% in the course of 2017 and 2018.[29] This corresponds to a 250,000 increase in unemployment. To the extent that this pause in firms' committing to permanent hiring reflects abstaining from new investment projects, it strengthens the case of a recession hitting the UK economy in 2016–2017.

This downturn in the UK's growth rate is also supported by the GfK index that measures consumer confidence, which shows an 11 point decline – the sharpest since 1990. Various market developments; developments such as Lloyds job losses announcement, mortgage approvals

---

[28] Bank of England, 'Inflation Report' (2016). http://www.bankofengland.co.uk/publications/Documents/inflationreport/2016/aug.pdf downloaded 11/11/2016.

[29] Bank of England, 'Inflation Report' (2016). http://www.bankofengland.co.uk/publications/Documents/inflationreport/2016/aug.pdf downloaded 11/11/2016.

declining to their lowest levels since 2008, British Airways reduced profits guidance and Foxton's postponement of new branch openings amongst fears of price corrections in the London professional and residential prices – point to a looming and potentially significant slowdown in economic activity.[30] On the other hand, there were good news over job creation from McDonald's, new investment programmes in the UK announced by GlaxoSmithKline Plc and an influx of tourists taking advantage of the low pound. The overall balance between 'bad' and 'good' news will be dictated by the willingness of international investors to push ahead with their investment projects in the UK.

Foreign Direct Investment – Bank of England – Interest Rates

A country's national account comprises the capital and the current account. The capital account registers capital flows. The current account measures net trade in goods and services, primary income and secondary income. FDI is the main component of primary income. The impact of the Referendum on the FDI trend is vital. A contentious issue prior to the Referendum, Brexit proponents claimed that FDI may marginally decline in the short run, but it will eventually recover once the Brexit shock is absorbed.[31] However, as mentioned earlier, the impact of the Referendum on FDI needs to be placed in a wider perspective. FDI has been reduced since 2011, in particular due to the low interest rate environment. In order for FDI to be maintained at steady levels, a minimum rate of interest of 2–3% is required. This is in order for a sufficient rate of return on investment and profits to allow their partial reinvestment.

Initially, the 0.5% rate of interest, set in 2009, was considered temporary in nature. It was thought that once the UK economy would return to its previous growth pattern, increases in the rate of interest would

---

[30] http://www.propertyweek.com/residential-and-development/100613.subject.
[31] https://www.theguardian.com › World › EU Referendum and Brexit.

follow suit. The need to increase the rate of interest to levels that will facilitate the reinvestment of profits has been debated over since 2011. The UK economy's strong performance in 2013–2015 placed pressure on the BE to review its interest rate policy. Forward guidance, introduced by the then new Governor of the Bank of England in 2013 and linking the base rate to reductions in unemployment, was quickly abandoned as unemployment was reduced below 7%, currently standing at 4.8%.

Maintaining the base rate to 0.5% prevented the UK economy's return to 'normality' – without the same punishment of savers, or risks of fuelling an asset bubble, that exist in tandem with ultra-low interest rate policies. The procession back to 'normality' could have been initiated in the second half of 2016/early 2017, had the Referendum result being different. However, the unexpected outcome and the impeding EU withdrawal have cause a significant reduction in the economy's growth rate, according to PMI data, leading to further reduction in the base rate, after 7 years, to 0.25%.

FDI has experienced a significant decline due to reductions in net terms – that is, income generated from UK companies' investments abroad minus income generated in the UK from foreign-owned companies. Primarily, income generated by UK companies in the Netherlands and other Eurozone countries. Leaving investment programmes aside, this decline also reflects disinvestment and the exceptionally low interest rate environment in the Eurozone, USA and Japan. Overall, the FDI in the last 5 years has fallen but not collapsed. But Brexit has the potential to lead to a dramatic, *permanent* decline in FDI. Indeed, FDI accounted for 79% of the £66 billion decline in the primary income balance between 2011 and 2014.[32]

The reason for this decline is twofold: firstly, due to a steady decrease in the value of UK earnings on investments by UK companies abroad – something now bolstered by the devalued pound – and, secondly, by an increase in earnings of foreign companies in the UK. The decline in income from UK companies abroad, from £105 billion in 2011 to

---

[32] Hamroush, et al., 'An analysis of Foreign Direct Investment, the key driver of the recent deterioration in the UK's Current Account' Office for National Statistics (2015).

£73 billion in 2014, can be attributed to a fall in the rate of return received on UK assets, and a reduction in the net worth of UK stocks. The depreciation of the pound could well cushion this decrease, as profits increase in pound terms. However, the same principle works in reverse for earnings generated in the UK by foreign companies – potentially a more dangerous problem in this context. Above all, the crucial factor is the actual trade agreement that the UK government will secure with the EU. Clearly, an agreement that could give rise to trade tariff and quotas will be harmful to FDI and could potentially be a blow to FDI volumes.

The reduction in the rate of interest in August has exacerbated these issues. Foreign companies engaged in FDI projects in the UK would have more of an incentive to shift away any profits made to countries with higher rates of return. The new governments' pledge not to abide to the balanced budget target could mitigate Brexit's adverse effects on FDI, but there are limitations to the extent of fiscal expansion that the government can engage in.

Given the importance of FDI for the UK's trade performance, the country's new trade deal with the EU is vital for determining the success of the pound's depreciation. This is because the EU remains the UK's biggest trade partner and export market, and due to the fact that many foreign companies are located in the UK, with its welcoming business environment and broad, previously unfettered access to EU markets. In sum, the pound's depreciation can only lead to a new sustainable equilibrium for the UK economy if there is a 'good trade' agreement with the EU. If this is not the case, then the costs resulting from the pound's depreciation could outweigh the expected benefits.

In particular, a series of interdependent factors will come into play. First, the increase in import prices would be higher than expected, leading to accelerating inflation from imported goods and services.[33]

---

[33] Nussbaum and Ryan, *Brexit Bites Back as Peugeot Joins Dell in Lifting Prices.* Bloomberg (2016). http://www.bloomberg.com/news/articles/2016-08-10/brexit-bites-back-as-peugeot-joins-dell-in-lifting-prices downloaded 10/08/16. Meakin, *Carney to Ignore Inflation Overshoot as Economists See Rate Cut.* Bloomberg (2016).

http://www.bloomberg.com/news/articles/2016-08-12/carney-to-ignore-inflation-overshoot-as-economists-see-rate-cut downloaded on 13/08/16.

Indeed, the Office for National Statistics in its September inflation report registered an annual increase of 6.5% in import prices while input costs increased by 4.3% in July after 32 months of declines.[34] If import push inflation exceeds the decline in inflation caused by lower demand (demand-pull inflation), this would lead to rates of inflation that the BE and the UK consumer would find hard to cope with. In this case, the BE will find it increasingly difficult to further stimulate growth by expansionary monetary policy.[35] Further QE would thereby be ruled out.[36]

Second, modern production processes, with their complex and global supply chains, are far more complicated than in even relatively recent decades, when production and manufacturing were predominantly still local.[37] IT developments and the growth of services in imports and exports make production in the UK simply a single step in a global supply chain. The pound's depreciation and the new trade deal with the EU will define the UK's companies' terms and conditions in this worldwide network. This is most pertinent for multinational corporations that have their headquarters in London. Relocating to other European cities such as Paris or London – or other cities outside the EU, such as New York or Tokyo – would be considered before the final print of the agreement is agreed and ratified. A prolonged negotiating process, which seems quite plausible at present, could add to this uncertainty.

Thirdly, much of the pound's decline effectiveness would depend on the foreign demand for UK exports. In this case, a weak growth trajectory for the EU economy would be a drag, as it would imply a

---

[34] Office for National Statistics, 'UK Consumer Price Inflation: Sept 2016' (2016).
 https://www.ons.gov.uk/economy/inflationandpriceindices/bulletins/consumerpriceinflation/sept2016 downloaded 11/11/2016.
[35] Bank of England, 'Inflation Report' (2016). http://www.bankofengland.co.uk/publications/Documents/inflationreport/2016/aug.pdf downloaded 11/11/2016.
[36] Giles, 'Harsh Realities of a Weakened Pound' *FT* (2016).
 http://www.ft.com/cms/s/2/9c746d04-4456-11e6-9b66-0712b3873ae1.html?siteedition=intl#axzz4GQotgOYv downloaded 07/08/2016.
[37] On this transition see for example. https://supernet.isenberg.umass.edu/articles/globalsupplychainoutsourcing.pdf and http://it.toolbox.com/blogs/everything-anything-supply-chains/foreign-exchange-risks-in-global-supply-chains-what-lies-in-store-36173.

lower growth projector for the UK.[38] In this case, trade dependence with China and India would be essential to support UK's growth. However, the short-term challenge would be to dictate the terms of trade with these two countries, while negotiating the new EU trade agreement. With the Chinese economy facing extreme challenges in the medium term due to debt built-up, the debate centres on the chances of a 'soft' versus a 'hard' landing for its economy. India therefore presents the only BRICS that the UK could rely on for a medium-to-long run boost to its exports. The likelihood is that a favourable trade agreement with India would be relatively easy to secure.[39]

Fourthly, the changing nature of UK exports in the last two decades means that far more services than manufacturing goods are exported. From 1998 to 2007, services exports grew from 30.2% to around 42.2%, while manufacturing exports declined by the same amount. This left the UK particularly exposed to the severity of the Great Recession (as discussed above) than other major economies with less reliance on financial services, such as France and Germany. In addition, as shown above, it implied that the subsequent recovery was slowest in relation to previous recession, as rebalancing the economy away from the services and financial sector has and continues to prove elusive.

Fifthly, and related to the first and second reasons above, many UK companies are importers and exporters at the same time. In particular, they (and Britain as a whole) are net importers of commodities. However, as most of these are priced in US dollars, the pound's depreciation increases input costs for UK factories dependent on importing commodities.[40] Sixth, overseas demand. With the IMF predicting a

---

[38] King, 'The UK's Balance of Payments Conundrum' *FT* (2016).
http://blogs.ft.com/the-exchange/2016/07/20/the-uks-balance-of-payments-conundrum/?siteedition=intl#recommended-h-504491470546859260 downloaded on 07/08/16.

[39] Campbell and Tetlow, 'Indian Business Welcomes UK Trade Deal' *FT* (2016). http://www.ft.com/cms/s/0/2e0eb278-4372-11e6-b22f-79eb4891c97d.html#axzz4FpTCFbuR downloaded 30/07/16.

[40] Gemma, 'UK Manufacturing Output Falls Sharply Following Brexit Vote' *FT* (2016). http://www.ft.com/cms/s/0/b832a75c-57e0-11e6-8d05-4eaa66292c32.html#axzz4FpTCFbuR downloaded on 01/08/16. Giles, 'Harsh Realities of a Weakened Pound' *FT* (2016). http://www.ft.com/cms/s/2/9c746d04-4456-11e6-9b66-0712b3873ae1.html?siteedition=intl#axzz4GQotgOYv downloaded 07/08/2016.

slowdown in international trade to less than 3% for 2016–2017, international demand for UK exports could be reduced despite the pound's drop in value.

All the above factors could limit the effectiveness of the pound's depreciation on export growth. Combined with an unsatisfactory or limited trade agreement with the EU, or a prolonged period of protracted negotiations, and a sustained period of low interest rates, will be detrimental to inward FDI in the UK. This would make it probable that the nation's current account would deteriorate even further, than its record levels of 5.2% in 2015.

Productivity

Brexit has the potential to derail the productivity catch up that the UK needs to undergo. Early indications point to a significant slowdown in business investment following the Referendum result, vital for reducing the cost of production.[41] Delaying investment programmes were also caused due to negative real interest rates as discussed above. This has inevitably impaired productivity growth. The UK economy's low productivity is not a new phenomenon. The growth rates achieved in 2013–2016 were against a background of a consumer credit boom, facilitated by exceptionally low interest rates of 0.5%. The export-recovery advocated by the former Chancellor of the Exchequer, George Osborne, never materialised. In the absence of government investment programmes, consumer expenditure provided the only major source of economic growth. However, increases in household's debt levels made this type of growth unsustainable. Coupled with the Referendum's outcome, the prospects for the UK economy from the next 2–3 years are not encouraging – as confirmed by the BE forecasts.[42]

---

[41] https://www.theguardian.com/business/2016/jul/28/health-check-of-key-sectors-post-brexit-vote-counter-growth-figure.
[42] http://www.independent.co.uk/news/business/news/bank-forecasts-two-years-of-steady-growth-with-inflation-hitting-target-740539.html.

Overall, the UK's economic recovery during 2013–2016 has led to a record number of people at work – exceeding 31 million in total – and as such has increased the participation ratio (people currently at work, divided by the number of people able to work) to 74.4%. However, two distinctive features of the recovery were the stubbornly higher youth unemployment rates and the low productivity, in particular in relation to France and Germany.[43] Despite its decline to its lower level since 2005, youth unemployment remained at 11.6% – far higher than any other age group. The combination of these factors leads to a position where more people are at work but with a higher average working age and lower productivity than workers in other major OECD countries.[44]

These conditions are in line with labour market patterns established throughout the recovery since 2013, featuring strong employment figures but low wage growth. While the productivity lag could be attributed to a number of factors, such as IT influences, overall skills and lack of retraining, the reduction in unemployment below the 5% benchmark implies that slack has been reduced and only a residual remains in the labour market. Therefore, future increases in growth can *only* result from higher productivity. This is particularly the case beyond 2019.

The above discussion raises the question of the nature of the UK recovery from 2013 to 2016 in the light of low(er) productivity rates. The appreciation in the value of the pound in relation to the Euro from 2013 to 2016 increased the cost of production per unit of output by international standards, and it reduces exporting firms' short-term profit margins. The decline in the value of the pound since June will help such firms increase their profitability by increasing productivity in the short run. However, as discussed above, there are factors that could limit the

---

[43] Hamroush, et al., 'An Analysis of Foreign Direct Investment, the Key Driver of the Recent Deterioration in the UK's Current Account' Office for National Statistics (2015).

[44] O'Connor, 'Workers Suffer Real-term Pay Cuts on a Par with Greece, Says TUC' (2016a). http://www.ft.com/cms/s/0/aabea3cc-533b-11e6-9664-e0bdc13c3bef.html#axzz4GQotgOYv downloaded 06/08/16. O'Connor, 'UK Jobless Fell Below 5% Before Brexit Vote' *FT* (2016b).
http://www.ft.com/cms/s/0/e943404c-4e5b-11e6-88c5db83e98a590a.html#axzz4GQotgOYv downloaded 06/08/16.

effectiveness of the pound's decline. Indeed, Mark Carney recognised in his interview on the 4 August 2016 that the deprecation in the pound would only be able to partially mitigate the current account deficit, reducing it by about half.[45] This implies a reduction of the current account deficit from 5.2% in 2015 to 2.5–2.7% in 2016–2017.

In the long run, increases in inflation will reduce productivity – in particular in relation to countries that maintain lower inflation. Thus, QE and reductions in the rate of interest were/are a short-term remedy to lower growth. However, improving productivity is a long-run target: which requires, amongst many things reforms in education to enable a highly skilled workforce, and the continuous integration of IT (such as digital skills) in the production process. Up to when these objectives are achieved, the growth pattern of the UK economy will remain fragile and subject to cyclical fluctuations. Indeed, the limits of monetary and exchange rate policies led the Governor of the BE to claim in August 2016, that

> The future potential of this economy and its implications for jobs, real wages and wealth are not the gifts of monetary policymakers. We cannot immediately or fully offset the economic impacts [of the vote to leave the EU]. The big issues for government are those that they have acknowledged, which is the importance of negotiations with European allies on the new relationship that will be developed, the importance of having a productivity plan [...] it's those decisions and those policies that will really be the determinants of long-term prosperity.

It needs to be borne in mind that the BE forecasts were based on the assumption of no changes in the UK's trade relations with the EU countries, apart from a reduction in the degree of trade openness, as establishing improved trade relations with non-EU countries would not fully mitigate trade losses with the EU. They were also assuming no changes in the government's economic policy. As a result, negotiations with the EU over a new trade deal present another major challenge in

---

[45] http://www.telegraph.co.uk/business/2016/08/03/ftse-100-to-open-lower-hsbc-gets-pummelled-and-next-faces-higher/.

Table 6.2 Summary of UK key economic features, 2013–2019, and two Brexit scenarios

	Impact of Referendum		Impact of Brexit	
Variables	2013–2016	2016–2019	Soft Brexit-post19	Hard Brexit-post19
Trade agreement	Common market	Common market	Access to CM	Limited access to CM
Interest rates	low i/r = 0.5%	low i/r for longer	i/r to 'normalise'	i/r to remain low
Value of pound	higher £	Lower £	Relatively higher £	£ declines further
Inflation	< 2% target	> 2% target	Inflation to target	Inflation > target
Real inter. rates	Negative	Negative	Positive	Negative
Foreign Dir. Inv.	Declines	Declines	Modest declines	Dramatic declines
Productivity	Low	Improved	Relatively stable	Deteriorate
Growth rates	Recovery	Lower short run	Modest = 2.2%	Lower than < 2%
Bal. of payments	Deficit	Narrowing	Deficit to stabilise	Potential Bal. Pa. Crisis

such a fluid environment. A summary of the UK key economic features since 2013, and the impact of the Referendum is presented in Table 6.2. Two Brexit scenarios, a 'soft' and a 'hard' one relating to the trade agreement that will be agreed and implemented post–2019, are also presented.

As it can be observed in Table 6.2, the worst-case scenario under a 'hard' Brexit involves a 'bad' trade agreement with the EU that would limit access to the Common Market. This will require interest rates to remain low for longer, and the UK pound would depreciate more in 2019 (this would improve productivity in the short run). As a result, inflation would be considerably higher than target, possibly leading to an upward revision by the Bank of England from the 2% inflation target in the short term. This would imply negative real interest rates for longer, with adverse effects on FDI, productivity and growth in the long run. A balance of payments crisis caused by a dramatic depreciation in the pound cannot therefore be ruled out. This is an unlikely scenario, but it should be bore in mind, while the exit negotiations take place, and the likelihood of a good trade agreement fades away. However, the EU has so far signalled that the best solution for both parties would be sought out.

Effects of Brexit on the European Union

The GDP of the EU exceeds €14.5 trillion, out of which €2.3 trillion is the UK's GDP (just below a fifth of EUs GDP). This is calculated on a pound to Euro exchange rate of €1.25. In terms of the EU budget, Brexit will reduce it from €141 billion to around €129 billion. As the current EU budget runs up to 2020, it is not entirely clear whether the UK is legally bound to pay its contributions up to 2020, should it depart earlier. Let it be as it may, the UK's departure from EU would cause prolonged negotiations among the remaining 27 countries over the EU budget for the 2020–2026 cycle.

In terms of the Eurozone, the UK's departure will significantly reduce the (already limited) effectiveness of QE of the ECB. The ECB's QE objectives are twofold – being both internal to the Eurozone and external to the rest of the world.

Internal Objectives

Firstly, by reducing the cost of borrowing money to stimulate lending in the Eurozone countries, Brexit will not have an immediate impact on this objective. It could have a long run effect to Eurozone companies that export to the UK, as they would experience a reduction in their exports to the UK, but that would depend on the post-Brexit trade arrangements with particular Eurozone countries.

Secondly, by penalising banks when keeping reserves with the ECB (negative deposit rates), Brexit will not have an immediate effect on this objective as well, unless it was followed by prolonged turmoil in financial markets. However, it would definitely be an additional factor prolonging the return to 'normality' – that is, the increase of the ECB's rate of interest to 2–3%. The rate of return on savings remains exceptionally low across the Eurozone (as is in the UK).[46]

Thirdly is the goal to reduce Eurozone countries' cost of servicing their national debt and thus alleviate the short-term expense of debt servicing on national budgets. Again, there is likely to be no major immediate effect on the Eurozone countries' servicing of national debt, unless Brexit is followed by broader turbulence in debt markets. With Italy due to hold a Constitutional Referendum in October, Italians Banks seem particularly vulnerable to contagion.

External Objectives

The aim of the ECB's QE programme is to reduce the value of the Euro against the other major currencies in order to enhance Eurozone's volumes of trade (exports) to international markets. The UK is the main trading partner of the Eurozone countries. This objective has already been undermined since the depreciation in the value of the pound – from €1.40 per pound in December 2015 to €1.15 in July, and lower since – has rendered EU exports to the UK far more expensive. As a result, even if a favourable trade agreement is reached between the two parties, the EU-27 will face lower exports as the UK provides the biggest export market to Eurozone countries. A further (potential) decline in the pound when Brexit materialises could render ECB's external objective obsolete. A relatively high value of the euro in relation to the dollar will also have an adverse impact on Eurozone exports to the USA. Trade relations with Russia and the slowdown in BRICS economic growth in all the members, save India, will imply that export-led recovery is not attainable, thus reducing the Eurozone's fragile growth potential. Thus, from an export perspective, Brexit would have a negative impact on UK exports to EU and Eurozone's exports to the UK, as both parties lose out.

---

[46] https://www.ft.com/content/3f3ac996-a4ea-11e5-97e1-a754d5d9538c.

Financial and debt markets could put additional pressure on the three internal objectives of the ECB's QE. If this realisation is ensued (in the extreme case) by a debt crisis in the UK following Brexit, this would most likely have negative repercussions on debt servicing for the Eurozone countries involved in the Eurozone debt crisis, in particular Greece and Portugal.

The Eurozone Banks: A Threat to the Future and Stability of the Eurozone?

The low interest rate environment has severely undermined Bank profitability in the EU, alongside the USA and Japan. However, the prospect of rising interest rates following the recovery of the USA and the UK economies through 2012–2016 had aided bank shares in returning to their 2008 heights by the first half of 2016. But the UK Referendum outcome sent a shockwave through financial centres around the globe – leading to the widespread reduction of growth forecasts, and playing a contributing role to the FED postponing increases to their base rate. In the UK, the BE reduced its base rate to 0.25%, with prospects for a further cut left open. This squeezed bank profitability even further and helps provoke a sharp fall in share prices – a fall which, in the Deutsche Bank, exceeded 40%.[47] In the EU, the loss has amounted to €510 billion by the autumn of 2016. To put that in perspective, the losses exceed the value of all bailouts the EU has offered to debt-ridden countries, or the value of the Italian stock market.[48] Banks in Germany and Italy have been hit particularly hard.

---

[47] https://www.theguardian.com/business/2016/sep/27/deutsche-bank-shares-fall-to-new-low-after-another-turbulent-day.
[48] Horta, *Europe's Tumbling Lenders Lose Almost Half Their Value in a Year*. Bloomberg (2016). http://www.bloomberg.com/news/articles/2016-08-02/europe-s-tumbling-lenders-lose-almost-half-their-value-in-a-year downloaded 02/08/16 70. Hale, et al., 'European Bank Shares Fall in Brutal Start to August' *FT* (2016). http://www.ft.com/cms/s/0/2412e9ee-5888-11e6-9f70-badea1b336d4.html#axzz4GClnsVJ4 downloaded 02/08/16.

The value of the European banking sector of the 600 Banks Index has been reduced from €1.3–1.4 trillion in June 2015 to €0.9 trillion in July 2016. This represents a reduction of 30–35% in the value, with Deutsche Bank and Commerzbank falling even sharper. While problems pre-existed the Referendum, its outcome played a pivotal role for this decline. Italian Banks have suffered the most since the outcome.

Deutsche Bank, Germany's biggest lender, is currently in the spotlight over (as with other international banks such as the UK's Royal bank of Scotland) – its part in the mis-sale of mortgage-backed securities. For this, it could face a fine of 14 billion USD, which it disputes with the US Justice Department. While accepting its role in this mis-selling, it argues that the fine is grossly excessive and that the scale is largely in retaliation for the fine of 13 billion Euros (plus back taxes to the Irish Government) that the EU Commission imposed on Apple for breaches of EU State Aid rules. Blame in part for the bank's troubles is pointed squarely at the ECB for its policy of maintaining such low interest rates, a view supported by Wolfgang Schäuble, Germany's finance minister when he stated that

I think for supervision, regulation and restructuring of banks in Europe we have a lot of institutions which are responsible for this. . . . It's not to the World Bank and other international organizations to supervise banks.[49] Deutsche has to address its failure to deal with its bad loan portfolio; to establish new strategies for growth and to strengthen its capital base. But its weaknesses are a symptom of Eurozone banks in general. Worst still is the Italian banking crisis which if not resolved could shake the Eurozone to the core.

Central to the crisis is the position of the nation's domestic banks. Italy is the only Southern Eurozone member state not in receipt of bailout funds from the EU. Pressure was placed on the Italian government in the autumn 2011 until the spring of 2012 to accept a bailout similar to the one received by Spain, but this was firmly rejected despite

---

[49] https://www.ft.com/content/53e8cc58-8e14-11e6-a72e-b428cb934b78.

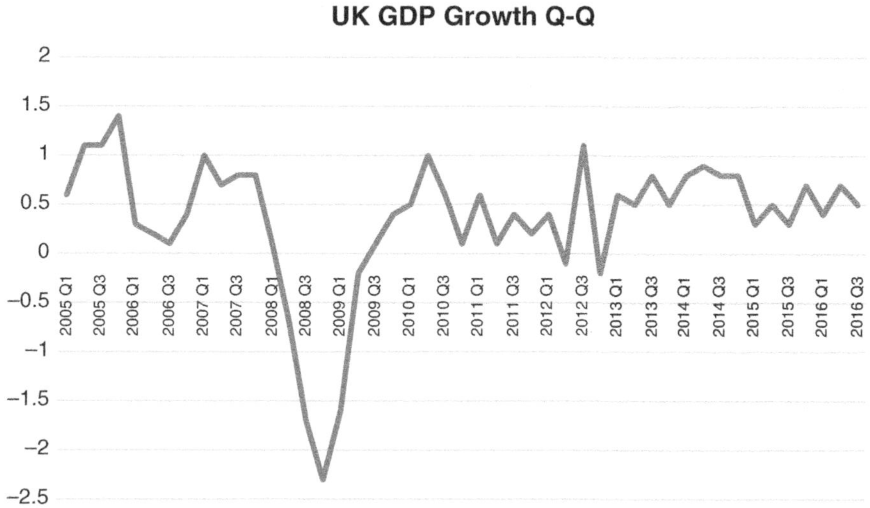

UK GDP Growth Q-Q

Fig. 6.1 UK GDP growth

Authors' own work, data downloaded from ONS 14/11/2016

a background of mounting debts reaching 133% of (Italian) GDP in 2015 and expected to exceed 135% in 2016 as shown in Fig. 6.1.

However, with financial institutions in Italy not exposed to 'toxic' assets,[50] it was decided in 2012 that no bailout was necessary as it was gauged that the Italian economy would resume its growth potential – an expectation which turned out to be wrong. However, resuming growth in Italy has proved elusive since joining the European Monetary Union in 1999. Since that year, the country has registered no real growth and has experienced a loss of competitiveness in excess of 30% in relation to Germany and the Netherlands.[51] Industrial production has declined dramatically, partly due to the inability to devalue in relation to its

---

[50] Debts whose value has fallen significantly or associated with financial instruments such as CDOs, Collateral debt obligations.

[51] Marsh, *Europe's Deadlock: How the Euro Crisis Could be Solved – and Why It Won't Happen*. Yale University Press (2013). Marsh, *The Euro: The Battle for the New Global Currency*. Yale University Press (2011).

Northern Eurozone partners and partly due to the nature of its products that are price sensitive. The country as a result has not recovered the export markets it held prior to the Great Recession.[52] Its youth unemployment rates in the South of the country are comparable to these of Greece and Spain. In the last couple of years, a strong dollar and ECB's QE have helped alleviate the country's problems but have not provided a long-term solution to its structural problems. In 2016, the first quarter growth of 0.3% was followed by a decline in the second quarter to 0% growth.[53]

As a consequence, the problems for the Italian banks are closely tied to the continued deterioration of the country's economy. With Italian debt at €2.2 trillion, the gradual slowdown of the economy and the defaults that come as a result, Italian banks are under immense strain as they find it increasingly difficult to raise the capital required to cover the losses. Further, the decisions taken in 2012 to ring-fence the single currency, ruled out state aid to domestic banks, and the only option available was the so-called bail-in rescue programme adopted in the case of Cyprus in 2013.[54] This involves drawing on bondholders and equity investors to cover the losses. As many bondholders and equity investors are households and 'small savers', this makes this option politically difficult to implement.[55] Such a solution has already come as a shock to small savers in regional banks around the country: a scenario that risks them losing access to their life-savings to support a bank's liquidity or capitalisation.

In terms of specific Italian bank institutions, the oldest one, Monte dei Paschi di Siena, has seen its share price drop a total of 80% from its

---

[52] Karagounis, et al., 'The Stability and Growth Pact, and Balanced Budget Fiscal Stimulus: Evidence from Germany and Italy' *Inter-economics*, 50(1), pp. 32–39 (2015).

[53] BBC (2016) 'Italian Economy Stagnates as German Growth Slows' http://www.bbc.com/news/business-37056800 downloaded 12/08/16.

[54] 'Bail-in' is an alternative to the bailout policy during the financial and Eurozone crisis, where failing banks' investors (depositors) take a hit rather than taxpayers.

[55] Robinson (2016) 'Italian Banks Reel But Monti Has No Regrets for Avoiding Bailout' http://www.bloomberg.com/news/articles/2016-08-09/italian-banks-reel-but-monti-has-no-regrets-for-avoiding-bailout downloaded 10/08/16.

January 2016 value. The bank holds a total of €47 billion of bad debt. Unione di Banche Italiane SpA has lost 62% of its value in 2016, and Uni Credit experienced massive losses as well.[56] The UK's Referendum outcome accelerated the pace of the slowdown in Italian banking shares. The outcome came at a background of €360 billion non-performing loans (NPLs), a fifth of the total. To put this number in perspective, it exceeds the total load of Greek debt. A further €85 billion is not yet included in bankbooks. If they were included, this would further reduce banks' already low capital ratios, placing them under immense pressure to accept recapitalisation on the basis of creditors' haircut.[57]

Further, the lack of an effective Eurozone Banking Union and a Eurozone-wide deposit insurance scheme implies that Italy runs the risk of running out of options. A viable solution could involve the creation of a 'bad' bank to absorb the NPLs, in a similar way that the Spanish banks were put back in a healthy state – and a tried and tested procedure also applied in the Banking Resolution procedure for Laiki bank (formerly known as Cyprus Popular bank) in the Cyprus financial crisis.[58] However, as mentioned, Spain had to receive extra-financial liquidity from the ECB, equal to €100 billion. At the time, Italy successfully distanced itself from bailout countries, despite the increases in the rate of interest charged for the Italian debt reaching 7%. Italy managed to do so, due to its small balance of payments deficit that rarely exceeded the 3% threshold since 1999. In the absence of modest growth though, the ratio or NPLs to total loans increased since 2012 leading to the current impasse. As Italy cannot be bailed out due to the size of its economy, the issue is potentially explosive for the

---

[56] Zega, *Traders Brace for More Turmoil in World's Worst Equity Market*. Bloomberg (2016). http://www.bloomberg.com/news/articles/2016-08-16/traders-brace-for-more-turmoil-in-worlds-worst-equity-market downloaded 17/08/16.

[57] Hale et al., 'European Bank Shares Fall in Brutal Start to August' *FT* (2016). http://www.ft.com/cms/s/0/2412e9ee-5888-11e6-9f70-badea1b336d4.html#axzz4GClnsVJ4 downloaded 02/08/16.

[58] See 'Cyprus and the Financial Crisis – The Controversial Bailout and What it Means for the Eurozone' (Theodore and Theodore), Chapter 5 (2015).

entire Eurozone. The entire Italian banking crisis is exacerbated by the exposure of depositors to the potential loss of their savings. When linking this to the political instability arising out of the forthcoming Referendum on the Constitution, it is not difficult to appreciate that Brexit is not the only source of uncertainty facing the EU, and the future of the Eurozone.

7

The EU and China, Russia and Security Strategy

The relationship between China and the European Union (EU) – at least on the surface – can be viewed as one built on mutual commercial interests developed over a number of years. Efforts by the EU to underpin trade by linking to continued progress on China's human rights and democratic reforms (copyright laws) continue to be monitored and are ongoing between the EU and Chinese government representatives.

This is all in marked contrast to the EU's relations with Russia. Europe has been dominated by Russia's occupation of the Crimea – for which the EU maintains a policy of economic sanctions[1] – also Russia's part in fuelling the crisis in the Ukraine, and its military sabre rattling, alarming the EU 'Visegrad' and Baltic States. Both the EU and China are keen to increase trade relations and continue to grow a viable strategic partnership. Establishing what is an EU perspective on this is sometimes clouded by the vested interests of individual member states. The shaping of EU–China relations has been influenced more by the EU heavyweights France and Germany and Britain – with its less

---

[1] Impact of EU sanctions on EU agri-food sector trade volumes, August 2014–July 2015, EU agri-food exports to Russia fell by 43%, from €11 to €6.3 billion.

protectionist approach in trade matters. EU enlargement has made this process more difficult when having to accommodate the larger E28 agenda.

The China of Deng Xiaoping (China's leader between 1978 and 1989) was linked to the opening up of China to economic reforms under the slogan of 'One Country, Two Systems'. Since gaining membership of the World Trade Organisation (WTO) in 2001, the country has never looked back and today ranks as the second largest economy in the world – giving it increasing influence and power to engage in world affairs and quite rightly a commensurate political status to match. How does this accord with EU foreign policy objectives? Common ground exists in those matters where China's foreign policy addresses issues of universal concern such as the environment, the further liberalisation of trade, international security and the fight against international terrorism.

Collectively, the EU sees China's growing power in accordance with its economic strength and ensuing political position in the world order holding both membership of the UN Security Council and the G20.[2] But individually in commercial terms, some EU states (as in the case of Italy and Portugal) have been concerned that they have not been able to compete against the flood of cheap textiles, clothing and footwear from China. The economic attitudes of Germany, France and Poland are inclined towards protectionism but not all to the same degree.[3]

Beijing has also exploited divisions (as does Russia) within the EU 28 members which identify separate categories, those who are more trade protectionist (France, Germany, Poland) from others more ideologically 'free-traders' (Denmark Netherlands, Sweden and the UK). The UK has led this camp evidenced when David Cameron, the former Prime Minister in a trade mission to China in 2013, tried to initiate a multi-billion Euro trade deal independent of the EU Commission's ongoing trade negotiations.[4] For the UK, its future relations with China may well

---

[2] 1 October 2016, the RMB officially received reserve currency status with a 10.92% weighting in the IMFs Special Drawing Rights. The Chinese RMB was finally included in the IMF's basket of reserve currencies in December 2015.

[3] Poland's new (PIS) government has taken on a protectionist approach.

[4] https://www.ft.com/content/235ff2da-3bbe-11e6-9f2c-36b487ebd80a.

take the bilateral route but this will depend on the outcome of the Brexit deal – to be negotiated after Article 50 (Lisbon Treaty) has been invoked. The UK remains in the Customs union with the other EU 27 until it actually *exits* the EU. Until then, as part of the EU, it is subject to EU trade policies, represented by the EU in the WTO.

There are concerns that the EU has succumbed – in dealing with China – to an approach of 'unconditional engagement', a policy that gives China access to all the economic benefits of trading, but even with nearly four decades of its 'New Open Door' policy, China still maintains barriers to entry to investors. Overall Brussels has been receptive to inward investment as long as it doesn't encroach on Europe's most sensitive industries such as technology and where intellectual property rights can be safeguarded. Criticism has hardened in 2016 to Chinese companies (linked to the Chinese state) getting access to strategically important technological industries prompting Berlin to push for EU protective measures. This protectionist reaction was sparked by a surge of Chinese deals culminating in a €4.5 billion acquisition of the robot maker Kuka, one of Germany's most innovative companies, by the Chinese appliance maker Midea with additional cases given below.[5]

Brussels is anxious not to give cause for further popular resentment against what is seen as unfair trade practices such as steel dumping, which have come to threaten many thousands of EU jobs. With French and German elections due to take place in the spring and autumn of 2017, respectively, it has not pushed on approving China's application for market economy status (MES).

In May 2016, the European Parliament voted against giving China MES by the end 2016 as provided for when it joined the WTO in 2001. Although China still falls under 'emerging' market status, it continues to be criticised for its protectionist policies and lack of reciprocity to its internal markets.

---

[5] http://digital.olivesoftware.com/Olive/APA/FinancialTimesUK/#panel=document.

Chinese Investment in the Eurozone

Chinese investment (foreign direct investment [FDI]) in the EU is important particularly in the struggling Eurozone economies of the south. At home, its growth and direct investment abroad are reshaping the world economy. Inward investment in Greece is a good case in point. The best example is its investments in the port of Piraeus (67% share by China's state-owned shipping company Cosco) which the cash-strapped Syriza government was previously reluctant to privatise. The geopolitical implications of Chinese investment in Europe do have its concerns. From an economic viewpoint, there are misgivings that Piraeus – one of the most important sea ports in the region – would serve as a platform for China to export and distribute its goods even more widely throughout Europe and the Mediterranean region, potentially competing with Europe's industrial base.

This strategy tracks Beijing's 'One Belt, One Road' (OBOR) project – a string of ports, logistics hubs and other trading infrastructure stretching all the way from Southeast Asia to the north of England. In their recently published book 'China's Offensive in Europe', Philippe Le Corre and Alain Sepulchre[6] assess the developing relationship between China and the EU suggesting there is no 'master plan' to take over Europe. Factors, which have influenced investment in Europe date back to the opportunities, post the 2008 financial crisis and the Euro-debt crisis, when China purchased bonds of Eurozone countries and started to invest in infrastructure.[7]

Chinese foreign investment is expected to grow throughout Europe in the years to come. The financial crisis spotlighted in Greece and the fall in the value of the Euro have helped China. Some of its leading corporations have created new partnerships within the EU, working to expand the country's power through finance and infrastructure.

---

[6] *China's Offensive in Europe* studies the trends, sectors and target countries of Chinese investments in Europe. Philippe Le Corre, a visiting fellow at the Brookings Institution, and Alain Sepulchre, a senior adviser with BCG in Hong Kong.

[7] http://euasiaegf.net/chinas-offensive-in-europe-is-there-a-master-plan-in-beijing/.

Serving as an example, Piraeus (already mainland Europe's mass migration entry point) can be identified as a crucial hub of China's objective for its new Silk Road, 'OBOR' connecting Europe to China via sea and land. This has raised issues of national security in Europe. It concerns the USA,[8] as some of the Chinese investments in Greece as elsewhere are perceived as part of a geopolitical plan rather than economic gain.[9] Views vary on this matter. Peter Mandelson, the former EU Trade Commissioner and Business Secretary in Gordon Brown's Labour administration, suggested, 'It would be commercially, globally suicidal for China if they were to invest on the one hand and then try to mess around with other countries' security the next' adding 'Nobody would trust Chinese investment again, nobody would want to do business with China again'.[10] On a separate note, China sees the USA as its ultimate competitor *not* Europe where it views its links in economic terms.

Other EU countries have become beneficiaries of Chinese FDI including the UK, which negotiated with the French company EDF Energy and Chinese state-backed company China General Nuclear Power (CGN) to regenerate the UK nuclear power industry. Delays by the government of Teresa May in July 2016 in giving the go-ahead to a deal with CGN and EDF – to construct the Hinckley nuclear power plant (in Somerset) – were viewed in business and political circles as a mistake although the contract was approved soon after.

Peter Mandelson who had formerly led EU trade delegations to Beijing during his term of office in Brussels believed that 'the UK has no choice but to preserve the China relationship as after Brexit the UK will be dependent on China's goodwill'.

'Out of the EU, we are probably more dependent on China's goodwill because we need to replace trade lost in Europe', Mandelson stated in a BBC Radio interview. 'We'll want to deepen our economic ties with China post-

---

[8] China–US rivalry in the South China seas.

[9] For Greece, a member of NATO, an investment of such strategic importance does raise issues of dependency national security and sovereignty but one that the Greek government can balance off against the economic benefits it brings to its crisis ridden economy.

[10] http://www.politico.eu/article/peter-mandelson-uk-has-no-choice-but-to-preserve-china-relationship/.

Brexit. It'll be a major foreign economic-policy priority for the country. I don't think that making any move in the meantime that makes that more difficult, and difficult enough it is going to be, is in Britain's interest'.[11]

Chinese direct investment in the Eurozone was up 37% in 2015, rising to $17.1 billion from $12.5 billion. Apart from Greece discussed above, Italy, one of the Eurozone's weaker economies, received the most investment of any EU nation from Chinese companies. That was largely down to a $7.9 billion deal between Pirelli and ChemChina. France holds second place with $3.6 billion of investment in the tourism industry and infrastructure sectors.[12]

Resistance to New FDI Deals

The UK government's delay in approving the Hinckley Nuclear power project is symptomatic of a growing resistance in Brussels, the USA and Australia, to the growing size and volume of Chinese acquisitions. Since the middle of 2015, nearly 40 billion dollars' worth of mergers and acquisitions have been put on hold because of competition and issues of national security. These investments don't include the proposed takeovers of Syngenta, the Swiss Agribusiness (44 billion dollars), and Aixtron, the German semiconductor company (670 million Euros), which are still being scrutinised by the regulators.[13] These concerns apart, genuine reciprocity (by the Chinese) for foreign investment will help to quell criticism. The OECD has China placed next to bottom in 'restrictiveness' towards FDI in a list of 59 countries ranked.[14]

China is now part of the global community and together with other major economic powers is prey to international market instability, exchange rates volatility and ongoing banking crises. The EU recognises the importance of China's increasing economic dominance which is now

---

[11] http://www.bloomberg.com/news/articles/2016-08-10/mandelson-urges-u-k-nuclear-deal-with-prized-partner-china.

[12] https://www.ft.com/content/c1155e72-e5e0-11e5-a09b-1f8b0d268c39.

[13] https://www.ft.com/topics/themes/Mergers_&_Acquisitions.

[14] http://www.oecd.org/corporate/mne/statistics.htm.

being utilised to gain access to European markets by way of inward investment.

The quid pro quo for the EU is not only economic but also continuing to insist that China engages in the introduction of political and social reforms. It is important for the EU to press on helping China establish an open democracy and civil society based on the rule of law. There will be set backs such as the latest crackdown on human rights lawyers, which sends out a signal that anyone using the legal system to right judicial wrongs or defend human rights will themselves be punished, prominent lawyers and activists have been imprisoned for 'subversion'.[15] There will be no improvement until the justice system is divorced from the communist party, separate advocacy rights for lawyers and establishing the independence of the judiciary.[16]

The EU's China Policy can be summarised as follows:

- To engage China further, both bilaterally and on the world stage, through an upgraded political dialogue.
- To support China's transition to an open society based upon the rule of law and respect for human rights.
- To encourage the integration of China in the world economy through bringing it fully into the world trading system, and supporting the process of economic and social reform that is continuing in China.
- To raise the EU's profile in China.[17]

China and the EU without Britain

The EU is China's largest trading partner but is concerned about the level of influence it can sustain if the UK leaves the EU. A Brexit could affect China's strategy in dealing with the EU, which has started to lean towards protectionist policies (see above). Without the support of

---

[15] https://www.ft.com/content/22b8a356-6470-11e6-8310-ecf0bddad227.
[16] Ibid.
[17] http://eeas.europa.eu/delegations/china/eu_china/political_relations/index_en.htm.

Britain, which has been a staunch advocate of an investment pact between the EU and China, it would have to make extra efforts to boost ties with EU countries. This is a view held by He Weiwen, co-director of the China–US–EU Study Centre China Association of International Trade, which is part of the Ministry of Commerce.

'The European Union [without the presence of Britain] is likely to adopt a more protectionist approach when dealing with China. [The cooperation between China and the EU] may become more difficult', he said. 'For Chinese companies which have set up headquarters or branches in the UK, they may not be able to enjoy tariff-free access to the wider European market after Britain leaves the EU'.[18]

Between 2000 and 2015, Britain was the top European destination for Chinese outbound direct investment, with cumulative investments of US$16.6 billion, according to the US-based Brookings Institution. It is also the second largest trading partner with China inside the EU.

CK Hutchison chairman Li Ka-shing, Hong Kong's richest man and leading investor in the UK, stated in an interview with Bloomberg two days before the June Referendum[19] that if Britain left the EU, it would be 'detrimental to the UK, and it will have a negative impact to the whole of Europe'. As a result, Li Ka-shing said he would scale back his investment in the UK which, according to Dealogic,[20] amounts to around US$50 billion in Britain since 1995.[21] 'China will probably not give up entirely on the UK, but it will treat it as what it will be: a medium-sized economy with a strong financial focus and not much of an industry left', said Philippe Le Corre, a researcher with the Brookings Institution and co-author of *China's Offensive in Europe*, a book published last month. This view is gaining ground. There is no doubt that London's financial centre would be important for Chinese investors

---

[18] http://www.scmp.com/news/china/diplomacy-defence/article/1978486/how-will-china-be-affected-if-britain-leaves-european.

[19] http://www.bloomberg.com/news/articles/2016-06-20/billionaire-li-ka-shing-warns-against-brexit-as-referendum-looms.

[20] Dealogic is a financial markets platform giving its clients integrated content, analytics and technology to finance firms.

[21] http://www.scmp.com/news/china/diplomacy-defence/article/1978486/how-will-china-be-affected-if-britain-leaves-european.

who would still use it as a renminbi (RMB) trading hub – but with uncertainty posed by Brexit negotiations, there is every chance that Frankfurt, Paris and Luxembourg could take business away from London.

China's Reserve Currency Status

China's RMB formally became a reserve currency on 1 October 2016 which follows years of lobbying by the Chinese authorities and coincides with the 67th anniversary of the start of communist rule. This means, the RMB is to be incorporated in the International Monetary Fund's (IMF) special drawing rights (SDR) – a reserve asset whose value was previously determined by a basket of just the dollar, Euro, yen and £ Sterling. This in practice means it falls behind the dollar (66%) and the Euro (20%) as the world's third reserve currency – dislodging £ sterling from that position. It should remove domestic opposition to currency reforms and pave the way for further restructuring of its economy from export – led to domestic growth. Reserve currency status for the RMBs (10.92% weighting) adds to its growing influence in trade with the EU and the rest of the world.

Christine Lagarde, IMF managing director, said that the inclusion of the RMB in the SDR basket was a recognition of the progress China had made in reforming its monetary, foreign exchange and financial systems as well as advances liberalising its financial markets.

'The extension of the SDR basket is a historical milestone for the SDR, for the fund but more importantly for China and the international monetary system', she said. 'It is an important step in the integration of the Chinese economy into the global financial and monetary system'.[22]

The EU's problems with mass migration, a faltering Eurozone and the instability caused by Brexit will require China to modify its own strategic outlook on Europe. In contrast, the EU looks to China to partner in building a safer and securer global economic environment – *a level playing field* between the two trading blocs working together to further

---

[22] https://www.ft.com/content/2baa6fec-86d2-11e6-bcfc-debbef66f80e.

their mutual interests, for innovation cooperation, including reciprocal admission to respective research and innovation programmes.

In summary, EU–China cooperation is developing on a wide front. The EU–China Strategic Agenda 2020 provides a common framework for this EU–China cooperation, highlighting new fields of collaboration increasing their roles and responsibilities as global players. Furthermore, foreign and security policy has become a major aspect of EU–China relations. The EU and China have played a constructive role in fighting piracy off the coast of Somalia (in the Horn of Africa) and overall in the fight against international terrorism. Conditions for successful cooperation activities of mutual benefit exist for both sides.

Trade Imbalances

A surge in imports led the EU's trade in goods deficit with China to a record €180 billion in 2015–2016, according to Eurostat data. Finland and Germany were the only two countries recording a surplus in trade in goods in 2015, while the Netherlands and the UK had the biggest deficits.[23]

The UK, according to this data, spent over €30 billion more on Chinese goods than it received through exports: though its €2.4 billion surplus in trade in services was the third highest in the EU (behind Germany and Ireland). Total service exports across the continent increased 24% to €36 billion, leading to a surplus of €10.3 billion. A surge in imports led the EU's trade in goods deficit with China to a record €180 billion last year, according to Eurostat data. Total service exports across the continent increased 24% to €36 billion, leading to a surplus of €10.3 billion. The union's surplus in services hit a new record but remained a fraction of total trade.[24]

---

[23] http://ec.europa.eu/eurostat/documents/2995521/7553974/6-12072016-BP-EN.pdf/67bbb626-d55f-4032-8c24-48e4c9f78c3a.
[24] Ibid.

The EU–Russia and Its Security Strategy

How safe is Europe? What governs the formulation and implementation of a pan-EU strategy to deal with the various concerns of member states? These questions are dominated not only by the migration crisis, terrorism but also by political instability caused by Russia – already in possession of the Crimea – flexing its military muscle in Ukraine and the Baltics. But the problem doesn't end there. To Anna Fotyga, a former Polish Foreign Minister and current MEP and Chair of the European Parliament Subcommittee on Security and Defence, it is the additional threat from the Middle East which causes the greatest concern; a view echoed by Csaba Hende, Hungary's defence minister who argues that 'currently in the view of Hungary, the international community's main enemy in the middle East is the radical jihadist group of ISIS....'[25]

The members of the Visegrad (V4) group have a uniform consensus to develop a defence and security agenda.[26] This initiative was enhanced during the Slovak presidency 2014–2015 to create a long-term vision for the security policy and defence cooperation of the V4 and intends to continue its implementation. These four EU states have one thing in common. Before 1990, they were all part of the communist bloc and bordered the frontiers of the Soviet Union.[27]

Being members of an enlarged EU cannot alone fully address security concerns. Membership of NATO provides a stronger safety net against Russian remilitarisation. The NATO – Russia Founding Act of 1997 – as with the earlier Treaty on Conventional forces in Europe aimed at limiting deployments in Europe and avoiding conflict through a shared vision of common and comprehensive security. Events in Crimea and Ukraine put paid to that.[28]

---

[25] http://www.debatingeurope.eu/2014/09/17/what-is-the-biggest-security-threat-to-europe/#.WBck9CT33Rc.

[26] www.visegradgroup.eu/other-articles.

[27] Poland Hungary, Slovakia and Czech republic.

[28] http://www.nato.int/nrc-website/media/59451/1997_nato_russia_founding_act.pdf.

Eastern Europeans, particularly the Baltics states, are increasingly nervous of Russia's intentions. This mood is vividly expressed by Witold Waszczykowski, the Polish Foreign minister, when he said that 'The political and military situation has not improved. The measures taken in Wales are not enough to provide security. The decisions in Warsaw will have to take a harder stance. This is an existential threat for the Baltic countries... the time of peace is over'.[29] The Estonians – and their southern neighbour Latvia – feel particularly exposed sharing a common border with Russia.[30] Baltic and other East European politicians voiced their concerns in discussions with the author in meetings held in Brussels at the Committee of the Regions (CoR).[31]

EU Security–NATO Relations

Events in Europe and the Middle East dictate the need for ever greater cooperation. Historically, relations between NATO and the EU were launched in 2001, building on steps taken during the 1990s to promote greater European responsibility in defence matters NATO–Western EU cooperation.[32]

With a shared membership, the NATO–EU 2002 declaration on a European Security and Defence Policy established the political principles underlying the relationship which gave the EU assured access to NATO's planning capabilities for its own military operations.[33]

In 2003, the so-called Berlin Plus arrangements set the basis for the Alliance to support EU-led operations in which NATO as a whole is not

---

[29] 2004 NATO summit. See also https://next.ft.com/content/1eadb32e-3e45-11e6-9f2c-36b487ebd80a.
[30] Lithuania's border with Russia is with the Kalingrad enclave on its western flank.
[31] Interviews held on 5 June with Eastern European politicians at the Committee of the Regions Brussels.
[32] At that time, the Western European Union (WEU) was acting for the European Union in the area of security and defence (1992 Maastricht Treaty). The WEU's crisis-management role was transferred to the European Union in 1999.
[33] Increased to 22 after the EU enlargement in 2004 and 2007 (Turkey has only a custom union agreement with EU), NATO has associated status with its' has a holding as part.

engaged.³⁴ In practice, this includes regular meetings to combat terrorism and proliferation of weapons of mass destruction.

Clearly, the NATO alliance and the EU share common interests and challenges – having, as they do, 22 states sharing membership of both institutions.³⁵ Put in place in the opening years of the Cold War, NATO provides the ultimate security umbrella for the region. Under Article 5 of the 1949 Treaty (4 April), it offers protection against military attack to any members – stating, according to the principle of collective security, that an attack against any one of the alliance is an attack against all.³⁶ This may give comfort to Baltic States nervous of Russian intentions post Crimea and Russian involvement in Eastern Ukraine, but it doesn't provide any 'trip wire' effect in deterring urban terrorism such as the Brussels and Paris bombings November 2015 and March 2016.

Visiting the European Council on Tuesday (28 June 2016), NATO Secretary General Jens Stoltenberg stressed the importance of the strategic partnership between NATO and the EU. He emphasised NATO's need of a strong EU and the European Global Strategy. The UK plays an important role in NATO and the government of Teresa May signals its desire to continue to support EU initiatives in equal measure post-Brexit.

Addressing the UK's vote on membership in the EU, the Secretary General suggested that the Brexit's result would take time to digest its ramifications. Jens Stoltenberg made reassurances that the UK's position within NATO remains unchanged. 'The UK is a strong and committed Ally, responsible for almost one quarter of defence spending among

---

³⁴ http://www.nato.int/issues/nato-eu/index.html.

³⁵ http://www.nato.int/cps/en/natohq/topics_49217.htm.

³⁶ The parties agree that an armed attack against one or more of them in Europe or North America shall be considered an attack against them all and consequently they agree that, if such an armed attack occurs, each of them, in exercise of the right of individual or collective self-defence recognised by Article 51 of the Charter of the United Nations, will assist the party or parties so attacked by taking forthwith, individually and in concert with the other parties, such action as it deems necessary, including the use of armed force, to restore and maintain the security of the North Atlantic area. http://www.nato.int/cps/en/natolive/official_texts_17120.htm.

European NATO Allies', he said.³⁷ The leave vote did however throw American foreign policy into a tail spin. How far this affects the 'special relationship' remains to be seen. A realignment of US policy may well be guided by the outcome of negotiations and to what extent relations with the EU both economically and politically pan out in the future. US foreign policy may well lean towards Germany to compensate for UK's EU exit.

Mr Stoltenberg was keen to underline that cooperation between NATO and the EU is as important as ever.³⁸ The EU's increasing role would be adding value in a number of ways and he outlined areas where cooperation could be enhanced, including maritime security and countering hybrid warfare.³⁹

What has been encouraging is the move to increase defence spending among NATO members. NATO and in particular the USA have been asking for increased expenditure for some time as fears increase over the migrant crisis and Russian belligerence. The V4 group was providing a united focus in Central Europe.⁴⁰

Fears that the UK Referendum leave vote would throw into jeopardy the EU's determination to handle security issues was unfounded as all member states, including the UK, had a common interest in pursuing effective measures. EU politician Anna Fotyga MEP, the Chairwoman of the EU Subcommittee on Security and Defence, is one who stated: 'Our peace and security, never to be taken for granted, are increasingly threatened by events on our doorstep and beyond. The Treaty on European Union provides the legal ground for effective action by Member States to tackle these threats in the EU's neighborhood....'

From the establishment of the EU Common Security and Defense Policy (CSDP) in 1999 to the 30 civilian and military missions carried out since, the EU has contributed to stability and helped maintain peace in the Balkans, the South Caucasus, Africa and the Middle East. In 2013

---

[37] www.nato.int/cps/en/natohq/news_132843.htm.

[38] http://www.nato.int/cps/en/natohq/news_132843.htm?selectedLocale=en.

[39] Hybrid warfare is a military strategy concept blending conventional, irregular and cyberwarfare.

[40] http://www.europarl.europa.eu/committees/en/sede/home.html.

EU leaders set out a roadmap for more effective capabilities and a new impetus to the CSDP, while underlining our important relationship with NATO.[41]

The whole question of European security went to the next stage at the NATO summit in Warsaw 8 and 9 July 2016. The Secretary General declared 2016 to be the first year '... with increased defense spending among European allies for the first time in many, many years'. Mr Stoltenberg added, 'We are faced with uncertainty, we are faced with more threats, more security challenges than in a generation, and we need unity, we need strength, we need stability'.[42]

NATO and the UK

Any doubts of the UK's commitment post-Brexit were dispelled by the Secretary General when visiting EU officials on the 28th at the Council of Europe he stated that 'The UK is the largest European provider of defense capabilities in Nato, [it has] the biggest defense spending, it has the biggest defense investments ... second only to the United States in the whole alliance ... a strong UK in a strong Europe is important for unity and stability'.[43] He went on to say, 'The EU was becoming increasingly important in almost all the challenges Nato had to deal with', Mr Stoltenberg added. The UK was the 'key' in developing the relationship between the two.[44]

At a NATO meeting on 20 May, foreign ministers' joined with the EU's high representative Federica Mogherini to stiffen up cooperation on a common security agenda. This was to coordinate activities against illegal trafficking, organise cyber defence measures and respond to illegal immigration in the Aegean. The EU had already delivered on economic sanctions against Russia for its annexation of Crimea, an effective set of

---

[41] http://www.europarl.europa.eu/committees/en/sede/home.html.
[42] http://uatoday.tv/politics/the-financial-times-nato-to-raise-defence-costs-as-uncertainty-rises-664462.html.
[43] http://www.nato.int/cps/en/natohq/news_132843.htm.
[44] en.censor.net.ua › News › World.

measures which had the result of imposing hardship on the Russian economy – as well as for the EU.[45] NATO being a defensive military organisation was not designed to execute measures of this kind.

Additionally, in line with the aims set out in the Lisbon treaty, Europe's first security strategy in more than a decade is to push for closer EU defence cooperation, paving the way for multinational headquarters, military procurement and deployments to help cope with 'times of existential crisis'. A draft version of the EU's 'global strategy' defence integration as 'the norm' that will boost the bloc's defence industry and better project Europe's foreign policy clouts in its neighbourhood.[46]

The paper, overseen by Federica Mogherini, the EU's foreign policy chief, was part of a multipronged political move towards the goal of a joint European military force, which was outlined in the Lisbon treaty but not implemented.[47]

The move came at a time of political uncertainty, posing both a threat and opportunity for the EU. Post-Brexit, Germany and France expressed a desire to progress an EU common defence strategy. This would call for a more 'structured cooperation', where willing EU states group military equipment, military forces personnel and decision-making power.[48]

In the past, the UK has been less keen to support security initiatives other than NATO options. The Germans and French – in particular – now wanted to send a clear message of EU solidarity. 'The Union only succeeds,' Mr Juncker added, with no apparent sense of irony, 'When everyone is pulling in the same direction'. His surprise appointment of Sir Julian King – the former ambassador to France – to become the new EU Counter Terrorism Security Commissioner indicated a desire to maintain close cooperation with the well-respected UK Security services even though the UK was leaving the EU, possibly before an EU Security

---

[45] Stats on the loss of trade.
[46] https://www.pressreader.com/usa/financial-times-usa/20160628/281651074412935.
[47] https://www.ft.com/content/ec4d06aa-3c32-11e6-8716-a4a71e8140b0.
[48] www.worldaffairsboard.com/showthread.php?t=66462.

Union was established.⁴⁹ Mr Juncker was quoted also as saying that: 'Security is one of the pressing challenges I have highlighted... In particular, three priorities were identified as needing to be addressed: tackling terrorism and preventing radicalisation, disrupting organised crime, and fighting cybercrime'.⁵⁰

Although Britain will want to show it will continue to carry its share of defence spending, there will be substantial concern in Europe that the Brexit vote may reflect an increasingly isolationist approach – coupled with a potential slowdown in the economy that may force new domestic priorities. However, Britain has expressed a commitment to lead one of the four NATO battalions that are due to be deployed as a 'tripwire'⁵¹ in the Baltic States. The Kaczynski government in Warsaw makes no attempt to hide its anti-Russian stance and leads NATO's eastern flank in its anti-Russian rhetoric reminiscent of a 'cold war' climate.

Russia's reaction by its deployment of nuclear-capable missiles, tanks and fresh troops in Kaliningrad – the Russian exclave on Poland's northern border (and Lithuania's NW border) – has increased tension in Poland and Lithuania. NATO's action in the Baltics provided a pretext for Russia to go a step further and deploy short-range nuclear weapons in Kaliningrad, moving Iskander-M missiles into the enclave on the 8 October 2016.

The Russian defence ministry spokesman, Igor Konashenkov, stated that deployment was part of routine drills. 'These missile units have been deployed more than once (in the Kalingrad region)... and will be deployed as part of military training of the Russian armed forces'.⁵²

The NATO meeting in Warsaw was clearly set in the context of not only Russian aggression in Ukraine but also terrorism in EU cities and the migration crisis at Europe's borders. In the somewhat foreboding

---

⁴⁹ http://www.independent.co.uk/news/world/europe/brexit-eu-terrorism-security-commissioner-julian-king-appointment-eu-security-union-jean-calude-a7168046.html.
⁵⁰ Ibid.
⁵¹ 'Trip wire' was part of military strategy when facing overwhelming Warsaw Pact forces before the end of the cold war in Europe.
⁵² https://www.theguardian.com/world/2016/oct/08/russia-confirms-deployment-of-nuclear-capable-missiles-to-kaliningrad?CMP=Share_iOSApp_Other.

tone of the high representative: 'We need a stronger Europe. This is what our citizens deserve, this is what the wider world expects. We live in times of existential crisis, within and beyond the EU'. 'Our union is under threat', it goes on. 'Our European project which has brought unprecedented peace, prosperity and democracy is being questioned'.

The 'urgent' need for security investment is another of these policy responses. 'Member states remain sovereign in their defence decisions', the paper states. 'Nevertheless to acquire and maintain many of these capabilities, defence co-operation must become the norm. The EU will systematically encourage defence co-operation and strive to create a solid European defence industry, which is critical for Europe's autonomy of decision and action'.[53]

This new tone of solidarity, backed up with symbolic NATO battalions and a fighter jet presence, is of particular importance to the frontline Baltic States. A number of Interviews were held to gauge views from politicians in the CoR based in Brussels in June 2016. Those representing regional and municipal constituencies in the Baltics and East European states expressed their security concerns stating the need to maintain vigilance resulting from border tensions with Russia.[54]

Nevertheless, conciliatory views are starting to be expressed not to close doors on relations with Russia. Europe must improve its relationship with Russia and should not let this be something decided by Washington, European Commission President Jean-Claude Juncker said on Thursday (8 October).[55] President of the EU Commission Jean-Claude Juncker, in a somewhat softening tone, said that tensions had to be eased, even if this was not necessarily a popular move. 'We must make efforts towards a practical relationship with Russia. It is not sexy but that must be the case, we can't go on like this', he said at an event in the southern German town of Passau.[56]

---

[53] Paper delivered by the High Representative, Federica Mogherini at NATO meeting 20 May.
[54] Interviews with the Authors 15 June 2016 during Plenary meetings held at the Committee of the Regions CoR, Brussels.
[55] www.bbc.co.uk/news/world-europe-34486157.
[56] http://uk.reuters.com/article/2015/10/08/uk-eu-juncker-russia-idUKKCN0S22MF20151008.

The political upheavals from the aftermath of Brexit will come to dominate the EU's agenda not only because of 'exit' negotiations but for the need to stabilise the European project itself. There are already political shifts in Europe that will support populist forces more in keeping with Putin's world vision. Marine Le Pen, leader of France's far-right National Front as with other right-wing leaders, is a Putin admirer having expressed her support for Russia in the Ukrainian crisis.[57] During the visit, Le Pen asserted her support for Russia in the Ukrainian crisis, blaming the EU for declaring a new 'cold war on Russia'. 'It's obvious that all changes now, be it in France or Germany or elsewhere, will be much more in favour of Russia', Mr Lukyanov said.[58]

Polish Reactions

A more contrasting approach to Russian relations was voiced at the July Warsaw NATO summit. Andrzej Duda, Poland's President (hosting the Summit), stated that the new battle group deployments in Poland, Estonia, Lithuania and Latvia were of 'breakthrough significance' and would allow NATO to negotiate with Russia from a position of strength. 'In the face of the changing situation in the security environment in our part of the world... it is necessary to strengthen the presence and potential of NATO'.[59]

Meanwhile, Antoni Macierewicz, Poland's Defence Minister, told Rzeczpospolita newspaper that Russia was 'the biggest threat' to world peace and praised Berlin for recognising the danger. Ms Merkel's speech to the German parliament also stressed the need for dialogue with Russia to secure 'permanent security in Europe'. But her strong comments on Russia's threat were in contrast with recent remarks by Frank-Walter Steinmeier, her foreign minister.[60]

---

[57] https://euobserver.com/eu-elections/123887.
[58] https://www.ft.com/content/098ba53c-41f6-11e6-9b66-0712b3873ae1.
[59] https://www.ft.com/content/b2d16102-4446-11e6-9b66-0712b3873ae1.
[60] Ibid.

The Effect of EU Sanctions

The EU joined the USA in imposing sanctions on Russia last year over its annexation of Crimea from Ukraine, which have been extended for a further six months with counter measures by Russia affecting the economies of EU member states such as Poland and Germany itself. But it is significant that despite Brexit, the UK government has signalled its intention to play a full part in Europe's security and in the fight against terrorism joining with Germany and France to renew economic sanctions against Russia.

These are proving to be costly to both sides (see Fig. 7.1). New sanctions are being urged to cover Russia's support for military and political support for the Syrian regime engaged in what is described as indiscriminating bombing of the Northern Syrian city of Aleppo (in October 2016). The Russians deny their involvement or complicity in this. Not all EU states agree with renewed sanctions.[61]

EU Policy Inconsistencies

Nord Stream 2 exemplifies certain inconsistencies in EU sanctions policy. Trade in natural gas was exempt and is linked historically – at least by Germany – 'as a means of keeping a window for political dialogue open and supporting future cooperation with the Russian government'.[62] Demand for gas has in fact declined and is not in harmony with the concept of the Energy Union – perceived as a project to promote a policy of European green energy.

Poland has orchestrated resistance to Nord Stream 2 with the support of eight other EU member states (the Czech Republic, Estonia, Croatia, Hungary, Lithuania, Latvia, Romania and Slovakia). In the words of

---

[61] https://www.theguardian.com/politics/2016/oct/20/may-european-leaders-stop-russian-atrocities-syria-brexit.

[62] http://europesworld.org/2016/07/19/explaining-germanys-contradiction-energy-union-nord-stream-2/#.WA3D5ySfzRd.

Konrad Szymanski, Poland's Minister for European Affairs, 'By supporting Nord Stream 2, the EU in effect gives succour to a regime whose aggression it seeks to punish through sanctions. This contradiction is unsustainable. This is why Poland and other central and Eastern European member states have called on the EU Commission to act as a guardian of EU treaties and to demand that Nord Stream 2, including its offshore sections, conform in full with EU law.'[63]

Cost of Sanctions

Figure 7.1 gives the Agricultural Food Exports Values to Russia from selected EU member states (in millions of Euros) as the decline between 2014 and 2015.

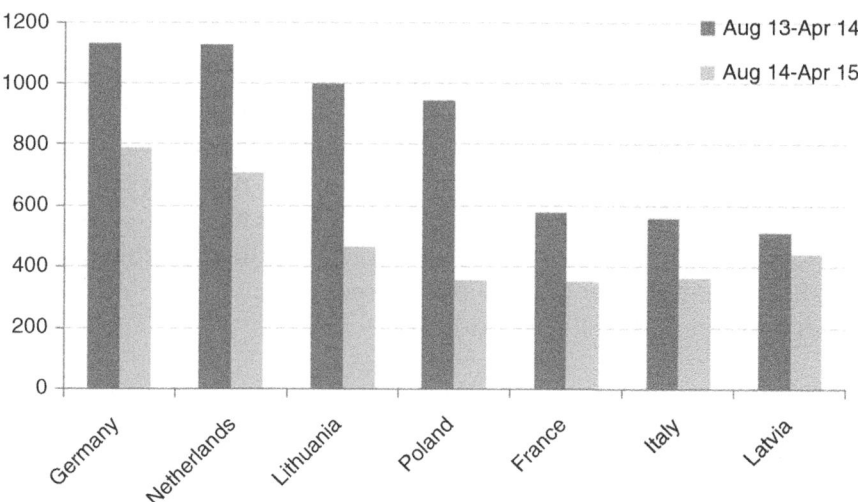

Fig. 7.1 The impact of sanctions on EU member states (in € million)

Data Source: The EU commission, DG agriculture, 2015

---

[63] https://www.ft.com/content/25a17928-96c3-11e6-a1dc-bdf38d484582.

EU agricultural food exports account for 7% of the total EU exports of goods. About 9% of these agri-food exports are bound for Russia, which is the second most important destination for EU agri-products after the USA. In 2013, overall EU agricultural exports to Russia totalled €11.3 billion. Russian retaliatory measures or 'countersanctions' covered about 43% of these. Exports worth approximately €5.1 billion (representing about 4.2% of total EU agri-food exports). However, the restrictions do not include other products such as wine, spirits, cereals, pasta, olive oil, beverages and a range of other products. Poland, the biggest producer of Apples and many other products as has Lithuania, suffered substantially from the embargo. Trade volumes, between August 2014 and July 2015, EU agri-food exports to Russia fell by 43%, from €11 to €6.3 billion.

Juncker said that these running tensions had to be eased, even if this was not necessarily a popular move. 'We must make efforts towards a practical relationship with Russia. It is not sexy but that must be the case, we can't go on like this', he said at an event in the southern German town of Passau.[64]

The political upheavals from the aftermath of Brexit may well dominate the EU's agenda. But there are already political shifts in Europe that will support populist forces more in keeping with Putin's world vision. Marine Le Pen, leader of France's far-right National Front as with other right-wing leaders, is a Putin admirer having expressed her support for Russia in the Ukrainian crisis.[65] During the visit, Le Pen asserted her support for Russia in the Ukrainian crisis, blaming the EU for declaring a new 'cold war on Russia'.

A Russian Perspective

Russia and the EU share the same continent. From high expectations in 1994, when an Agreement on Partnership and Cooperation was signed, economic and political and economic relations will continue to

---

[64] http://uk.reuters.com/article/2015/10/08/uk-eu-juncker-russia-idUKKCN0S22MF20151008.
[65] https://euobserver.com/eu-elections/123887.

deteriorate while economic sanctions and political discord over Syria and other conflicts apply. Russia was concerned that the Transatlantic Trade and Investment partnership (TTIP), between the EU and the USA (still under negotiation), will inevitably put Russian exports to the EU at further risk. The EU – Canada Comprehensive Economic and Trade Agreement (CETA) agreement with Canada was after some opposition from one of Belgium's regions (Wallonia) finally signed on 30 October 2016.

Of more concern to Russia will be if there is closer economic integration of EU with the USA via a TTIP agreement, as this may decrease Europe's reliance on Russia's energy supplies with potentially greater access through TTIP to free exports (including oil) from the US.[66]

---

[66] http://www.russia-direct.org/opinion/how-ttip-will-impact-russias-interests-europe.

8

The EU, Taxation and the Multinationals

Brussels is taking a robust approach in leading the fight against tax avoidance by the world's multinationals in an effort to stem the flow of tax revenues escaping to offshore tax havens. This crusade doesn't restrict or violate the autonomy of states supremacy over taxation policy. Neither is it a back door to tax harmonisation per se (which is not part of EU law) – at least not yet.

The EU's tax strategy is clarified in a Commission document: 'Tax policy in the European Union – Priorities for the years ahead' (COM (2001) 0260). Subject to compliance with EU rules, member states are at liberty in choosing a tax system considered most appropriate.[1] Central to EU policy is the abolition of tax hurdles which interfere with the smooth operation of the Single Market, across borders. Hence, actions to eliminate tax evasion, improve VAT compliance and tax fraud are considered within its legitimate remit – particularly where tax avoidance breaches EU state aid rules.[2] The coordination of

---

[1] www.europarl.europa.eu/atyourservice/en/displayFtu.html?ftuId=FTU_5.11.1...
[2] https://www.ft.com/content/7fd897de-6e03-11e6-a0c9-1365ce54b926.

tax policy ensures that domestic regimes support wider EU policy objectives, set out recently in the Europe 2020 strategy for smart, sustainable and inclusive growth.[3]

The Commission has been active in the removal of cross-border tax hurdles for EU citizens[4] such as those faced in cross border, e.g. discrimination, double taxation, difficulties in claiming tax refunds and difficulties in obtaining information on foreign tax rules.[5] Long-standing reform to tackle tax evasion was introduced through the Savings Taxation Directive (2003/48/EC) and directives providing for mutual assistance between tax administrations.[6] The 2003 Directive was replaced by Directive 2014/107/EU to strengthen actions to prevent tax evasion.[7]

The EU Directives back domestic authorities in collecting tax on interest from citizens holding bank accounts in other member states. The 2014 Directive widens this scope to cover not only interest income but also from dividends and other types of capital income. It created an information exchange system for tax regimes to assist in identifying individuals that receive deposit (savings) income from banks in another member state. It provides for the *automatic* exchange of information to enable states to collect data on income from savings of non-residents and automatically transfer this data to their tax regimes where the individual lives.[8]

---

[3] http://eur-lex.europa.eu/legal-content/EN/TXT/?uri=celex%3A52010DC2020.

[4] http://www.europarl.europa.eu/RegistreWeb/search/simple.htm?reference=COM_COM%282010%290769.

[5] The Commission has also become more proactive in taking legal action where member states' national tax rules or practices do not comply with the Treaty.

[6] *eur-lex.europa.eu* › EUROPA › EU law and publications › EUR-Lex.

[7] http://ec.europa.eu/taxation_customs/individuals/personal-taxation/taxation-savings-income/repeal-savings-directive-line-with-international-eu-developments_en.

[8] The EU has savings taxation agreements with third countries: Switzerland, Andorra, Monaco, Lichtenstein and San Marino. Likewise, the aim of these agreements is to assist member states in recovering tax revenue that may be due from citizens who have savings accounts in these countries.

Corporation Tax – EU Initiatives on Tax Avoidance and Its Wider Implications

'Member States cannot give tax benefits to selected companies, this is illegal under EU state aid rules'.[9] This was a statement made by Margrethe Vestager, the EU Competition Commissioner in a landmark ruling (30/8/16) demanding Apple to repay €12 billion in corporation tax (CT) arrears to the Irish government. The verdict was based on a claim that Dublin had, in effect, offered illegal state aid allowing Apple to pay annual tax rates of less than 1% on its European profits for over 10 years.

The ruling prompted criticism at the very heart of the US Administration when the US Treasury accused Brussels of 'overriding national tax authority'[10] adding that 'The Commission's actions could threaten to undermine foreign investment, the business climate in Europe, and the important spirit of economic partnership between the US and the EU.'[11]

The war of words seems set to continue with a US treasury commissioned white paper published on the 24th of August 2016 stating that

'This shift in approach appears to expand the role of the [competition directorate] beyond enforcement of competition and state aid law … into that of a supranational tax authority that reviews member state' decisions on corporate tax.[12]

The US Treasury department has also said the 'commission's pursuit of retroactive recoveries is not only in tension with the G20's efforts to emphasize tax certainty, but also sets an undesirable precedent that could lead to other tax authorities … [seeking] large and punitive retroactive recoveries from both US and EU companies.'[13]

---

[9] europa.eu/rapid/press-release_IP-16-2923_en.htm.
[10] https://www.ft.com/content/e8c333ec-7698-11e6-bf48-b372cdb1043a.
[11] https://uk-mg42.mail.yahoo.com/neo/launch?.partner=bt-1&.rand=48bq6pn01m4ic#mail.
[12] https://www.ft.com/content/1081af60-69f3-11e6-a0b1-d87a9fea034f.
[13] http://www.eurofinance.com/news/2016/08/30/eu-tax-bomb-ignited-apple-ruling-what-treasury-needs-to-know.

The fear here was that other countries would follow suit. It was justified when on the 16th September the Japan authorities' claimed that Apple owed it 118 million dollars retrospectively in taxes after a ruling the company was liable for withholding taxes on royalties paid from its local Japanese iTunes unit. The Japanese tax authority argued that the iTunes unit which sends part of its profit made from Japanese clients to its Apple base in Ireland had failed to pay a withholding tax on these earnings.[14]

Margrethe Vestager, the EU's competition commissioner, continued to assert that Apple should have realised it had a tax deal that was 'too good to be true' and has dismissed claims that she acted retrospectively to change Irish law. 'The state aid rules apply since 1958,' she said. 'It has never been a secret that tax exemptions could be state aid, and that, if so, they'd have to be paid back. The only secrets were the tax rulings themselves.'[15] In the meantime, Apple and the Dublin government will appeal against the EU's decision with the support of the USA. The tax authorities in the USA are progressing their own claim against Apple for unpaid taxes.

In terms of US CT levels, the high level of CT in the USA (highest in the G20) has played its part in American companies exploring ways to mitigate their CT liabilities by establishing headquarters abroad with Ireland (12%) being a favoured EU destination. The situation is unlikely to change soon, although the steps suggest that some US multinationals are addressing the matter to their own government.[16]

The American tax code, in particular, is in need of reform, a point accepted by both sides in Congress. It is one of only six members of the OECD group of rich countries that taxes overseas income earned by domestic businesses, which has led to situation today where billions of dollars are placed abroad in 'tax havens' by the likes of Apple, Amazon,

---

[14] http://www.independent.co.uk/news/business/news/apple-tax-japan-penalty-iphone-maker-forced-to-pay-fine-a7310846.html.
[15] http://www.irishtimes.com/business/economy/corporate-america-rallying-to-apple-s-side-in-its-eu-tax-battle-1.2794003.
[16] www.sbs.ox.ac.uk.Docs.Policy_Papers.

Google, Facebook and numerous other US companies denying the Internal Revenue Service (IRS) revenues which in turn would bolster the economy for urgently needed investment in infrastructure projects.[17]

Unpopular with Who?

The EU's actions may be unpopular with multinationals – now threatening to move business elsewhere. But EU citizens are less than sympathetic being aware of their own governments' problems – to increase tax revenues for urgent public spending needs. The populist agenda sweeping Europe has identified a linkage between the multinationals and their hold on the global economy which benefits the big players and is increasingly perceived by the electoral to be rigged in their favour.

Citizens have become aware and critical of large corporations stockpiling profits, with impunity, in tax havens – through complex tax avoidance measures – to mitigate tax liabilities. Although not a main issue in the Brexit decision, leave voters in the UK felt a sense of alienation from globalisation symbolised in their view by banks and multinationals whose interests are propped up by Brussels and neo-liberal regimes.

This is an urgent concern shared with other international authorities, i.e. to curb the ability of the multinationals on CT avoidance. The latest attack from Brussels focuses on new targets such as Amazon, Google, Facebook. Amazon, in particular, is being investigated for what is being suggested that it is full tax liabilities in Luxembourg.[18]

Others such as McDonalds and Starbucks, the coffee franchise chain, are being probed for benefiting from illegal state aid. In the case of McDonalds, Luxembourg, the home state of Jean-Claude Junker, Head of the EU Commission, stood accused of permitting the US fast food

---

[17] https://www.americanprogressaction.org/issues/economy/reports/2011/11/17/10718/could-tax-reform-boost-business-investment-and-job-creation/.
[18] The French tax authorities are claiming €1.6 billion in *back taxes* from Google with Michel Sapin the French Finance Minister ruling out any settlement and said the amount Google would have to pay would be 'way bigger' than the UK deal.

chain of paying no tax on its European royalties in Luxembourg (or in the USA).

The matter was again expressed by Margrethe Vestager Competition Commissioner in a statement when she said that Luxembourg had acted against the spirit of a US–Luxembourg double taxation treaty. 'A tax ruling that agrees to McDonald's paying no tax on their European royalties either in Luxembourg or in the USA has to be looked at very carefully under EU state aid rules,' she said. 'The purpose of double taxation treaties between countries is to avoid double taxation – not to justify double non-taxation.'[19] The ruling against McDonalds follows that made in October 2015 against both Luxembourg and the Netherlands when the Commission instructed both states to recover tens of millions of Euros in unpaid taxes from Fiat, the Italian car manufacturer, and Starbucks both accused – as with many other companies – of aggressive tax avoidance measures.[20]

For the present, it ferments increase uncertainty for these companies' tax liabilities in their European trading relations – and for their future investment plans – unable to gauge future tax commitments. For member states such as Ireland, this could put at risk its long-held economic model based primarily on foreign direct investment (FDI) if as a result of the Apple ruling further investigations being conducted result in the EU issuing similar verdicts. Multinationals with their 'port' base in Ireland currently enjoy corporate tax levied at 12.5%.

Luxembourg as a Tax Haven

Luxembourg is not on the EU's published (June 2015) blacklist of the world's 30 leading tax havens. But this does not stop it earning a well-deserved reputation for 'tax haven' status in facilitating beneficial (tax) arrangements for multinationals, many of whom set up bases and European Headquarters there.

---

[19] https://www.ft.com/content/2708caa2-99ce-11e5-9228-87e603d47bdc.
[20] https://www.ft.com/content/2708caa2-99ce-11e5-9228-87e603d47bdc.

Smallest of the member states,[21] it has developed a sophisticated array of tax loopholes for companies such as Vodafone and GSK in the UK and Amazon in the USA to mitigate their tax liabilities when it receives revenues directly and or when they are diverted to foreign branches of Luxembourg companies in place such as Ireland and Switzerland. As with Ireland, the EU Commission checks whether these deals are anticompetitive and in breach of state-aid rules.[22] The OECD BEPS Project discussed below aims to establish a single set of consensus-based international tax rules to bring states into line. The importance of this has been expressed by the President of the European Commission, Jean-Claude Juncker, who was the prime minister of Luxembourg between 1995 and 2013.

In a speech in Brussels in July, EU Commission President Juncker promised to 'try to put some morality, some ethics, into the European tax landscape,' stating Luxembourg was not a tax haven. Previously, at the G20 Summit in 15 November 2014 (In Brisbane), he commented – without addressing any role as Prime Minister in Luxembourg: 'What we are intending now is not a full-fledged tax harmonization on each and every detail, but eliminating from our national tax legislations the open gates for tax evasion... I'm in favour of tax competition but I'm also in favour of a fair tax competition in Europe.'[23]

It is not intended here to dwell on each case as investigations are ongoing with some cases several years to run. They involve multinationals which have engineered selective tax deals with individual member states. This is becoming a global issue for sovereign states worldwide and not just in the EU. The OECD is therefore separately working on a strategy to provide guidance to over 100 countries and tax jurisdictions. This will inform on tax avoidance strategies that exploit gaps and

---

[21] 2586 square kilometre (same as a medium-sized county in Britain).
[22] 'This is the real harm that tax havens like Luxembourg cause. They turn "tax competition" into a global race to the bottom, depleting the contributions of major corporations and leaving citizens to pick up the tab.'
[23] https://www.icij.org/project/luxembourg-leaks/pressure-juncker-g20-summit-over-lux-leaks-revelations.

disparities in tax rules to artificially move profits to low or no-tax locations.[24]

Whatever solutions are finally decided, legal arguments will still rage over the methodology for profits' calculation. For example, in the EU Commission's case against McDonald's, it focused on the payment of royalties from franchisees operating in Europe to a company called McDonald's Europe Franchising in Luxembourg. The Luxembourg authorities asserted that 'Luxembourg considers that no special tax treatment nor selective advantage have been granted to McDonald's. Luxembourg will fully co-operate with the commission in the investigation.'[25]

The payment of royalties to low tax jurisdictions – attributable to branding and intellectual know-how – is a theme of other investigations by Brussels, as many (multinational) companies claim that intellectual property was created outside the EU and should therefore be deducted from taxes due on European profits.

The Transfer Pricing System

Companies have been able to mitigate their corporate tax liabilities through the 'transfer price system', a scheme by which multinational corporations can claim that they 'buy' and 'sell' partially completed goods from one country to another. The way it works is that a multinational company producing a product in one country for sale in another transfers it to an associate entity in the second country which in turn conducts the sale with the client. The selling price where the transfer *arises* splits the profits. The 'split' can be directed so that the greater profit arises in the jurisdiction with the lowest tax rate. Where

---

[24] https://www.google.co.uk/search?q=The+OECD+is+separately+working+on+a+strategy+to+provide+guidance+to+over+100+countries+and+tax+jurisdictions+This+will+inform+on+tax+avoidance+strategies+that+exploit+gaps+and+disparities+in+tax+rules+to+artificially+move+profits+to+low+or+no-tax+locations.&ie=utf-8&oe=utf-8&client=firefox-b&gfe_rd=cr&ei=IVUTWP77L9DO8ge_vKT4CQ.

[25] https://www.ft.com/content/2708caa2-99ce-11e5-9228-87e603d47bdc.

also companies are purporting they buy and sell partially completed goods from one country to another, the issue is on how to determine market value.

Brussels has been trying to form a common approach in dealing with this and to introduce common tax rules. Pierre Moscovici, the EU Commissioner for Tax Affairs, has set out to establish a Common Consolidated Corporate Tax Base or CCCTB as part of a harmonisation strategy but this is opposed by the UK (and others) advocating tax competition. In the UK, George Osborne, the former UK Chancellor, announced in his last budget (before his departure following the UK Referendum) a clear indication to lower UK corporate tax from 20% to 17% or less by 2020 challenging Dublin's hegemony on this.

The ultimate aim in the formation of the CCCTB is to reach agreement with member states on the central principle of where company profits *arise*. The initiative is not new but a relaunch. What will be the benefits?

It is a fair and competitive corporate tax framework for the EU. Cross-border companies will only have to conform to one, single EU system for calculating their taxable income, rather than many different national rules.[26] The case made by Apple, the world's largest corporation (by market capitalisation), was that the greater part of its profits originates from its Irish Dublin subsidiary where CT is 12.5%. They argued that although commercial activity was initiated or conducted in London or Paris, actual 'value added' takes place in Dublin. The same line was taken by Google, the search engine company, in its ongoing case with the EU. Some definitive ruling will eventually take form on where the *transaction* took place to establish where the taxation should take effect.

The OECD/G20 BEPS Project would create a single set of consensus-based international tax rules to protect tax bases so increased certainty and transparency tax authorities and taxpayers alike.[27] An OECD formula may hopefully gain support with an agreement on how to divide a

---

[26] https://ec.europa.eu/taxation_customs/business/company-tax/common-consolidated-corporate-tax-base-ccctb_en.

[27] www.oecd.org/tax/beps/.

company's tax base so it better reflects where the economic activity actually takes place and where the profit should be taxed.[28]

The EU's relationship with those multinationals conducting business in the Single Market is of vital concern to all parties: to establish a level-playing field so that member states do not obtain unfair tax advantages. The temptation for regimes to lower CT rates is inevitable, especially in smaller (economically) member states like Ireland competing for foreign investment from multinationals – counting reduction in taxes is offset by increased employment which FDI can generate.[29]

In the UK, the new UK Chancellor Philip Hammond intends to take a pragmatic approach but has revised his predecessor's (George Osborne) intention to lower the UK's corporate tax rate down to 17% by 2020 – the UK – already the lowest rate in the G20 – seeing no great value in risking falls in corporate tax receipts. This seems prudent with the level of uncertainty for the post-Brexit economy.[30]

The European Commission's decision against Apple's tax deal in Ireland highlights the growing antipathy to tax avoidance. EU leaders such as Sweden's prime minister has made clear, aggressive tax cuts by the UK would needlessly antagonise even those governments inclined to approach Brexit negotiations in a constructive spirit.[31] This does not escape the fact that post-Brexit, the UK could become a fiscal heaven for multinationals as EU rules would only be binding if it remained part of the Single Market.

---

[28] Another 36 jurisdictions have signed up to new rules on corporate tax avoidance as a global crackdown on aggressive tax planning picks up speed.

In a boost for a project that aims to capture as much as $240 billion, a year in lost tax revenue around the world, business centres such as Singapore and Hong Kong have agreed to back the base erosion and profit shifting (BEPS) initiative, originally developed by the G20 group of big economies and the OECD. A large group of developing countries, including Nigeria, Egypt and Kenya, also signed up to BEPS at a 2-day meeting that kicked off in Kyoto, Japan yesterday. With the number of signatories now at 82, the gathering is aimed at expanding the framework across the globe.

[29] Ireland's low corporate taxation status may be under threat from post Brexit, UK, seeking inward investment.

[30] http://www.telegraph.co.uk/business/2016/09/11/chancellor-dismantles-key-osborne-pledge-to-cut-corporation-tax/.

[31] https://www.bloomberg.com/news/articles/2016-08-30/apple-s-14-5-billion-eu-bill-may-pressure-u-s-on-tax-overhaul.

Reflections on Corporate Tax Strategies

Some member states – and those of the Eurozone South in particular – will have difficulties in attracting inward investment (FDI), especially from multinationals except where flexible labour laws and low costs prevail. But for most, it is often a matter of striking a balance – not at the expense of eroding the national tax base.[32] Clearly, FDI supports increased employment in distressed areas, helping to alleviate inter alia high levels of youth unemployment – in countries such as Greece and Spain.

Lower rates are an important driver for company relocation even, e.g. enterprises in recession struck Greece. Greek companies have engaged in relocation to Bulgaria; its northern neighbour sporting the EU's lowest CT rates. Bulgaria's CT of 10% marks Greece at 26% (in 2014) very uncompetitive, especially when lower wage costs are taken into account.[33] In 2015, this rate was increased to 29%, encouraging continued relocation to Bulgaria, although Greek Small and Medium Enterprises (SMEs) had been investing there since the 1990s when the Greek economy was expanding.[34]

In a recent statement (25 May 2016), the Greek Ambassador to Bulgaria, Dimosthenis Stoidis, said that '...about 2,000 Greek companies relocated to the neighboring country in 2015 explaining that the outflow of Greek businesses does not cause great concern to the Greek economy, because this was not accompanied by great transfer of major capital.'[35]

Greece, with its high levels of CT, is just one case in point. But it illustrates the view cogently expressed by Joseph Stiglitz when he said '...Competition among jurisdictions can be healthy, but they can also be a race to the bottom. Capital goes to the jurisdiction that taxes it at the lowest rate, not where its marginal productivity is the highest.

---

[32] http://ec.europa.eu/news/2016/07/20160705_2_en.htm.
[33] Bulgaria has a fixed exchange rate with the Euro of 1.94 Lev to the Euro.
[34] <www.tradingeconomics.com> greece (Corporate Tax Rate in Greece is reported by GSIS, Greece).
[35] http://greece.greekreporter.com/2016/05/25/almost-2000-greek-companies-relocated-to-bulgaria-in-2015/.

To compete, other jurisdictions must lower the taxes they impose on capital. Thus, the scope for redistributive taxation is reduced.'[36]

Given that the outcome of the OECD BEPS, G20 initiative, was designed to meet states' concerns about the potential for multinationals to locate profits where they gain more favourable tax treatment, it is hoped that its recommendations will eventually be implemented.[37]

---

[36] Professor Joseph Stiglitz, 'The Euro and Its Threat to the Future of Europe' (2016).

[37] http://www.ey.com/Publication/vwLUAssets/EY-the-g20-oecd-beps-project-is-nearing-comple tion/$FILE/EY-the-g20-oecd-beps-project-is-nearing-completion.pdf.

9

Conclusion

Europe's political, economic and social troubles are legion. They now encompass everything from mass migration, deflation and Eurozone debt to Brexit and the surge of anti-establishment populists. Beset as the region is by crisis, the disconnect between the political class/elite and popular consensus is a fissure at the heart of the entire European project – a godsend both to right-wing attacks on the creditability of the European Union (EU) itself and leftist critiques of the political and financial infrastructure of European society.

The EU was founded on the principle of a super-national entity: one with a common destiny, but which recognised the varying traditions and identities of its members, and that would set the path for a closer economic union and partnership between nations – at first. Making the peoples of the continent more prosperous and avoiding the tragedy of another wholesale European conflict were foremost in the minds of the founding fathers of the European Economic Community (EEC).

In the light of the social and economic convulsions of the last decade, this project for a unified Europe has come increasingly under attack. When looking through the prism of an increasingly hostile and Eurosceptic electorate, it is hard to see much remaining support for

9 Conclusion

further integration, especially on the political front. This is despite the paradox that an 'ever closer union' seems the only way of keeping the Eurozone economically intact.

Our analysis, however, bears out that the picture may be more complex than many suppose. For one thing, membership of the European club is still valued by most of the electorates of Europe. Countries fought hard to meet *Acqui Communitaire* (Accession requirements) criteria to join. A real sense of pride emanated from European electorates on their accession (Witnessing the actual celebrations in Nicosia when, e.g. Cyprus joined 1 May 2004 was a moving event). Even Freedom of Movement could be accommodated until evidence of strains and electoral opposition in host states compounded by mass external migration tipping the balance against it.

Membership has brought enormous benefits in developing the EU's regions through the European Regional Development Funds. Both this and European Social funding provided support on a scale that national governments (even in France, Italy or the UK) simply could not afford (or follow different partisan priorities). Brussels has initiated proposals to enhance workers' rights and progressive consumer protection legislation. EU infrastructure projects have built bridges, roads and helped industries grow with billions of Euros allocated for research, development and innovation schemes.

Critics of the EU have singled out a lack of democracy in the workings of the EU – a term referred to as the 'democratic deficit'.[1] But does it make laws? No, although it does make proposals (many of which come via national political leaders) which are then deliberated, amended and passed or rejected by the elected representatives of national governments and directly elected members of the European Parliament.[2] It has political leadership functions as well as administrative. As the civil service of a super-national organisation, it represents the EU in trade agreements like the EU – Canada Comprehensive Economic and Trade Agreement (CETA) signed with Canada and TTIP negotiations with the USA (discussed in Chapter 8).

---

[1] A term used by the British political scientist Professor David Marquand in 1979.

[2] MEPs are elected by proportional representation.

Lack of transparency is as much the fault of EU member states not informing its electorate sufficiently – through the educational system – on what it stands for and merits of membership. Ignorance of the EU is almost universal. A filtered version of the relevance of its various institutions, and on how control is devolved, is also widespread.

With the creation of the Eurozone from 1999, and the enlargement of the EU since 2004, it has become even more important to explain its importance to EU citizens. Rejecting the status quo, however, falls short of member states questioning their support for the Union per se.

Are EU 'bureaucrats' in the EU Commission all powerful and unaccountable – as is perceived to be the case?[3] Do they represent the forces of the neo-liberal ruling elite present in so many governments of the member states? Many would say *yes*, a perception held even by 'Remainers' in the UK. Populist forces go further by demanding reforms; the return of power to domestic national governments and the reversal of shared sovereignty surrendered for membership of the club.

But perceptions of remoteness, bureaucracy and perceived lack of transparency are often criticisms that can be levelled at any 'Whitehall' (London) style state institution – whether, e.g. Fonction Publique Francaise (in Paris) and the Deutscher Beamtenbund (in Berlin).

Demands for Change

EU Commission President Junker's State of the Union address (14 September 2016) and statements by EU President of the Council, Donald Tusk, at the Bratislava Summit (16 September 2016) could be taken as first steps at a charm offensive. Success will only depend on follow through with realistic proposals on key issues – jobs, migration control, security, including reforms necessary to improve the functioning of the union and membership of the single currency. Years of

---

[3] Legislative proposals do emanate from the Commission but they have to be considered by the Council of Ministers in conjunction with MEPs who are elected directly by EU citizens.

austerity, ill-conceived and unpopular refugee policies make this axiomatic for Europe's future political stability.

The UK Brexit vote and the rise of populism are stirring this demand for action. The response to the UK's departure has caused dismay in Eastern Europe, with many fearing it may lead to a kind of federalism and deeper integration favoured by the Brussels elite – which would now be fiercely resisted.[4]

The Visegrad group provide the Vanguard, arguing for repatriation of power back to national parliaments following leave voters in Britain. A move in this direction would answer critics of the 'democratic deficit' and make the EU more democratically accountable. In this light, elections (General and presidential) in 2017 – in the Netherlands, France, Germany – offer a wakeup call for Europe's mainstream parties to act swiftly. Neutralising dissenting voices with policies that meet aspirations by correcting the status quo helps them as well as Brussels to remain in power.

As we have discussed, the debt crisis has shown that some level of fiscal integration and debt mutualisation is probably the only way for its ultimate survival. Eurozone leaders are finding it more difficult with each bailout rescue to balance their economic decisions with the political implications they create. Economists have long been familiar with a concept known as 'moral hazard' – a scenario which creates incentive for individuals to act recklessly by insulating them from the consequences of their actions. By insuring risk, governments create perverse incentives that make banks less cautious and less willing to appropriately price such risk. In the case of the Eurozone, instead of the banks making effective provisions in the event of financial trouble, the government assured cheap credit, backed as it was by both low interest rates and the supportive financial structure of the EU and then the Eurozone. But the nature of the bailouts, which shifted the burden of reckless lending away from the banks and onto the vulnerable economies of the EU, gave the

---

[4] Interviews 15 June 2016 with regional and municipal politicians representing Eastern Europe constituencies.

implications of moral hazard a whole new dimension and has burned through much of the popular faith in the common European project.

The new members of central and Eastern Europe have embraced the principle of free movement and have for the most part been the main beneficiaries of it – having migrated in large numbers to the UK, Germany and other North West richer states for higher paid jobs and better living standards. But sharing these privileges (which they pay for in their contributions to the EU budget) with the current influx of non-EU migrants from Syria, Iraq, Afghanistan and other Muslim countries is quite another matter. Germany's EU neighbours such as Poland, Hungary, the Czech Republic and Slovakia have not signed up to the Brussels relocation quota scheme. Instead, they are taking a tough line. The Bratislava summit 16 September 2016 was an opportunity for Angela Merkel to admit the need to address the growing concerns of members – particularly those of the Visegrad group who vehemently opposed her refugee policies and uncontrolled migration particularly through the refugee crisis of 2015–2016. She attempted to assuage criticism by saying: 'We have to show with our actions that we can get better', the German chancellor said. The bloc had to improve 'in the domain of security, internal and external security, the fight against terrorism, the cooperation in the field of defence', as well as defence and jobs, she added.[5] So far, this call has been largely unheeded. The migration crisis was an opportunity to band the members of the EU closer together in common policy but, as we have shown, has only managed to drive them further part.

The expansion of the EU itself in the 2000s, in the context of the weak macroeconomic picture since the Great Recession, has been riven with political consequences, and a huge spur to the opposition to open immigration policies now seen in Britain and France (and culminating in Brexit). Even if the arguments against the East European expansion rest on valid economic reasoning, the very nature of the EU rendered the expansion inevitable. Joining the EU has offered both the former

---

[5] https://www.theguardian.com/world/2016/sep/16/bratislava-summit-donald-tusk-urges-eu-leaders-not-to-waste-brexit-crisis?.

dictatorships of the Mediterranean littoral and Eastern Europe's former communist satellites admission to the democratic club of 'old' Europe and for this they and the world should be thankful. The EU has been instrumental in gaining them recognition as parliamentary democracies based on the rule of law – with the added bonus of funding their fledging economies.

How could financial assistance be refused when there was no dispute that they were significantly poorer than the southern EU countries? The authors here have argued in favour of the overall process of Eastern EU enlargement, despite the potential problems that could arise as a result.

With the benefit of hindsight, was the entire EU expansion to the East a mistake? No. If the East was to be brought in from the economic cold, living standards could be raised and their economies would come to be less reliant on Moscow. There are obvious difficulties in integrating 11 new countries, with a population exceeding 100 million, political culture, history and economic condition far different to their western neighbours. But then again, is this not what the EU is all about? And were there no cultural differences and different political histories among the old EU 15? It is true that five out of the original six EEC countries (France, West Germany, Belgium, the Luxemburg and the Netherlands) together with the UK, Ireland and Denmark that joined the EEC in 1973 share a similar political background and history based of parliamentary democracies since the end of WWII. But the enlargement of the East had echoes of the Mediterranean enlargement of the 1980s – when Greece joined in 1981, followed by Spain and Portugal in 1986 – that integrated almost 60 million more people into the EEC, many of whom had lived in the shadows of monarchy, fascism or dictatorial rule. Similar fears about mass migration or the economic 'drag' of those nations were raised at the time. But that integration was broadly successful, at least until the Euro crisis almost 30 years later.

Even if the arguments against the East European expansion rest on valid economic reasoning, the very nature of the EU rendered the expansion inevitable. Joining the EU offered these three countries not only funds from EU institutions but, above all, it helped consolidate the rule of law based on democratic processes. How could Germany reject integrating these countries to the EU, when it had to undergo its own process of integrating East Germany in the re-unified country in the early 1990s? And how could financial assistance be refused when there was no dispute that they were significantly poorer than the southern EU countries?

All these feeds into the issue of the migration crisis, which, as we argued, have become perhaps the biggest existential threat to the political will and unity of the region going forward. Initially, the humanitarian response in Europe, particularly in Germany, to the plight of the refugees was positive. But in most countries, the mood has changed. Many in the EU are developing a growing resistance to their frontiers becoming 'open borders' to a continued flood of migrants encouraged by the success of those already being accommodated. In communities, especially but not exclusively in rural communities', there is a genuine fear that Europe will be overwhelmed in terms of the changing demographics and the increased burdens on their benefit and welfare systems. This is most felt in those jurisdictions already facing austerity measures affecting their own poor – in particular, the bailout countries of the Mediterranean littoral. But these concerns are also being seen even in more prosperous northern Europe in village communities with ageing and declining populations facing the prospect of absorbing quotas that would change the world as they have always known.

As the crisis in Europe has evolved, so have the challenges brought to it by dissident members. The Greek authorities in the spring of 2015 asserted that they aim at striking a deal with the Troika that would ensure access to the Troika bailout funds without meeting the obligations that come along with it, as these were worsening the country's devastating debt–recession spiral. As outrageous as this idea may have sound to North Eurozone authorities, in particular Germany, Finland, Netherlands and Austria, there was a 'Keynesian' economic rationale to it. As the financial assistance to Greece comes with draconian fiscal consolidation, it reduces the country's growth potential rendering further cuts unavoidable. If the help comes without the scale of the cuts North Eurozone countries insisted on, it would boost growth, and as such it could generate the resources necessary for debt repayment. However, this logic is anathema to neo-liberal economists and politicians – in particular, in Germany's Christian Democratic Union (CDU) party, as they are perceived to encourage fiscal laxity. As a result, Greece was not allowed to participate on the ECB's Quantitative Easing (QE) programme. This led to a deterioration in the country's public finances and an increase in the deficit, raising the need for a third bailout. As such, Greece capitulated without a battle.

In the UK, the battlefield is not the Eurozone but EU membership. Greece, the most troubled member of the EU until Brexit, is one of the smaller Eurozone countries – whereas the UK is the second largest EU economy after Germany (arguably third to France since the summer of 2016, with the rapid devaluation of the pound). Given that the UK is not in the Euro, the danger is that the deterioration in the country's public finances in the short run would not manifest itself in the balance of payments, but in a gradual but steady erosion in the value of the pound and the overall macroeconomic environment. This could lead to higher inflation and lower tax revenue, rendering the need for a trade deal essential. Again, the battle could be lost before it is fought. The pound's depreciation of over 15% to date renders a currency crisis within reach and not just a hypothetical scenario, as was the case in the aftermath of June the 23rd. The ensuing inflationary pressures make the work of the Bank of England very difficult indeed. A 4% inflation in the summer of 2017 (while exit negotiations are under way) could prompt an increase in the rate of interest. However, if growth is subdued to the overall uncertainty, stagflation (that is inflation together with low growth) could prevail for, at least, the duration of the negotiations. As a result, an increase in the rate of interest could postpone recovery, or, in the absence of an increase in the rate of interest, inflation would remain above target (2%) for longer, with the adverse effects on consumers who have been accustomed since 2008 to stagnant-to-declining wages. It is very likely now that some form of 'stagflation', the curse of the British economy in the 1970s, will return to Britain.

The ongoing crisis, of which Brexit is the latest and most novel manifestation, exposes a deep contradiction at the heart of the Europe – between the Eurozone's need for successful integration and voters' (and protestors') overwhelming rejection of it. If such populism continues to rise, it would not be a large leap from here for a member of the single currency to win a democratic mandate to quit it altogether – a Lehman-like event which would not only reignite the worst of the crisis but put the survival of the entire European project in the balance. Political upsets can be much harder to put to rights than economic ones, and it would not take much to bring another party like Syriza to power or at least hold the balance of power – as was feared in the snap presidential election in Greece in December 2014, which sent markets tumbling.[6] Nor would it take much now to elect a Brexit emboldened, largely anti-EU right-wing party such as the National Front in France – or its rising equivalents in Hungary and Poland. After Brexit, the French and German 2017 elections may well determine the future course of the EU. Reforms started now will help to price in a safe landing in April for the French and September for the German elections. The guiding principle for the Commission is for closer union to be 'off' the table.

The possibility of such populism being satiated by a return to economic growth in the EU also appears dubious. Unemployment levels in the EU remain extreme, at over 25 million people in 2015–2016 – three-quarters of whom are in the Eurozone.[7] Debt remains dangerously high and, with the region teetering on the edge of deflation, could rapidly worsen. The region may well be trapped in a 'lost decade' similar to that of Japan in the 1990s. But politically, the EU would be far less likely to survive such an experience intact than Japan: a nation-state which had centuries to form a cohesive identity.

Brexit has exerted immense political pressure in the EU and the Eurozone. It most certainly provides additional support for national-centric parties already on the rise in the EU/Eurozone. The developments discussed in this book render the agreement and implementation of new initiatives in the Eurozone (fiscal union, debt mutualisation etc.) almost impossible for the foreseeable future. It would take, at a minimum, until the spring of 2019 for the specific details of Brexit and post-Brexit arrangements to be fully demarcated. This will pave the way for a prolonged period of uncertainty. In this environment, renegotiating the EU's budget alone (as one of its main net contributors

---

[6] http://www.ft.com/cms/s/0/4db45c9c-7f95-11e4-b4f5-00144feabdc0.html#axzz3Lxt5XLDc.
[7] From the Eurostat employment figures from the European Commission, for which see http://ec.europa.eu/eurostat/statistics-explained/index.php/Main_Page.

will no longer be a member state) could prove a Herculean task, let alone undertaking new initiatives.

In essence, this reflects the unsustainable status quo in the UK–EU relations, where the EU's main financial centre is located in the UK, which has not joined the Euro. Our analysis therefore points to the partial relocation of European capital markets from London in the period leading up to the formal withdrawal of British membership. This, of course, will substantially impact on inward investment (FDI) to the UK from third parties, e.g. China, India, Brazil and Japan, in order to re-export to other EU markets. While only a limited number, set by the UK authorities, of EU workers could be employed in the UK – in contrast to the openness of the Single Market arrangements – the decline in the UK's growth potential will increase unemployment in the UK.

Although there is substantial criticism of the EU in Eastern Europe, overall sentiment is quite different, with all major polls showing a substantial majority in favour of remaining. Furthermore, it is already paving the way for the centrifugal political forces riveting through the EU, with many other countries' electorates requesting a Referendum on either EU membership or other specific issues of importance to them. Such requests may not be satisfied by the current authorities but could be potentially encouraged by more right-wing governments. As we discussed, the 2017 elections in France will be a crucial next step in this process.

Ultimately, this is an issue where democracy converges somewhat destructively with economics. The battle to save the Euro has led to the unprecedented centralisation of authority in the EU over banking, budgets and welfare. It has produced the steady accretion of powers to the ECB, the European Commission and the European Parliament. Bailout terms have been dictated from the top, and voters in stricken countries have largely lost the ability to define the policy of their own governments. This transfer of powers is the result of economic failure, not success, and enforced without the endorsement of the public. The chances of it being accepted or tolerated are slim. Resentment and hostility towards Brussels, the Eurozone and the EU itself will continue to rise. Such sentiments, sharpened, are brandished as vigorously in France now as they are in Brexit Britain, or the austerity-afflicted

'PIGS'. And in Eastern Europe, they are on the march. What final form the seismic shifts in the EU and Eurozone will take is still unclear. But without any doubt, economic stagnation will continue to be the legacy of the financial crisis, the Euro trap and the bailouts, and political fragmentation is inevitable. The only question is how much.

Timeline of the European Union

The Treaty of Rome 1957
This established the European Economic Community (EEC). The Treaty came into force in **1958**. It also established the European Atomic Energy Community (EURATOM).

1973: The Treaty of Accession, bringing the UK, Ireland and Denmark into the EEC.

1979: The establishment of the European Monetary System (EMS), including the Exchange Rate Mechanism.

1979: The European Parliament was established.

1981: Greece joined the EEC.

1986: Spain and Portugal joined the EEC.

1986: The Single European Act was signed coming into force in 1987.

1990: West and East Germany re-unified, bringing East Germany into the EEC.

1990: Stage 1 of European Monetary Union (EMU) began, with the removal of all restrictions on capital movements. (UK had removed exchange controls in October 1979).

1990: The UK joined the Exchange Rate Mechanism.

Timeline of the European Union

1993: The Treaty of Maastricht was ratified.

1994: Stage 2 of EMU began, creating the advisory European Monetary Institute, followed by the launch of the European System of Central Banks. Monetary Policy.

1995: Austria, Sweden and Finland joined the EU, under the Treaty of Corfu (signed in 1994).

1997: Stability and Growth Pact signed.

1997: The Treaty of Amsterdam was signed coming into force in 1999.

1999: Stage 3 of EMU began, with the creation of the Euro and the *locking-in* of 11 countries states exchange rates.

2001: The Treaty of Nice was signed and came into force 2003.

2002: The Euro replaced Member States' own currencies with euro notes and coins introduced.

2004: The Accession Treaty entered into force and the EU enlarged to include 10 new Member States: Cyprus, the Czech Republic, Estonia, Hungary, Latvia, Lithuania, Malta, Poland, Slovakia and Slovenia.

2007: Romania and Bulgaria join the EU, taking membership to 27 states.

2007: Treaty of Lisbon signed 13 December 2007 and came into force 1 December 2009

2008: Collapse of Lehman Brothers and the global financial crisis.

2010: European Financial Stability Facility (EFSF) replaced by the European Stability Mechanism (ESM).

2010: The first Greek bailout.

1993: The Treaty of Maastricht was ratified.

1994: Stage 2 of EMU began, creating the advisory European Monetary Institute, followed by the launch of the European System of Central Banks. Monetary Policy.

1995: Austria, Sweden and Finland joined the EU, under the Treaty of Corfu (signed in 1994).

2013: Croatia joins the EU on the 1 July as the 28th member.

2013: Ireland exits the bailout programme.

2016: Cyprus exits its bailout programme.

2016: UK Referendum 23 June resulting in a vote to leave the EU.

Bibliography

Artis, M. (2000). 'Should the UK Join EMU?' *National Institute Economic Review* 171, 70–81.

Artis, M. (2003) 'Is there a European Business Cycle?' CESifo Working paper 1053, Leibniz Institute for Economic Research, University of Munich, www.cesifo-group.de/portal/pls/portal/docs/1/1189526.PDF.

Artis, M., & Zhang, W. (1997) 'International Business Cycles and the ERM: Is there a European Business Cycle?' *Oxford Economic Papers* 51, 1–16.

Atkins, R. (2016) 'Austria's Main Parties Face Electoral Rout' 23/04, *FT*.

Atkins, R. (2016) 'British Debate Resonates with Eurosceptic Swiss' *FT*.

Bank of England. (2014) 'Stress Testing the UK Banking System: Key Elements of the 2014 Stress Test' April 2014.

Bank of England. (2015) 'Official Bank Rate History' http://www.bankofengland.co.uk/boeapps/iadb/Repo.asp.

Bank of England. (2016) 'Inflation Report' http://www.bankofengland.co.uk/publications/Documents/inflationreport/2016/aug.pdf downloaded 11/11/2016.

Bannerman, C. D. MEP. (2016) *Time To Jump: A Positive Vision of a Britain Out of the EU and in EEA Life*. Epsom, United Kingdom: Bretwalda Books.

Baskaran, T., & Hessami, Z. (2013) 'Monetary Integration, Soft Budget Constraints, and the EMU Sovereign Debt Crises' University of Konstanz, Department of Economics Working Paper Series 03.

Bibliography

BBC. (2016a) 'UK's Economic Growth for 2014 Revised up' http://www.bbc.com/news/business-32126975.

BBC. (2016b) 'China's Economic Slowdown Deepens' http://www.bbc.com/news/business/economy, downloaded 14/08/16.

BBC. (2016c) 'Italian Economy Stagnates as German Growth Slows' http://www.bbc.com/news/business-37056800 downloaded 12/08/16.

Berstain, H. (2016) 'European Union Referendum – Potential implications for Greater Manchester of the UK leaving the EU' Report on briefing to Greater Manchester Leaders on the EU referendum and the potential implications of an 'out' vote, Greater Manchester Combined Authority.

Blanchard, O., Amighini, A., & Giavazzi, F. (2013) *Macroeconomics: A European Perspective*. London, United Kingdom: Prentice Hall.

Blanchard, O., Furceri, D., & Pescatori, A. (2014) 'A Prolonged Period of Low Real Interest Rates?' C. Teuling & R. Baldwin. eds *Secular Stagnation: Facts, Causes and Cures*. London: Centre for Economic Policy Research.

Boltho, A., & Carlin, W. (2013) 'EMU's Problems: Asymmetric Shocks or Asymmetric Behavior?' *Comparative Economic Studies*, 55 (3), 387–403.

Bongardt, A., & Torres, F. 2016 'The Political Economy of Brexit: Why Making It Easier to Leave the Club Could Improve the EU' *Inter-economics*, 51 (4), 214–219.

Brooks, R. (2016) *The Great Tax Robbery*. London, United Kingdom: One World Publications.

Cadman, E. (2016) 'Carney Issues Stark Warning with Package to Ease Brexit Downturn' *FT*, http://www.ft.com/cms/s/0/0d729692-5a1a-11e6-9f70-badea1b336d4.html#axzz4GQotgOYv downloaded 05/08/2016.

Cadman, E. (2016) 'UK Turns in Strong pre Brexit Growth' *FT*, http://www.ft.com/cms/s/0/0de0953e-53d5-11e6-befd-2fc0c26b3c60.html#axzz4FM7PSkZh downloaded on 27/07/2016.

Campbell, P., & Tetlow, G. (2016) 'Indian Business Welcomes UK Trade Deal' *FT*, http://www.ft.com/cms/s/0/2e0eb278-4372-11e6-b22f-79eb4891c97d.html#axzz4FpTCFbuR downloaded 30/07/16.

Centre for Economic Policy Research. (2015) 'Rebooting the Eurozone: Step I – Agreeing a Crisis Narrative' *Policy Insight*, 85.

Cesaratto, S. (2013) 'The Implications of TARGET2 in the European Balance of Payments Crisis and Beyond' *European Journal of Economics and Economic Policy: Intervention* 10 (3), 359–382.

Changinikolaou, P. (2016) 'Audits for Registered only Companies in Bulgaria and Cyprus by the Ministry of Economics Kathimerini' http://www.kathimerini.gr/870963/article/oikonomia/epixeirhseis/elegxoi-gia-eikonikes-epixeirhseis-se-oylgaria-kai-kypro-apo-to-ypoik downloaded 15/08/16.

Commission of the European Communities, European Commission. Annual Economic Reports and Reviews: (1995) 'Convergence Report 1994' (1995a) 'One Currency for Europe: Green Paper on the Practical Engagements for the Introduction of the Single Currency' (1995b) 'Report on Convergence in the European Union in 1995'.

Commission of the European Communities, European Commission. Annual Economic Report and Reviews (1998) 'Report on Progress Towards Convergence and the Recommendation with a View to the Transition to the Third Stage of Economic and Monetary Union, Part-1: Recommendation'.

Confederation of British Industry Report (2015) 'CBI Makes Case for being in a Reformed EU' http://news.cbi.org.uk/news/cbi-makes-case-for-being-in-a-reformed-eu/ downloaded 14/08/2016.

Congdon, T. (1998) *A Maoist Leap Forward? The Single Currency and European Political Union*. London, United Kingdom: The Selsdon Group: 1–8.

Copeland, L. S. (2008) *Exchange Rates and International Finance*. London, United Kingdom: Prentice Hall.

Crafts, N., & Toniolo, G. eds. (1996) 'Economic Growth in Europe Since 1945' Centre for Economic Policy Research, Cambridge University Press.

Crawford, M. (1996) *One Money for Europe? The Economics and Politics of EMU*. London: Macmillan.

Currie, D. (1997) 'The Pros and Cons of EMU' Research Report, The Economist Intelligence Unit.

Darvas, Z., & Merler, S. (2013) '−15% to +4%: Taylor-Rule Interest Rates for Euro Area Countries' http://www.bruegel.org/nc/blog/detail/article/1151-15-percent-to-plus-4-percent-taylor-rule-interest-rates-for-euro-area-countries, downloaded 25/04/2016.

De Grauwe, P. (2011) 'The Governance of a Fragile Eurozone' *Australian Economic Review*, 45 (3), 255–268.

De Grauwe, P. (2014) 'Should We Worry About Deflation?' *The Economist*, http://www.economist.com/blogs/freeexchange/2014/01/deflation-eurozone-1, downloaded 24/04/2014.

De Grauwe, P. (2016) 'European Monetary Unification: A Few Lessons for East Asia' *Scottish Journal of Political Economy* 63 (1), 7–17.

Delors Committee. (1989) *Report on Economic and Monetary Union in the European Community*. Luxemburg: Office for Publications of the European Communities.

Dinan, D. (1999) *Ever Closer Union: An Introduction to European Integration*. London, United Kingdom: Macmillan Press Ltd.

Dreyer, O., & Gerlach, S. (2016) 'Germany's Idiosyncratic Views Test Cohesion of Eurozone' 12/05, *FT*.

Duke, S. (2016) 'Europe's Attack on Google is the Latest Skirmish in a High-stakes Battle with America's Technology Titans' 24/04, *The Sunday Times*.

Editorial. (2016) 'The Guardian View on Interest Rates: Time for the Treasury to Act' *The Guardian*, https://www.theguardian.com/commentisfree/2016/aug/04/the-guardian-view-on-interest-rates-time-for-the-treasury-to-act downloaded 05/08/16.

Editorial. (2016) 'China's Biggest Economic Challenge' *Bloomberg*, https://www.bloomberg.com/view/articles/2016-08-25/china-s-biggest-economic-challenge downloaded 26/08/2016.

Editorial. (2016) 'Lights, Camera, Rate Cuts: Brexit Demands an All-action Blockbuster from the Bank' *The Guardian*, https://www.theguardian.com/business/2016/jul/31/mark-carney-bank-blockbuster-brexit-lights-camera-rate-cuts downloaded 31/07/16.

Eichengreen, B. Wyplotz (2016) 'Minimal Conditions for the Survival of the Euro' *Inter-economics*, 51(1), 24–28, 10.1007/s10272-016-0569-z.

Eijffinger, S., & De Haan, J. (2002) 'European Monetary and Fiscal Policy'.

Europa. http://eur-lex.europa.eu/summary/chapter/taxation/2101.html?root=2101 downloaded 12/08/16.

European Commission, Eurostat, Statistical Books (2011) 'External and Intra-EU Trade: A Statistical Yearbook, Data 1958–2010' http://ec.europa.eu/eurostat/documents/3217494/5729733/KS-GI-11-001-EN.PDF/9e06d19b-bdce-49e0-a766-65fbbfc78081 downloaded 14/08/2016.

European Commission, Statistics (2016) http://trade.ec.europa.eu/doclib/docs/2006/september/tradoc_113366.pdf downloaded 31/07/16.

Eurostat. (2003) *Fifty Year of Statistics on Europe*. Luxemburg: Office for Official Publications.

Evans, P. A. (2016) 'Italy much Choose between the Euro and its own Economic Survival', *The Telegraph*, http://www.telegraph.co.uk/business/2016/05/11/italy-must-chose-between-the-euro-and-its-own-economic-survival/ downloaded 03/08/2016.

Feldstein, M. (1992) 'The Case Against EMU', *The Economist*, 13/06/1992: 12–19.
Feldstein, M. (1997) 'EMU and International Conflict' *Foreign Affairs* 76, 60–74.
Fergal, O. (2016) 'U.K. Hiring Plunges as BOE Warns That Unemployment Will Rise' *Bloomberg*, http://www.bloomberg.com/news/articles/2016-08-04/u-k-hiring-plunges-as-boe-warns-that-unemployment-will-rise downloaded 05/08/16.
Flassbeck, H., & Lapavitsas, C. (2015) *Against the Troika Crisis and Austerity in the Eurozone*. London, United Kingdom: Verso.
Friedman, M. (1953) *The Case for Flexible Exchange Rates in Essays in Positive Economics*. Chicago: University of Chicago Press.
Friedman, M. (2002) 'Milton Friedman: EU to Collapse within 10 Years' *EU Observer*, 17th July 2002, http://euobserver.com/news/6944.
Gemma, T. (2016) 'UK Manufacturing Output Falls Sharply Following Brexit Vote' *FT*, http://www.ft.com/cms/s/0/b832a75c-57e0-11e6-8d05-4eaa66292c32.html#axzz4FpTCFbuR downloaded on 01/08/16.
George, S. (1996) *Policy and Politics in European Union*. Oxford, United Kingdom: Oxford University Press.
Giles, C. (2016) 'Harsh Realities of a Weakened Pound' *FT*, http://www.ft.com/cms/s/2/9c746d04-4456-11e6-9b66-0712b3873ae1.html?siteedition=intl#axzz4GQotgOYv downloaded 07/08/2016.
Giles, C., & Fray, K. (2016) 'Eight Charts Showing Sof UK Economy before Bank of England Rate Decision' *FT*, http://www.ft.com/cms/s/0/fd522642-5596-11e6-9664-e0bdc13c3bef.html#axzz4GQotgOYv downloaded on 07/08/16.
Glover, J., & Sirletti, S. (2016) 'Monte Paschi Capital Wiped Out in European Bank Stress Test' downloaded on 30/07/16.
Gros, D. (2010) 'Adjustment difficulties in the GIPSY Club' Centre for European Policy Studies Working Document, No 326. Brussels: Centre for European Policy Studies.
Gros, D. (2012) 'Macroeconomic Imbalances in the Euro Area: Symptom or Cause of the Crisis?' Centre for European Policy Studies Policy Brief, No. 226. Brussels: Centre for European Policy Studies.
Gros, D. and Mayer (2010) 'Towards a Euro(pean) Monetary Fund' CEPS Policy Brief No. 202. Brussels: Centre for European Policy Studies.
Gros, D., & Thygesen, N. (1998) *European Monetary Integration: From EMS to EMU*. Third, Edition. London: Longman.
Guest, R. (2011) 'The Global Financial Crisis and Undergraduate Macroeconomics' *The Australian Economic Review* 44 (1), 113–120.

Hale, T., Blackden, R., & Noonan, L. (2016) 'European Bank Shares Fall in Brutal Start to August' *FT*, http://www.ft.com/cms/s/0/2412e9ee-5888-11e6-9f70-badea1b336d4.html#axzz4GClnsVJ4 downloaded 02/08/16.

Hamroush, S., Taylor, C., Luff, M., Wales, P., & Hardie, M. (2015) 'An Analysis of Foreign Direct Investment, the Key Driver of the Recent Deterioration in the UK's Current Account' Office for National Statistics.

Hardie, M., Jowett, A., Marshall, T., & Wales, P. (2013) 'Explanation Beyond Exchange Rates: Trends in UK Trade Since 2007' *ONS*.

Hinarejos, A. (2013) 'Fiscal Federalism in the European Union: Evolution and Future Choices for EMU' *Common Market Law Review* 50, 1621–1642.

Horta, S. (2016) 'Europe's Tumbling Lenders Lose Almost Half Their Value in a Year' *Bloomberg*, http://www.bloomberg.com/news/articles/2016-08-02/europe-s-tumbling-lenders-lose-almost-half-their-value-in-a-year downloaded 02/08/16.

HM Treasury (2003) *The Five Tests Framework: EMU Study*. London, United Kingdom: Stationery Office.

HM Treasury (2003) *The United States as a Monetary Union; EMU Study*. London, United Kingdom: Stationery Office.

Hughes, A., & Saleheen, J. (2012) 'UK Labour Productivity since the Onset of the Crisis – An International and Historical Perspective' International Economic Analysis Division, Bank of England Quarterly Bulletin, Q2, http://www.bloomberg.com/news/articles/2016-07-29/monte-paschi-capital-wiped-out-in-european-bank-stress-test.

IMF. (2016) 'Currency Composition of Official Foreign Exchange Reserves' COFER, http://data.imf.org/?sk=E6A5F467-C14B-4AA8-9F6D-5A09EC4E62A4&sId=1408202905739 downloaded on 31/07/16.

Institute of Fiscal Studies (2016) 'Brexit and the UK's Public Finances' IFS Report 116, https://www.ifs.org.uk/uploads/publications/comms/r116.pdf downloaded 11/11/2016.

Issing, O. (2000) 'Europe: Political Union though Common Money?' *Economic Affairs*, Occasional Paper 98.

Jones, S. (2016) 'Investors Yank More From U.K. Funds on Brexit Than During Crisis' http://www.bloomberg.com/news/articles/2016-08-02/investors-yank-more-from-u-k-funds-on-brexit-than-during-crisis downloaded 02/08/2016.

Karagounis, K., Syrrakos, D., & Simister, J. (2015) 'The Stability and Growth Pact, Rand Balanced Budget Fiscal Stimulus: Evidence from Germany and Italy' *Inter-economics* 50 (1), 32–39.

Keynes, J. M. (1931) *The Economic Consequences of Mr. Churchill*. Essays in Persuasion, Macmillan, London.

King, S. (2016) 'The UK's Balance of Payments Conundrum' *FT*, http://blogs.ft.com/the-exchange/2016/07/20/the-uks-balance-of-payments-conundrum/?siteedition=intl#recommended-h-504491470546859260 downloaded on 07/08/16.

Klein, C. M. (2016) 'What if Greece got Massive Debt Relief but no One Admitted it?' (Part-2), *FT*.

Krugman, P. (2012) 'Crash of the Bumblebee' *The New York Times*, July 29, 2012: A19.

Lapavitsas et al. (2012) *Crisis in the Eurozone*. London, United Kingdom: Verso.

Lavoie, M. (2015a) 'The Eurozone: Similarities to and Differences from Keynes's Plan' *International Journal of Political Economy* 44 (1), 3–17.

Lavoie, M. (2015b) 'The Eurozone Crisis: A Balance-of-Payments Problem or a Crisis Due to a Flawed Monetary Design?' *International Journal of Political Economy* 44 (2), 157–160.

Lucarelli, B. (2012) 'German Neomercantilism and the European Sovereign Debt Crisis' *Journal of Post-Keynesian Economics* 34 (2), 205–224.

Marsh, D. (2011) *The Euro: The Battle for the New Global Currency*. Yale, USA: Yale University Press.

Marsh, D. (2013) *Europe's Deadlock: How the Euro Crisis Could be Solved – And Why It Won't Happen*. Yale, USA: Yale University Press.

Mazower, M. (2016) 'Berlin should be Careful what it Wishes for' *FT*.

McKinsey Report (2015) *The Future of the Euro, An Economic Perspective on the Eurozone Crisis*. Germany: McKinsey & Company, Inc.

Meakin, L. (2016) 'Carney to Ignore Inflation Overshoot as Economists See Rate Cut' *Bloomberg*, http://www.bloomberg.com/news/articles/2016-08-12/carney-to-ignore-inflation-overshoot-as-economists-see-rate-cut downloaded on 13/08/16.

Micossi, S. (2015) 'The Monetary Policy of the European Central Bank (2002–2015)', CEPS Special Report, 109.

Minsky, H. (1992) 'The Financial Instability Hypothesis' Levy Economics Institute, Working Paper No. 74.

Moore, E. (2016) 'UK Debt: Gilt Complexities' Record-low Rates Have Made Government Bonds Hugely Attractive to Many Investors—But for How Long?' *Financial Times*, http://www.ft.com/cms/s/0/4d593a76-734d-11e6-bf48-b372cdb1043a.html#axzz4KJu29utQ downloaded 15/09/2016.

Nechio, F. (2011) Monetary Policy When One Size Does Not Fit All. Federal Reserve Bank of San Francisco, http://www.frbsf.org/economic-research/publications/economic-letter/2011/june/monetary-policy-europe/ downloaded 25/04/2015.

Noel, M. Sir (2016) 'EU Goes Far Beyond the Normal Nature of a Treaty Organisation' 06/05, *FT*.

Nolan, D. (2003) 'Ireland's Rapid Economic Convergence: The Role of Government Policy and European Union Structural Funds for Ireland's Boom Economy During the 1990s' http://www.celtic-irish.co.uk/news/wp-content/uploads/irish-economy.pdf.

Noonan, L., & Atkins, R. (2016) 'Swiss Banks Seek New Role as Secrecy is Eroded' 22/04, *FT*.

Nugent, N. (1999) *The Government and Politics of the European Union*. 4th Edition. Basingstoke: Palgrave.

Nussbaum, A., & Ryan, C. (2016) 'Brexit Bites Back as Peugeot Joins Dell in Lifting Prices' *Bloomberg*, http://www.bloomberg.com/news/articles/2016-08-10/brexit-bites-back-as-peugeot-joins-dell-in-lifting-prices downloaded 10/08/16.

O'Brien, F. (2016) 'U.K. Inflation Rate Surges to Highest in Almost Two Years' http://www.bloomberg.com/news/articles/2016-10-18/u-k-inflation-rate-surges-to-highest-in-almost-two-years downloaded 18/10/2016.

O' Connor, S. (2016a) 'Workers Suffer Real-term Pay Cuts on a par with Greece, Says TUC' http://www.ft.com/cms/s/0/aabea3cc-533b-11e6-9664-e0bdc13c3bef.html#axzz4GQotgOYv downloaded 06/08/16.

O'Connor, S. (2016b) 'UK Jobless Fell Below 5% Before Brexit Vote' *FT*, http://www.ft.com/cms/s/0/e943404c-4e5b-11e6-88c5-db83e98a590a.html#axzz4GQotgOYv downloaded 06/08/16.

O'Rourke, K., & Taylor, M. A. (2013) 'Cross of Euros' *Journal of Economic Perspectives* 27 (3), 167–192.

Office for National Statistics (2016) '*UK Consumer Price Inflation: Sept 2016*' https://www.ons.gov.uk/economy/inflationandpriceindices/bulletins/consumerpriceinflation/sept2016 downloaded 11/11/16.

Organisation for Economic Cooperation and Development (OECD), 'Global Growth Warning: Weak Trade Financial Distortions', Interim Economic Outlook, September 2016.

Padoa-Scioppa, T. (2000) *The Road to Monetary Union in Europe*. Oxford, United Kingdom: Clarendon Press.

Pancevki, B., & Campbell, M. (2016) 'Migrants March into Storm of Hatred' 25/10, *The Sunday Times*.
Peet, J., & Guardia, A. L. (2014) 'Unhappy Union – How the Euro crisi-and Europe-Can Be Fixed (Economist Newspaper)'.
Pento, G. M. (2013) *The Coming Bond Market Collapse, How to Survive the Demise of the US Debt Market*. Hoboken, New Jersey, USA: Wiley.
Pfanner, E. (2016) 'Brexit Knocks British Airways and Foxtons as Confidence Dives' http://www.bloomberg.com/news/articles/2016-07-29/brexit-knocks-british-airways-and-foxtons-as-confidence-dives downloaded 30/07/2016.
Pringle, R. (2014) *Escaping the Grip of Global Finance*. London, United Kingdom: Palgrave Macmillan.
Research on Money and Finance (2011) 'Breaking Up?: A Route out of the Eurozone Crisis', Lapavitsas, C., Kaltenbrunner, A., Lindo, D., Meadway, J., Michell, J., Panceira, J. P., Pires, E., Powell, J., Stenfors, A., Teles, N., Vatikiotis, V., RMF Occasional Report 3, November, 2011.
Rhodes, W. (2016) 'Eurozone Must Complete Banking Union to Avert Crisis' http://www.ft.com/cms/s/0/5eb51992-5413-11e6-9664-e0bdc13c3bef.html#axzz4FpTCFbuR downloaded on 30/07/16.
Robinson, E. (2016) 'Italian Banks Reel But Monti Has No Regrets for Avoiding Bailout' http://www.bloomberg.com/news/articles/2016-08-09/italian-banks-reel-but-monti-has-no-regrets-for-avoiding-bailout downloaded 10/08/16.
Ryan, C. (2016) 'Brexit Sees UK Consumer Confidence Fall Most since 1990' http://www.bloomberg.com/news/articles/2016-07-28/brexit-sends-u-k-consumer-confidence-falling-most-since-1990 downloaded 30/07/2017.
Sandbu, M. (2016) 'Italy Fears Brexit Would Damage Whole of Europe' 19/04, *FT*.
Sanderson, R. (2016) 'Monte dei Paschi Board Backs Private Sector Rescue Plan' *FT*, http://www.ft.com/cms/s/0/1d47b04a-5586-11e6-9664-e0bdc13c3bef.html#axzz4FpTCFbuR downloaded on 30/07/16.
Sibert, A. (2010) 'The EFSM and the EFSF: Now and What Follows' Directorate General for Internal Policies, Policy Department A: Economic and Scientific Policies, Economic and Monetary Affairs.
Simitis, C. (2014) *The European Debt Crisis*. Manchester, United Kingdom: Manchester University Press.
Sladkowska, B. and Strzelecki (2016) 'More Poles Are Now Moving to Germany Than the U.K' *Bloomberg*, http://www.bloomberg.com/news/articles/2016-09-18/more-poles-are-now-moving-to-germany-than-the-u-k downloaded on 18/09/2016.

Smith, D. 'In or Out, We Need a Euro With Stronger Foundations' 24/04, *The Sunday Times*.
Strobel, F. (2005) 'Leaving EMU: A Real Options Perspective' *Applied Economics* 37, 1449–1453.
Stiglitz, J. (2015) 'GDP per Capita in the UK is Lower than it was before the Crisis. That is not a Success' *Guardian*, http://www.theguardian.com/books/2015/may/24/joseph-stiglitz-interview-uk-economy-lost-decade-zero-growth 25/05/16.
Stiglitz, J. (2016) *The Euro and its Threat to the Future of Europe*. London, United Kingdom: Allen Lane Publishers.
Stockhammer, E. (2013) 'The Euro Crisis and Contradictions of Neoliberalism in Europe' *Economic Discussion Papers*, 2, Kingston University.
Strobel, F. (2005) 'Leaving EMU: a real options perspective' *Applied Economics* 37, 1449–1453.
Syrrakos, D. (2010) 'A Reassessment of the Werner Plan and the Delors Report: Why did they Experience a Different Fate?' *Comparative Economic Studies* 52 (4): 575–588. doi:10.1057/ces.2010.12.
Syrrakos, D. (2016) 'The Franco-German Alliance and its Role in the Process of European Monetary Integration, 1944–2010 – Lessons for Today' *Olsztyn Economic Journal* 11 (2), 119–135.
Syrrakos, D. (2017) 'On the Greek National Debt' *Economic Review* 34 (5), 8–11.
Szasz, A. (1999) *The Road to European Monetary Union*. London, United Kingdom: Macmillan Press Ltd.
Tetlow, G. (2016) 'Weaker UK Services Sector Adds to Pressure for BoE Action' *FT*, http://www.ft.com/cms/s/0/3015854e-5964-11e6-8d05-4eaa66292c32.html#axzz4GHJ6egKO downloaded 03/08/2016.
Theodore, J., & Theodore, J. (2015) *Cyprus and the Financial Crisis – The Controversial Bailout and the Implications for the Eurozone*. London, United Kingdom: Palgrave.
Treaty on European Union (1992) *Maastricht Treaty*. Luxemburg, Office for Publications of the European Communities.
Ungerer, H. (1997) *A Concise History of European Monetary Integration: From EPU to EMU*. Connecticut, USA: Quorum Books.
Varoufakis, Y. (2016) *And the Weak Suffer What They Must*. London, United Kingdom: Vintage Publishing.
Ward, J., & Tartar, A. (2016) 'A Guide to the Winners and Losers as Brexit Sends Pound Plunging: Exporters and Tourists Rejoice while British

Consumers Feel the Pinch' http://www.bloomberg.com/news/articles/2016-10-19/a-guide-to-the-winners-and-losers-of-the-post-brexit-pound-plunge downloaded 19/10/2016.

Wickers, M. (2008) *Macroeconomic Theory: A Dynamic General Equilibrium Approach*. Princeton, USA: Princeton University Press.

Wolf, M. (2016a) 'After Brexit, Britain would Sacrifice Access for Independence' *FT*.

Wolf, M. (2016b) 'Do not let Migration Determine Britain's Place in Europe' *Financial Times*, April 28, 2016.

Wolf, M. (2016c) 'Germany is the Euro-zone's Biggest Problem' *FT*.

Wolf, M. (2016d) 'Myths and Fantasies in the case for Brexit' *FT*.

Wolf, M. (2016e) 'Sovereignty and Power Are Not the Same' 04/05, *FT*.

Wyplosz, C. (2016) 'The Eurozone Crisis: Too Few Lessons Learned' http://voxeu.org/article/eurozone-crisis-too-few-lessons-learned downloaded 26/09/2016.

Zega, R. (2016) 'Traders Brace for More Turmoil in World's Worst Equity Market' *Bloomberg*, http://www.bloomberg.com/news/articles/2016-08-16/traders-brace-for-more-turmoil-in-world-s-worst-equity-market downloaded 17/08/16.

Index

A
Afghanistan, 77, 207
Africa, 30, 48, 74, 77, 79, 81, 84, 176, 180
  north, 74, 77
Agreement on Partnership and Cooperation (1994), 188
Air Berlin, 130
Air France-KLM, 130
Air Operator certificate (AOC), 130
Aixtron, 172
Albania, 122
Aleppo bombings, 186
Alitalia, 130
Al Jazeera, 76
Al-Khalifa, Nasser, 75
Allen & Overy, 125
Amazon, 194–195, 197
Amiri, Amin, 101
Ankara, 121
AOC, 129–130

Apple, 162, 188, 193–194, 196, 199, 200
  Ireland, 196, 200
  Japanese iTunes unit, 194
Arab Spring, 75
Argentina, 24–25, 31
  fixed exchange rate - USA (1991), 24
  inflation (1989), 31
Argentinean peso, 24, 32
ARM Holdings, 146
  See also Sale to Japanese firm (Softbank)
Artis and Zhang, 49
Asia, 57, 79, 130, 170
  Southeast, 170
Australia, 92, 118, 172
Austria, 8, 16, 17, 37, 58, 65, 66, 70, 78, 80, 209
  agreement with Brussels, 80
  Freedom Party, 80

Austria (*cont.*)
  Green party, 80
  Presidential Elections (22nd of May 2016), 80
  refugee policy, 80
  taxation, 37
Autumn Statement, 99
Avramopoulos, Dimitris, 59

B

Bagdad, 85
Bahrain, 75
Bailout, 4, 21, 36–45, 56, 58, 107, 162, 163, 165, 206, 209, 210, 212
  programme, 45
  state rescue, 55
  terms, 212
Balkans, 86, 180
  land routes, 76
Baltic States, 61, 64, 179, 183, 184
  frontline, 184
Bank of England (BE), 31, 34, 134, 135, 139, 141, 142, 145, 147, 148, 149, 150, 151, 153, 155, 157, 158, 161, 210
Baumbast case, 63
BDI, 123
Beijing, 168, 171
  One Belt, One Road (OBOR) project, 170
Belfast, 118
Belgium, 8, 12–18, 51, 60, 64, 66, 68, 189, 208
  Wallonia, 189
Benelux, 60
Berlin, 169, 185
  Wirtschaftstag (21st of June), 107

Bernanke, Ben, 50, 134
Bienkowska, Elzbieta, 108
Bijstand, 70
Black Wednesday, 34
Bloomberg, 148, 174
Bosnia, 120
Brandon-Bravo, Joel, 131
Bratislava, 106
  crisis summit (16th of September, 2016,)112
Brazil, 212
Brexit, 1, 4, 30, 47, 55, 56, 58, 66, 72, 87–131, 133–166, 169, 171, 173, 175, 179, 181, 182, 183, 185, 186, 188, 195, 200, 206, 210, 211, 212
  advocates, 149
  campaign, 106
  deal, 92, 169
  effects on FDI, 152
  hard Brexit, 116–117, 124, 129
  June statement, 91
  negotiations, 89, 94, 99, 104, 127, 129, 175, 200
  outcome of the EU Referendum (23 June 2016), 30
  post Brexit, 56, 90, 97, 101–103, 147, 149, 159, 171, 179, 181–182, 200, 211
  soft Brexit, 66, 114–118
  vote, 30, 72, 91, 97, 103, 115, 129, 145, 183, 206
BRICS (Brazil, Russia, India, China and South Africa), 48, 154, 160
Britain, 66, 69–71, 73, 87–88, 91–94, 96–100, 103–106, 110–112, 114–115, 117,

119–121, 123–126,
128–129, 135, 154, 167,
172–175, 183, 206–207,
210, 212
Blair government, 65, 74, 83
Business Bank, 102
Conservative Government, 73
economy, 122, 124, 210
government, 93, 98, 109
referendum, 105, 136, 174
royal Crown, 95
trade deficit, 144
visa regulations changes, 131
British Airways, 127–128, 150
Broadbent, Ben, 148
Brookings Institution, 174
Brown, Gordon
Labour administration, 171
Brussels, 40, 56, 71–73, 76–78, 80,
83, 85, 87, 89, 97, 107–108,
111–112, 114–115, 120,
124, 126, 169, 171–172,
178–179, 184, 191, 193,
195, 197–199, 204,
206–207, 212
agreement, 85
annual contribution, 115
bombings (March 2016), 83, 179
change(s) in policy, 115
deal, 124
dispute, 108
elites, 87, 206
neo-liberal elite, 89, 112
relocation quota scheme, 207
Brzeski, Carsten, 80
Bulc, Violeta, 130
Bulgaria, 3, 15, 29, 58, 62, 65, 67,
74, 201

C

Calais Impasse, 82
Calmy-Rey, Micheline, 72
Cameron, David, 73, 87–89, 91,
94, 168
Tories, 91
Canada, 116, 118, 121,
189, 204
Capital markets union (CMU),
107, 112
Carney, Mark, 157
Carolan, Damian, 125
Catalonia, 105
CCCTB (Common Consolidated
Corporate Tax Base), 199
CDS (Credit Default Swaps), 42
CETA (Comprehensive Economic
and Trade Agreement)
agreement (30th October
2016), 189, 204
CGN (China General Nuclear Power
Group), 171
Chad, 77
ChemChina, 172
China, 46, 48, 50, 92, 130, 154,
167–189, 212
Companies, 169–172
(*see also* Kuka, Midea)
economic dominance, 172
economy, 154
foreign policy, 168
growth rate decline, 48
investors, 174
Silk Road, 171
trade mission (2013), 168
Churchill, Winston, 23
CK Hutchison, 174
Cold War, 179, 183, 185, 188

Cologne
  riots (New Year's Eve, 2015), 81
Commerzbank, 162
Committee of the Regions (CoR) (Brussels, June 2016), 111, 178
Common Agricultural Policy (CAP), 32, 115
Common Market, 135, 144, 148, 158
  UK's position, 144
Commonwealth nations, 92, 118
Comprehensive Economic and Trade Agreement (CETA), 121
Congdon (1998), 28
Conservative Conference (2016), 92, 114
Corporation tax (CT), 193–195
Crimea, 167, 177, 179, 181, 186
Crisis, 35, 36, 86, 203
  Cyprus financial crisis, 165
  debt, 4, 35, 50, 58, 59, 206
  economic crisis in Greece, 40
  EMU debt, 52
  euro, 208
  Euro debt, 8, 20, 56, 170
  Europe, 2, 170, 209
  Eurozone, 1, 3, 22, 57, 88
  Eurozone debt, 3, 8, 9, 11, 22, 39, 74, 161
  Eurozone's economic, 76
  financial, 50, 134, 170, 213
  global financial (2008–9), 1
  Italian banking, 55, 165, 166
  migration, 1, 57, 77, 83, 89, 207
  migration crisis at Europe's borders, 183
  refugee, 76, 107, 112
  (see also New York Post)
  sovereign debt, 9, 45
  Ukraine, 167, 186, 188
  US subprime mortgage (2007–8), 8
Croatia, 29, 58, 83, 186
CSDP (Common Security and Defense Policy), 180
CT (Corporation Tax), 200–201
Currency devaluation, 9, 23
Customs Union, 32, 136, 169
Cyprus, 3, 8–9, 12, 21, 55, 56, 61, 65, 165, 204
  bailout, 45
  Turkish invasion (1974), 65
Czech Republic, 29, 61, 64, 77, 84, 186, 207
  government, 85

D

Davis, David, 90
Davutoglu, Ahmet, 85
Dealogic, 174
Debt, 42, 56, 142
  bank, 49
  debt forgiveness, 56
  debt-to-GDP 13, 16
  Greek, 24, 36–37, 41, 42, 44, 165
  Irish debt (2011–14), 38
  Italian, 39, 164–165
  management programmes (2010–12), 43
  Portuguese, 39
  ratios, 47
  Southern Euro, 56
  Spanish, 39
  UK, 134
Delors Report (1989), 34

Denmark, 7, 17, 18, 87, 111, 168, 208
Deutche and Societe General, 125
Deutsche Bank, 161–162
Deutscher Bearntenbund
 style state institution., 205
 (*see also* Berlin)
Deutschmark, 20, 32
Dijsselbloem, Jeroen, 107
Draconian monetarist principles, 36
Draghi, Mario, 54
Dubai, 130
Dublin, 125, 193–194, 199
 Regulations, 76
Duda, Andrzej, 78, 185

E

East Asian investors, 117
EasyJet, 127–130
ECB (European Central Bank), 3, 4, 12, 15, 16, 19, 20, 26, 29–30, 36, 37, 39, 40, 53, 54, 162, 165, 212
 financial lines, 39
 QE program, 160, 210
 rate of interest, 165
Economic depression, 44
Ecorys, 100
EDF Energy, 171
EEC, 60, 63, 68, 203, 208
 Member State, 63
 state, 63
EIB (European Investment Bank), 102–104
EIF (European Investment Fund), 102–104
Emirates airlines, 130
Energy Union, 186

England, 77
 English Conservative, 91
 Micro businesses in the north, 101
 North, 91, 170
 North East, 83
Erasmus (Exchange programme), 98–100
Erdogan, Recep Tayyip, 85–86
Estonia, 61, 64, 178, 185
Etihad airlines, 130
EU-China, 176
 Strategic Agenda 2020, 176
EU-IMF audit, 40
Euro, 7, 10, 13, 26, 29, 32, 38, 39, 41, 43, 44, 46, 48, 49, 54, 90, 133, 136, 140–141, 145, 156, 159, 175, 212, 213
 fall in the value, 170
 value, 54
Europe, 1, 23–24, 47–48, 54, 57–62, 64, 67–79, 83–86, 87, 88, 92, 94, 100, 105, 106, 107, 110, 111, 117, 120, 121, 123, 128, 149, 170–171, 174, 175, 177, 180, 183–185, 188, 203, 206, 210
 borders, 60
 business climate, 193
 Central Europe, 79, 180
 Central Europe accession states, 79, 81, 180
 Chinese foreign investment, 170
 Council of Europe, 181
 Eastern Europe, 64, 77, 178, 206, 207, 208, 212–213
 Eastern Europe accession states, 58, 62
 economic integration, 61

Europe (*cont.*)
  electorates, 204
  flow of migrants, 85–86
  Germany's economic
    dominance, 48
  implications of Chinese
    investment, 170
  industrial base, 170
  national security, 170
  Parliament, 105, 108
  political shifts, 188
  populist agenda, 195
  profits, 198
  reliance on Russia, 189
  single market, 119–126
  trading relations, 196
  Treaty on Conventional
    forces, 177
European
  Art 8 of the European court of
    Human Rights, 63
  aviation industry, 130
  business cycle, 49
  capital markets, 212
  defence industry, 184
  East accession states, 64
  Eastern labour, 62
  East expansion, 207–208
  Economic Area, 116
  economy, 48
  financial infrastructure of
    society, 203
  financial system, 5
  foreign investment for
    airlines, 130
  funding, 98
  Global Strategy, 182
  green energy, 186
  immigrants, 71
  integration, 64
  intra-European borders, 64
  liberal consensus, 111
  markets, 173, 175
  Members of the Parliament, 109
  modern electoral history, 80
  Parliament, 109,
    204, 212
  principal banks, 41
  project, 76, 110, 184, 185, 203,
    207, 211
  recession, 18
  royalties, 194
  security, 182
  value of the banking sector, 162
  Western and South trading block, 3
European Central Bank (ECB), 19,
    53, 135, 143, 162
European Commission (EC),
    11–13, 22, 44, 63, 66, 70,
    96, 99, 130, 184,
    192, 197,
    200, 212
  case against McDonald's, 198
  Commission's decision against
    Apple, 200
  (*see also* Apple's tax deal in
    Ireland)
  lawyers, 96
  leaked report, 44
European Common Aviation
    Area, 128
European Community (EC), 60
European Constitution
  rejection by the French and the
    Dutch electorates (2005 and
    2006), 29

Index   235

European Court of Justice
    (ECJ), 62–63, 68, 92, 110,
    119, 122
European Economic Area
    (EEA), 115, 119–120, 126
European Economic Community
    (EEC), 1, 32, 60–61, 68,
    203, 208
European Financial Stability Facility
    (EFSF), 37
European fiscal union, 29
European Free Trade Association
    (EFTA), 32, 103
European Investment Bank, 103, 104
European monetary integration
    (1970s and 1980s), 17
European Monetary System
    (EMS), 33, 49
European Monetary Union
    (EMU), 2, 13, 16, 19, 27,
    33, 35, 47, 52
    institutions, 50
    member countries and model, 50
    products, 47
    South countries, 47
    trade, 46
European Parliament
    vote against China MES, 169
European Regional Development
    Funds (ERDF), 101, 204
European Social Funding
    (ESF), 101, 204
European System of Central Banks
    (ESCB), 41
European Union (EU), 1, 7, 17, 20,
    24, 27, 30, 41, 46, 57, 61,
    66, 80, 87, 104, 109, 134,
    140, 155, 159, 166, 167,
    170, 174, 180, 185, 191,
    196, 199, 203, 213
agricultural food exports, 188
aid recipients, 52
Air Operating licences (AOC), 129
appointment of judges, 108
authorities, 52
banking union, 107
benefits of membership, 91
Berlin Plus arrangements
    (2003), 178
budget, 114, 117, 159, 207, 211
Cap EU immigration, 120
centralization of power in
    Brussels, 107
Central members, 111
China Policy, 173
China relations, 167
Chinese investment (FDI), 170
Common Asylum framework, 59
common defense strategy, 182
Common Security and Defense
    Policy (CSDP) (1999), 180
corporate tax framework, 199
customs union, 120
democratic principles, 108
Directive 2014/107/EU, 192
Eastern, 69, 111, 207
economy, 131, 155, 210
electorate, 30
enlargement, 61, 168, 205, 208
exports to the UK, 160
external border, 84, 112
external refugee problem, 121
external tariff barriers, 116
financial integration, 136
financial structure, 206
financing programme, 41

European Union (EU) (*cont.*)
  funding, 97–99
  (*see also* Horizon 2020, Erasmus Plus)
  infrastructure projects, 204
  intra-EU immigration, 3
  intra-EU migration, 68–69
  intra-EU mobility, 69
  intra EU routes, 129
  intra-EU trade, 8
  laws, 62, 69, 82, 120, 127, 187
  leaders, 40, 97, 106, 107
  legislation, 109, 120, 126
  Leichenstein model, 122
  markets, 129–130, 133, 152, 212
  mass migration problems, 175
  members health treatment, 131
  member states, 40, 57, 64, 123, 130, 144, 205, 207
  negotiations, 88–90, 92–94, 97
  new trade agreement with UK, 143
  non-EU migrants, 73, 207
  open borders policy, 84
  pan-EU strategy, 177
Europe's Mass Migration entry point, 171
Eurostat, 10, 57, 67, 69, 176
Eurozone, 7–9, 11–13, 15–17, 19–20, 22, 24–26, 27–56, 107, 136, 140, 151, 159–162, 164–166, 175, 201, 205, 209–213
  Banking Union, 165
  banks, 161
  BRICS economic growth, 160
  Chinese direct investment, 172
  creation (1999), 205
  debt to Brexit, 203
  debtor and creditor countries, 4
  Eurogroup, 107
  (*see also* The finance committee of the Eurozone)
  exports to the UK, 160
  exports to the USA, 160
  financial infrastructure, 19
  governments, 41
  growth export-orientated model, 48
  products, 145
  prolonged recession (2011), 49
  recovery, 127
  statistical financial regimes, 20
  Trade relations with Russia, 160
  wide deposit insurance, 165
Exchange rate
  fixed, 35
  fixed regime, 23, 29–34, 43
  flexible, 33
  free-floating, 31
  international, 20
  policies, 33
  'quasi' fixed regime (1979), 32–33
  stability, 13
  volatility, 33
Exchange Rate Mechanism (ERM), 13

F

Facebook, 195
Farage, Nigel, 65
Far Right and Neo-Nazi groups, 76
Federal Reserve Bank, 26, 50, 53
The finance committee of the Eurozone, 107

Financial Conduct Authority
  (FCA), 124
Financial crash (2008), 49
Financial shocks (1999-2008), 8
Finland, 8, 16, 17, 66, 176, 209
Fintech, 124
Fiscal
  conditions, 13
  consolidation, 17, 47
  cuts, 5, 47
  discipline, 19
  expansion, 152
  goals, 40
  integration, 17
  integration, 206
  laxity, 210
  performance, 13
  policies, 25, 55
  shock, 43
  union, 40, 53
Fonction Publique Francaise
  style state institution, 205
  (*see also* Paris)
Foreign direct investment (FDI), 83,
  117, 142, 150, 170, 196
Forex, 89
Fotyga, Anna, 177, 180
Fox, Liam, 90
Foxton, 150
Franc, 32
France, 4, 8, 16–18, 22, 30–32, 35,
  50–53, 58, 60, 62, 64, 65,
  67, 68, 69, 77, 81, 82, 101,
  111, 125, 129, 130, 134,
  136, 137, 138, 143, 154,
  156, 167, 168, 172, 182,
  186, 187, 188, 204, 206,
  207, 208, 210, 211, 212

  banks, 39, 42
  bombings in Paris (13th
    November 2015), 83
  centre-left government, 35
  elections, 169, 211–212
  exports to the UK, 32
  monetarist paradigm, 51
  National Front (rightwing EU
    party), 4, 82, 211
  Nord-Pas-de-Calais regions, 82
  Parliament, 135
  position in the Euro, 22
  unemployment, 18, 135
Frankfurt, 125, 175
Freedom of Movement (FOM), 89,
  114, 204
Free Trade Agreement (FTA), 121
Free Trade Area, 32
Free Trade Association, 59
Friedman, Milton (2002), 28

G

G20, 168, 193,
  197, 200
G7 economies, 147
GCC, 7
Germany, 3, 4, 8, 15–16, 18, 19, 20,
  21, 22, 23, 26, 31, 32, 36,
  37, 38, 46, 47, 48, 50, 51,
  52, 53, 56, 58, 60, 62, 64,
  65, 66, 67, 69, 70, 75, 76,
  77, 79, 80, 81, 82, 83, 84,
  85, 88, 101, 107, 137–138,
  143, 154, 161–163,
  167–169, 176, 180, 182,
  185, 186, 206–210
  anti-Muslim demonstrations, 76

Germany (*cont.*)
  (*see also* Far Right and Neo-Nazi groups)
  authorities, 16, 47–48
  banks, 23, 42, 165
  CDU party, 209
  East, 208
  economy, 2, 46, 54
  elections, 169, 211
  exports, 48–50, 145
  government, 76
  immigrants, 3
  industrial orders, 47
  Right Wing (AfD), 4, 76
  surpluses, 38
  Syrian asylum applications, 76
  taxation, 37
  unemployment, 81
  West, 208
GfK index, 149
Gibraltar, 106
GlaxoSmithKline Plc, 150
Golden Dawn (Greece), 4
Goldman Sachs, 10, 26
Gold Standard, 23
Google, 195, 199
Gorecki, Jan, 111
Gove, Michael, 126
Great Depression, 138
Great Recession, 35, 53, 138, 139, 154, 164, 207
Greece, 3, 4, 8, 9, 12, 13, 16, 19, 21, 22, 23, 24, 25, 35, 37, 38, 40, 42, 43, 44, 45, 46, 51, 52, 55, 56, 60, 61, 64, 68, 76, 78, 84, 85, 86, 112, 161, 164, 170, 171, 172, 201, 208–211
  account deficit (2008), 35
  Aegean, 60, 85
  authorities, 209
  camps, 86
  Chinese investments, 171
  conservative Greek government, 35
  economy, 10, 37, 55, 201
  exports, 55
  financial assistance, 209
  first Greek bailout (2010), 38
  government, 35
  government bonds, 36, 41
  Greek (second and third) bailout, 37
  Hellenic Postbank, 36
  impasse in Greek finances, 36
  Loan Facility, 37
  national strike, 36
  recovery, 43
  sovereign credit, 42
  sovereign debt rating, 40
  Syriza government, 4, 170, 211
  unemployment, 18–21
Grexit, 25, 36, 41
GSK, 197
Gulf, 74–75, 130

H

Hames, Tim, 102
Hammond, Philip, 90, 98, 104, 200
Hende, Csaba, 177
Hill, Jonathan, 104
Hinckley (in Somerset) nuclear power plant, 171
Hitachi, Fujitsu, Renault-Nissan, 117

Hobsons, 100–101
Hofer, Norbert, 80
Holland, 70, 82, 111
Hollande, Francois, 82, 94
Horizon research funding, 99
Horn of Africa, 176
Hoyer, Werner, 104
HSBC, 126
Hungarian Times, 77
Hungary, 28–29, 58, 61, 64, 76–79, 108, 111, 177, 186, 207, 211
    Orbans government, 108

I

IAG, 127, 128, 130
Iceland, 32, 72
IFS, 148
IMF (International Monetary Fund), 22, 25, 36, 40, 41, 43, 44, 45, 50, 54, 55, 56, 148, 154
    financing programme, 41
    negotiating mission to Athens, 36
    rules, 43
    special drawing rights (SDR), 175
    UK revisions, 147
Immigration, 89, 112
    illegal immigration (Aegean), 181
    internal and external, 2
    Muslim, 81
    policies, 82
Index of Permanent Positions, 149
India, 92, 146, 160, 212
ING-DiBa, 80
International Organization for Migration, 86

International PPP comparisons, 147
International Swaps and Derivatives Association (ISDA), 42
Investment banks, 125
Iraq, 74, 77, 207
    training camps, 83
Ireland, 3, 8, 9, 11, 12, 15, 16, 18, 23, 37, 38, 40, 45, 46, 47, 51, 52, 55, 61, 62, 63, 65, 66, 69, 87, 105, 118, 176, 194, 196, 197, 200, 208
    Anglo Irish Bank, 38
    bailout, 36–38, 45
    Bank of Ireland, 38
    economy, 15, 45
    government, 38, 193
    housing market, 38
    taxation, 37
    unemployment, 23
IRS revenues, 195
ISIS, 59, 78, 177
InFacts analysis, 119
Islamic state (ISIL), 83
Israel, 103
Issing (2000), 28
Italy, 3, 8, 12–18, 22, 32, 39, 45, 51, 55, 60, 62, 67–69, 76–78, 84–86, 165–168, 172, 204
    banks, 162, 164
    Constitutional Referendum (October), 56, 160
    economy, 164, 172
    government, 55, 162
    Lampedusa, 75
    participation to the single currency, 18

J

Japan, 147, 151, 161, 194, 211–212
  Japanese companies, 117
  tax authority, 194
Japanese investors, 117
Joint European Resources for Micro to Medium Enterprises (Jeremie), 101
Jordan, 74
Joussen, Fritz, 131
JP Morgan, 126
Juncker, Jean-Claude, 59, 182–183, 184, 188, 195–197

K

Kaliningrad, 183
Ka-shing, Li, 174
Kenny, Enda, 118
Keynesian policies, 29
King, Sir Julian, 182
Kobosko, Michael, 108
Konashenkov, Igor, 183
Krikorian, Mark, 77
Kuka, Midea, 169
Kuwait, 75

L

Lagarde, Christine, 45, 54, 175
Laiki bank, 165
Latvia, 61, 64, 178, 186
Lebanon, 74
Le Corre, Philippe, 174
  See also China's Offensive in Europe
Lehman Brothers, 210
Leipzig, 81
Le Pen, Marine, 185, 188
Libor, 89
Libya, 41
  The fall of the Gaddafi regime, 75
Liechtenstein, 64, 72
Lithuania, 61, 64, 183, 186, 188
Lloyds, 149
London, 112, 124–125, 136, 150, 153, 175, 199, 212
  financial centre, 174
  financial services, 124
  investment banks, 125
  meeting, 118
  residential property market, 148
  strongest financial market, 8
  style state institution, 93, 205
  (*see also* Whitehall)
Lord Hill, 112
Lord Kerr, 96
Low interest rates, 20
Lowry, Rich, 79
Lufthansa, 130
Lukyanov, Fyodor, 185
Luxembourg, 60, 64, 67, 106, 175, 195–198, 208
  US-Luxembourg double taxation treaty, 196

M

Maastricht Treaty, 1, 3, 7, 13–16, 18, 33, 51–53, 64
  criteria, 51
  debt criterion, 13, 16
  rules, 10
Macedonia, 85
Mali, 77
Malmström, Cecilia, 71

Malta, 3, 61–65
Mandelson, Peter, 171
   See also BBC Radio interview
Market Economy Status (MES), 169
Mass emigration, 68
Mass riots, 45
May, Theresa, 91–95, 104, 114, 118, 171, 179
McDonald's, 150, 195
McKinsey Report (2015), 46
Mediterranean, 23, 76, 84, 208, 209
   corruption, 46
   enlargement (1980s), 208
   region, 170
Merkel, Angela, 76–78, 85, 123, 185, 207
   chief economic advisor, 52
Middle East, 57, 74–75, 79, 84, 177–180
Migrants, 57–58, 86
   assimilation of Muslim, 81
   economic, 58, 112
   mass migration, 64–65
Minford, Patrick, 115, 121
Mogadishu, 85
Mogherini, Federica, 181, 182
Moldova, 122
Monetary Policy Committee, 19, 20, 29, 45, 141, 145
   expansionary, 31
   international destabilization, 50
   system, 46
   unification, 52
Monetary union, 17–19, 27–29, 33, 51–53, 107
   development, 34
   establishment, 34

Monte dei Paschi di Siena, 55, 164
Moscovici, Pierre, 199
Moscow, 208
MT criteria, 16
Mundell, Robert, 136

N

National Institute of Economics and Social Research, 148
NATO, 178–181, 185
   alliance, 179
   meeting in Warsaw, 183
   members, 180
   Summit in Warsaw (8-10 July 2016), 97, 106, 181
   Western European Union cooperation, 178
NATO-EU (2002)
   European Security and Defence Policy (ESDP), 178
NATO – Russia
   Founding Act of 1997, 177
Nazi, 79
Nell, Jacob, 125–126
Neo-Liberal ruling elite, 205
Netherlands, 8, 15–20, 58–60, 64, 70, 151, 163, 168, 176, 196, 206, 208–209
   taxation, 37
   welfare benefits, 70
   (see also Bijstand)
New York, 54, 153
New York Post, 80
New Zealand, 92, 118–119
NHS, 62, 90
Nice terror attacks, 129

Nicosia, 204
1949 Treaty (4 April), 179
　Article, 179
Nobel prize-winning economist, 56
Non Performing Loans (NPL), 56
Nord Stream 2, 186–187
North American Free Trade Area (NAFTA), 32, 93
Northern Ireland, 118
　Good Friday, 105
　(*see also* Peace settlement)
North Korea, 123
Norway, 32, 64, 72, 100, 114, 119–120, 128, 148
　association, 123
　EEA model, 120
　EU payments, 119
　(*see also* InFacts analysis)
　Norwegian model, 126
NPL, 165
Nugali, Osama, 75

O

O'Brien, David, 129
OECD, 10, 156, 172, 194, 197, 199
　BEPS Project, 197
　G20 initiative, 202
O'Leary, Michael, 128
Oman, 75
Orbán, Viktor, 78
Osborne, George, 88, 104, 137, 155, 199–200
Oxford university, 104

P

Pakistan, 77

Panama papers, 73
Papandreou, George, 10
Paris, 125, 153, 175, 199
　bombings (March 2016), 179
　terror attacks, 129
Parliamentary elections, 109
　political experiment observers, 107
　post Brexit, 149
　preassure on banks, 125
　(*see also* Deutsche and Societe General)
　regulations, 115, 119, 127
　relations with China and Russia, 167–168
　Research, Development and Innovation schemes, 204
　sanctions on Russia, 186
　Savings Taxation Directive (2003/48/EC), 192
　Security Union, 182
　southern countries, 22
　State Aid rules, 162
　tax strategy, 191
　Turkey deal (20th of March 2016), 85
　UK-EU trade arrangement, 133
　unemployment levels, 211
Passau, 184, 188
Peace settlement, 105
PIGS (Portugal, Ireland, Greece, Spain), 9, 213
Piraeus, 36, 170
　(*see also* Europe's Mass Migration entry point)
Pirelli, 172
PMI, 151
Podemos (Spain), 4

Poland, 3, 8, 12, 15, 28–29, 61–67, 74, 77–81, 107, 111, 168, 185–188, 207, 211
   central Statistical Office, 62
   Constitutional Court, 108
   Government's reforms, 108
   Justice party (PIS), 108
   Polish Plumber, 62
Political negotiation, 45
Political union, 28
PORTUGAL, 3, 8, 9, 12, 13, 14, 16, 18, 20, 22, 23, 38, 45, 46, 51, 56, 61, 64, 68, 161, 168, 208
   bailout (May 2011), 40
   financial assistance from the EU, 39
   taxation, 37
Posted Workers Directive (1996), 68
Pound sterling, 90, 129, 134, 143, 145
   decline in the value, 156
   depreciation, 152–155, 210
   fall, 134
   fluctuations, 140
PSI (Private Sector Involvement), 41
Purchasing Managers' Index (PMI), 151
Purchasing Power Parity measurements, 146
Putin, Vladimir, 185, 188

Q
Qatar, 75
Qatar airlines, 130
QE, 134, 135, 157, 159
   programme, 53–54, 143

Qualified Majority voting (QMV), 109
Quantitative Easing (QE), 53, 134, 142, 161

R
Refugees, 57–58, 75, 78
   invasion, 78
   quotas, 78
   sexual attacks, 81
   Syrian, 76, 81, 85
   Syrian asylum, 84
Renminbi (RMB), 175
Renzi, Matteo, 56
Romania, 3–4, 29, 58, 65–67, 74, 186
   migrants, 62
Royal bank of Scotland (RBS), 162
Russia, 111, 177, 178, 183–189
   aggression in Ukraine, 183
   annexation of Crimea, 181
   economy, 183
   exclave on Poland's northern border, 183
   intentions post Crimea, 179
   involvement in Eastern Ukraine, 179
Ryanair, 127, 129–130
   UK operating licence, 129

S
Sale to Japanese firm, 145
Sarkozy, Nicolas, 81
Saudi Arabia, 75
Schäuble, Wolfgang, 162
Schengen Agreement, 59, 64, 72, 76
   borders, 59

Schengen Agreement (*cont.*)
  rules, 64
  zone, 112
Scotland, 105, 118
  push for independence, 105
Second World War, 1
Sepulchre, Alain, 170
  See also China's Offensive in Europe
Serbia, 76, 83, 85, 120
Shelton, Andrew, 131
Sinclair-Jones, Ruth, 99, 100
Singapore, 117
Single currency, 49, 210
Single market, 7, 32–33, 48, 58, 91, 107, 115, 116, 134–135, 148, 200
Slovakia, 61, 64, 77, 78, 79, 81, 186, 207
  Bratislava Summit (16th September 2016), 106
  government, 81
  presidency (2014-15), 177
Slovenia, 61, 64, 76
Small and Medium Enterprises (SMEs), 23, 101, 105
SNP, 118
SNP campaign for Scottish independence (2014), 88
Somalia
  piracy, 176
  (*see also* Horn of Africa)
Soros, George, 34
South Korea, 117
Spain, 3–21, 39, 42, 45–47, 51–52, 60–67, 69, 76, 105, 111, 135, 162, 164–165, 201, 208
  banks, 38–39, 165

Cajas (Savings banks), 55
  emergency financial assistance, 45
  government, 40
  housing market, 39
  national debt, 47
  unemployment, 21
Stability and Growth Pact (SGP), 15, 17, 52–53
  fiscal constraints, 29
Standard and Poor's (S&P), 42
Starbucks, 195–196
Steinmeier, Frank-Walter, 185
Stiglitz, Joseph, 56, 201
  See also Nobel prize-winning economist
Stoidis, Dimosthenis, 201
Stoltenberg, Jens, 179, 180, 181
Sturgeon, Nicola, 118
Swansea university, 103
Sweden, 8, 17, 18, 58, 61, 66, 69, 77, 168, 200
Switzerland, 64, 72–73, 100, 114, 120, 123, 197
  neutrality, 72
Syngenta, 172
Syria, 74–77, 85, 189, 207
  refugees, 75
  Syrian civil war, 76
  training camps, 83
Szijjártó, Peter, 77
Szymanski, Konrad, 187

T

Teeven, Fred, 70–71
Thessaloniki, 36
Thomsen, Poul, 36, 44
Tokyo, 153

Transatlantic Trade and Investment partnership (TTIP), 189, 204
Travelzoo UK, 131
Treaty of Amsterdam, 64
Treaty of Lisbon, 1, 93, 94, 95, 169, 182
  Article 49, 96
  Article 50, 93, 94, 95, 96, 97, 114, 127, 169
Treaty of Rome, 1, 32, 58, 61, 68, 105
Troika, 3, 22, 35, 38, 42, 43, 54, 55, 209
  arrangement, 43
  bail-out funds, 209
  bailout policies, 4–5
Trump, Donald, 93
TUI, 131
Turkey, 60, 67, 74, 76, 85–86, 89, 103, 120
  agreement, 60
  AK party, 85
  Coup d'Etat on the (15th of July), 85
  exports, 121
  external tariff, 122
  general election (1st of November), 85
Tusk, Donald, 106–108, 112, 116, 205
Tyrie, Andrew, 124

U
Ukraine, 177
Uni Credit, 165
Unione di Banche Italiane SpA, 165
United Arab Emirates, 75, 130

United Kingdom (UK), 3–4, 18, 22, 23, 30–35, 49, 58, 61–63, 65–67, 69, 71–74, 82, 87, 89, 90, 92–94, 96, 99, 100–104, 106, 110, 112, 114–131, 133–161, 169, 171–174, 176, 179–186, 195, 197, 199, 200, 205–208, 210, 212
  banks, 143
  Birmingham, 92, 123
  (*see also* Conservative Conference)
  Blair government, 74, 83
  British Council, 99–100
  Bulgarian migration, 74
  Cameron's government, 87
  Conservative party, 87, 91
  domestic inflation, 147
  domestic routes, 128
  ECAA Agreement, 128
  economic recovery, 137–138
  economy, 2, 5, 10, 21–23, 25, 30, 31, 37, 39, 43–46, 48, 50, 54, 55, 79, 88, 90, 97, 101, 122, 124, 126, 131, 133–166, 168–170, 173–175, 182, 183, 195, 200, 201, 210
  EU withdrawal, 151
  exports, 20, 25, 27, 30–32, 46, 48, 54, 55, 116, 121, 134, 135, 136, 138–140, 153–155, 159, 160, 176, 187–189
  FDI projects, 152
  financial institutions, 142–143
  free-trade agreement with the EU, 116

United Kingdom (UK) (*cont.*)
  general election (May in 2015), 82
  government, 4, 10, 11, 12, 23, 28–30, 35, 36, 38, 40, 41, 47, 48, 53–55, 60, 62, 65, 73–76, 80–88, 90–93, 95, 98, 101–102, 107–112, 114, 115, 117, 118, 120, 122, 131, 142, 148, 152, 167, 170–172, 179, 183, 186, 193–195, 200–206, 212
  High Court's ruling (3rd of November 2016), 95
  Higher Education Funding Council, 101
  Hinckley delay, 172
  House of Commons, 95, 144
  House of Lords, 95, 110
  Houses of Parliament, 82, 87, 95
  Independence party (UKIP), 65, 82, 88, 91
  inflation, 30
  influence in Brussels, 97
  investment projects, 150
  Japanese businesses in the UK, 117
  (*see* also Hitachi, Fujitsu, Renault-Nissan)
  Labour party, 92
  Leave campaign, 82
  national debt, 142
  negotiations with Brussels, 72
  net worth of UK stocks, 152
  new EU trade agreement, 154
  New Labour government, 4
  new trade deal with the EU, 153
  nuclear power industry, 171
  post electoral system, 82
  Project Fear, 88
  (*see also* SNP campaign for Scottish independence (2014))
  public finances, 71
  recession, 138
  Referendum, 95, 133, 136–138, 140, 144, 160, 161
  Referendum impact on the economy, 136–137, 144
  Referendum impact on the FDI, 150
  referendum (June), 87, 128, 180
  Referendum outcome, 147–149, 161, 165
  Romanian migration, 74
  Security services, 182
  Supreme Court, 95
  trade dependence, 154
  (*see also* China and India)
  trade performance, 152
  trade relations with the EU countries, 157
  Treasury, 99
  Treasury Committee, 124
  vote, 87, 106, 112
  Whitehall departments of state, 93
United Nations (UN), 77
  law, 82
  Security Council, 168
United States of America (USA), 48–50, 53–54, 73, 77, 102, 124, 137–138, 143, 147, 151, 160–161, 171–172, 180, 186, 188–189, 204
  Administration, 193

American banks, 42
companies, 193
Corporation Tax (CT) Levels, 193
economy, 164
Federal Reserve, 54, 139, 141
financial markets, 54
government, 53
Justice Department, 162
multinationals, 194
national fiscal automatic stabilisers, 53
Obama administration, 48, 50
officials, 75
tax authorities, 194
tax code, 194
treasuries, 134
treasury, 193
treasury department, 193
University College London, 71
US dollar, 24, 53, 54, 133, 141, 146, 154, 175

V
Van Der Bellen, Alexander, 80
VAT compliance, 191
Venice Tribunal, 107–108
Vestager, Margrethe, 193, 194, 196
Villeroy de Galhau, François, 125
Visegrad, 77, 167
  group, 180, 206–207
  leaders, 107
  states, 111
  V4 group, 177

Vodafone, 197

W
Wales, 91
Wall Street Journal, 43
Warsaw, 97, 178
  Kaczynski government, 183
Washington, 184
Waszczykowski, Witold, 178
Weiwen, He, 174
Whitehall, 93, 205
Wilders, Geert, 81
World Bank, 54, 162
World Trade Organisation (WTO), 114, 168–169
  model of international trade, 116
  rules, 32
World War II (WWII), 66, 208
  post-WWII, 4
World War I (WWI), 23

X
Xiaoping, Deng, 168

Y
Yellen, Janet, 50
Yemen, 41
Yen, 175
Yorkshire, 101

The manufacturer's authorised representative in the EU is Springer Nature Customer Service Centre GmbH, Europaplatz 3, 69115 Heidelberg, Germany. If you have any concerns regarding our products, please contact ProductSafety@springernature.com

Printed and bound by CPI Group (UK) Ltd, Croydon, CR0 4YY

23/03/2026

02076662-0008